D0966273

EXTRAORDINARY WOMEN OF THE MEDIEVAL AND RENAISSANCE WORLD

EXTRAORDINARY WOMEN
OF THE MEDIEVAL AND RENAISSANCE WORLD

A Biographical Dictionary

Carole Levin
Debra Barrett-Graves
Jo Eldridge Carney
W. M. Spellman
Gwynne Kennedy
Stephanie Witham

GREENWOOD PRESS
Westport, Connecticut • London

Library of Congress Cataloging-in-Publication Data

Extraordinary women of the Medieval and Renaissance world : a biographical
dictionary / Carole Levin . . . [et al.].
    p.   cm.
    Includes bibliographical references and index.
    ISBN 0–313–30659–1 (alk. paper)
    1. Women—History—Middle Ages, 500–1500—Biography—Dictionaries.
    2. Women—History—Renaissance, 1450–1600—Biography—Dictionaries.
    I. Levin, Carole, 1948–
    HQ1143.E93   2000
    920.72'03—dc21   99–055218

British Library Cataloguing in Publication Data is available.

Library of Congress Catalog Card Number: 99–055218
ISBN: 0–313–30659–1

First published in 2000

Greenwood Press, 88 Post Road West, Westport, CT 06881
An imprint of Greenwood Publishing Group, Inc.
www.greenwood.com

Printed in the United States of America

The paper used in this book complies with the
Permanent Paper Standard issued by the National
Information Standards Organization (Z39.48–1984).

10 9 8 7 6 5 4 3 2

To the students at the State University of New York at New Paltz, the University of Nebraska at Lincoln, the College of Santa Fe, The College of New Jersey, the University of North Carolina at Asheville, the University of Wisconsin-Milwaukee, and the College of St. Mary who have studied medieval and Renaissance women with us. Just as our subjects were extraordinary, so are our students.

CONTENTS

ACKNOWLEDGMENTS

As the coordinating author, I, Carole Levin, put the team for the book together. I want to thank all my fellow authors; each brought fine scholarship and great joy to this project. It was a pleasure to work with them. Special thanks go to Jo Eldridge Carney and Debra Barrett-Graves for their help with discovering sources for the illustrations and with editing. They and the others were all wonderful colleagues and collaborators. Many people generously helped us as we worked on this project. First and foremost, we wish to thank our editor, Barbara Rader. Her vision and enthusiasm made the book happen. Dan Ehnbom used his expertise and friendship to help us with the illustrations. We also wish to thank Delia Baltera, Clif Bridges, Jessica Buser, Patrick Delin, Allan Donsig, Tim Elston, Stuart Fisher, Emily Greenwald, Margaret Hannay, Mark Hinchman, Shawn Holderby, Elaine Kruse, Michael Medwick, Michele Osherow, Lisa Roberts, Christa Setteducati, Bill Shields, and Joe and Julie Silvestri for all their help and support. Ruth Elwell's expertise provided the index.

The librarians at our home institutions as well as the staff at the Folger Shakespeare Library were generous and helpful. We would especially like to thank the staff of the Fogelson Library at the College of Santa Fe and the staff of the Love Library at the University of Nebraska at Lincoln. We appreciate the support we received from our home institutions. The University of Nebraska at Lincoln provided research support for both Carole Levin and Stephanie Witham, who was awarded the Human Rights and Human Diversity Graduate Fellowship and the Warren F. and Edith R. Day Student Aid Fund award. The College of New Jersey provided research support for Jo Eldridge Carney.

INTRODUCTION

In the 1920s the writer Virginia Woolf lamented the fact that she had no earlier role models and speculated that even if Shakespeare had a sister who also aspired to be a writer, her fate would be a tragic one. Woolf imagined that her "Judith Shakespeare" might run away to London to be a playwright and end up a suicide buried at some crossroads.[1] In fact, though Shakespeare did not have such a sister, there were many strong and powerful women of the medieval and Renaissance world with a wide range of aspirations and achievements. Some of these women indeed had tragic lives, whereas others flourished, but there are many women of great accomplishment in the medieval and Renaissance world. Because of the recovery work that scholars have accomplished over the last few decades, a number of medieval and Renaissance women have become well known to a wide audience.[2] When I first began to teach the history of European women two decades ago, one of my assignments on the first day was to have the class come up with a list of famous European women of the medieval and Renaissance period. All too often, the blackboard stayed for the most part blank. Now it would be filled with the names of queens, religious leaders, warriors, and writers such as Elizabeth I, Isabella of Castile, Joan of Arc, Lady Jane Grey, Eleanor of Aquitaine, Hildegard of Bingen, Heloise, Margery Kempe, Julian of Norwich, and Christine de Pizan.

This book moves beyond some of these more familiar women to discuss a range of "unsung" women who were nonetheless extraordinary for one reason or another. We deliberately chose not to include women of the time who are most famous today because information on them can be easily obtained. Some of the women included here are fairly well known, whereas others are quite obscure. A number of them were highly known and well praised in their own lifetimes, but their fame has faded over the centuries. Because of the sources available to us we include more women who were literate and thus privileged, but we attempted to have as broad a range as possible in terms of status and backgrounds. The women on whom we focus are ones who deserve more attention. These seventy short biographies are about women who frequently moved beyond the conventional ideology of the time that told women to be "chaste, silent, and obedient."[3]

The period of the Middle Ages and Renaissance included major political, religious, and social changes and cultural shifts. The influence of the Catholic Church weakened during this period. In the eleventh and twelfth centuries there was greater emphasis on education, particularly for those in the Church but also among the laity. There developed a literature written not in Latin but in the vernacular, the language of the people. In the fourteenth and fifteenth centuries, the development of humanism, the belief that the ancient Greeks and Romans had a moral wisdom compatible with and helpful to Christianity, profoundly changed many people's values, allowing them to concentrate on this world as well as the next. A more personal sense of self began to emerge, together with concepts of national identity and national monarchies. The Protestant Reformation and Catholic revival of the sixteenth century had political, social, and economic implications as well as religious ones. Cities began to develop as places of culture and power. As part of that process different European nations were "discovering," exploring, and subjugating "New World" territories. Spain's enormous empire in central and South America and Portugal's immense territories in Africa led to the development of the slave trade, which spread to other European nations. These explorations helped to encourage growth in trade and in the evolution of more sophisticated capitalistic systems. The invention of the printing press and movable type in the middle of the fifteenth century meant that information could be distributed at a much faster rate; people read aloud to each other, and literacy rates increased dramatically. In the sixteenth and seventeenth centuries these changes in turn led to political unrest and revolutions.

Some women responded actively to the changing world around them despite the messages they were hearing. Traditionally, women were told to obey their fathers and then their husbands; to be virgins and then chaste wives; to prefer silence to speech and self-expression. During the Middle Ages and Renaissance, many learned men described woman's nature as morally weak and intellectually feeble; they claimed not only that women were unworthy of education but education would be positively dangerous for them. For many writers and commentators, an assertive woman was an abnormal one.[4] Yet in spite of these prevailing attitudes, a number of women during this time period were able to become highly educated, reading and translating works from many different languages, though few parents were as supportive of their daughters' education as Thomas More (see Margaret More Roper). Elizabeth Cary's mother was so distressed by her daughter's intellectual interests that she forbade the servants to give the child candles so she would not be able to read at night; Elizabeth managed to procure them anyway and read a wide range of texts that prepared her for her own writings as an adult. Many of the women were able to establish themselves as writers or artists, and some of them, such as the court artists Levina Teerlinc and Sofonisba Anguissola, were able to support themselves through their work. Their writing encouraged some of the extraordinary women of this period to live their lives as they, rather than society, prescribed. The Venetian poet Veronica Franco was a "cortegiana onesta," an "honored courtesan," who had upper-class lovers and wrote about the pains and pleasures of love.

Some women, such as Diane de Poitiers, mistress and confidante of Henry II of France, also refused to accept the moral dictates of the time and achieved power, autonomy, or satisfaction as courtesans or mistresses instead of wives. Other women moved beyond the confines of their society by assuming political power themselves. Margaret of Anjou, queen consort of England, and Nzinga, an African queen in what is now modern-day Angola, actually led their soldiers in the field. While some women achieved great success in the political realm, others profiled here, such as Juana of Castile, known as the "Mad," and James I of England's cousin Lady Arbella Stuart, had their lives destroyed because of their proximity to power.

This work includes not only women who were extraordinary in a public sphere but women who as wives, mothers, daughters, and friends demonstrated the courage to live their lives in ways that went beyond the ordinary expectations of the times. In fourteenth-century Italy, Margherita Datini learned to read and write at the age of thirty so that she could correspond with her husband, a merchant who often traveled. Distressed at having no children, she finally agreed to raise her husband's illegitimate daughter as her own, giving her the education she herself had been denied as a child. Thomas More's daughter Margaret More Roper and his adopted daughter Margaret Giggs Clement put themselves in danger to ensure that their father's body was treated with dignity after Henry VIII ordered his execution in 1535. Maria de Salinas, companion to Catherine of Aragon, flouted Henry VIII's command so that she could be with her beloved queen as Catherine lay dying.

Some women put themselves at risk for their religious beliefs. In the late Middle Ages the Catholic Church struggled against what it perceived as heretical movements that finally brought about the Protestant Reformation, the breaking apart of the Catholic Church in the West. Although Martin Luther did not intend such a break when he posted his ninety-five theses denouncing abuses of the Catholic Church on the church door in Wittenberg in 1517, this was the result. In this time of religious upheaval, women as well as men showed remarkable bravery in staying true to their beliefs, whether they were Catholic or Protestant. While Katherine von Bora (Luther) was smuggled out of a convent at great risk because of her Protestant beliefs, Caritas Pirckheimer struggled against the Lutheran authorities to keep her convent from being shut down. Catherine Willoughby fled England with a small child in the mid-1550s to avoid religious persecution. Women such as Anne Askew and Marguerite Porete died because of their refusal to deny their religious beliefs.

This is a book about extraordinary medieval and Renaissance women, but *medieval* and *Renaissance* are problematic terms. Most of the women profiled here lived between the tenth and the seventeenth centuries. While in Italy the Renaissance arrived in the fourteenth and fifteenth centuries, in England and France the Renaissance came as late as the sixteenth and seventeenth centuries.

We also wanted to be flexible about the terms *medieval* and *Renaissance* not only chronologically but geographically. Although most of the women included in this book are Western European, we have deliberately included others so that we would have a global perspective. Profiled are politically powerful women in Eastern Europe, Asia, and Africa such as Jadwiga of Poland; Raziya, the Sultan, in India;

Melisende, Queen of Jerusalem; and Nzinga, Queen of Angola, in Africa.

Because this work focuses on women in history who have been largely "unsung" and who represent a wide range of backgrounds, some originally intended subjects have had to be omitted because of insufficient information. A few extraordinary women have been included, however, even if complete biographical information was not available. For example, Jacqueline Félicie worked as a physician in Paris in the early fourteenth century, and for practicing medicine without a license—as a woman she could not be licensed—she was brought before the Inquisition. The transcripts noted in the profile provide the only information we have about Félicie; after her trial, she disappears from recorded history.

The purpose of this collection is to make the lives of these extraordinary women available to a wider audience and to encourage further studies of their lives and of the lives of other medieval and Renaissance women. In numerous ways the lives of the women profiled here were remarkable and provide lessons for later generations. As we enter a new millennium, women and men of today need to know about and celebrate the courageous and impressive lives of women who have lived before them.

Carole Levin

NOTES

1. Virginia Woolf, *A Room of One's Own* (1929; New York: Harcourt Brace Jovanovich, 1991).

2. Two pioneers of medieval and Renaissance women's history were Eileen Power, *Medieval Women*, ed. M. M. Postan (Cambridge: Cambridge University Press, 1975), and Ruth Kelso, *Doctrine for the Lady of the Renaissance* (Urbana: University of Illinois Press, 1956). More recently, Natalie Davis and Joan Kelly transformed the field. For Kelly, see *Women, History, & Theory: The Essays of Joan Kelly* (Chicago: University of Chicago Press, 1986). For Davis, some very important early essays were collected in *Society and Culture in Early Modern France* (Stanford: Stanford University Press, 1975). Davis's bibliography is long and stellar. For an important recent work, see *Women on the Margins: Three Seventeenth-Century Lives* (Cambridge MA: Harvard University Press, 1995). For those who would like to read more on women in the Middle Ages and Renaissance, see the selected bibliography.

3. For more on these strictures for women, see Suzanne K. Hull, *Chaste, Silent, and Obedient: English Books for Women, 1475–1640* (San Marino: Huntington Library, 1982).

4. Linda Woodbridge, *Women and the English Renaissance: Literature and the Nature of Womankind, 1540–1620* (Urbana: University of Illinois Press, 1984), 214; Tim Stretton, *Women Waging Law in Elizabethan England* (Cambridge: Cambridge University Press, 1998), 44.

NOTE TO THE READER

The cross-references to notable women who appear as individual entries themselves are in boldface their first time of appearance in an entry. In the back matter, under "Notable Women by Title, Occupation, or Main Area of Interest," the reader will find that many entries are listed under more than one heading, as many of these women served multiple roles and occupations in their public and private lives. Note, however, that not all of these associations are necessarily listed in the initial entry description—just the one or ones of major importance in describing the individual. Lastly, under "Notable Women by Country or Region," also in the back matter, some women are listed under more than one country or region, owing to their birth in one and influence in another. If no parentheses follow the entry's name, she is listed only by her birth country. In the case of a dual listing, the country or region of birth is indicated in parentheses followed by an asterisk (*) and the country or region of influence is in parentheses followed by a dagger (†).

EXTRAORDINARY WOMEN OF THE MEDIEVAL AND RENAISSANCE WORLD

AKKA MAHĀDĒVĪ
(Mahadeviyakka)
(fl. ca. Twelfth Century)
India
Saint and Poet

In the early medieval period of India's history, a populist, devotional movement known as *bhakti* ("devotion") arose, one opposed to the practices associated with ritualized Hinduism. The movement, with its worship primarily focused on the major trinity of Hindu deities— Brahma, the creator; Viṣṇu, the preserver; and Śiva, the destroyer— opened the path of devotion to all believers, regardless of caste or sex. Women, in particular, fully embraced the new *bhakti* movement as a means of expressing their faith.

The rise of the *bhakti* religious movement known as *Vīraśaivism* ("militant or heroic Śaivism or faith in Śiva") occurred during the eleventh and twelfth centuries. The Śaivite ("Śiva-worshipping") saint Basavanna (ca. 1106–1167) became the movement's acknowledged leader. Basavanna presided over a community of devotees also referred to as *lingāyatas* ("those who wear the *linga*, the symbol of Śiva"). The *lingāyatas* spread their message of faith through their *vachanas* ("sayings" or "utterances").

Preeminent among the *bhakti* poet–saints of the *vachana* tradition is the remarkable woman known as Akka Mahādēvī. The daughter of a devoted Śaiva couple, Akka Mahādēvī was born in the village of Udutadi, India (located today in southern India, in the region of Karnataka near the modern-day village of Shimoga). Around the age of ten, Mahādēvī was introduced to Śiva worship by a local guru, or spiritual teacher. Śiva is the supreme god of *vachana* poems, the "auspicious" deity to whom the poet–saints express their personal devotion.

From the time of her religious initiation, Akka Mahādēvī fully devoted herself to the worship of Śiva, or *Chenna Mallikārjuna*, as Śiva was called in her hometown village temple. In giving her sole love to

Śiva, or *Chenna Mallikārjuna*, Akka Mahādēvī openly rejected the roles society tried to force on her as a woman. One popular account from Akka Mahādēvī's early life relates that Kauśika—a local king, a Jain, and, therefore, a *bhavi* ("nonbeliever")—happened to see her and fell instantly in love with her. He planned to make her his wife; however, as Kauśika was a non-Śaiva, Akka Mahādēvī received his proposal with abhorrence. Accounts vary as to whether or not Kauśika succeeded in making Akka Mahādēvī his wife; however, accounts agree that she ultimately renounced all family and community ties.

Her desire focused instead on leading a life of complete surrender and intense devotion to *Chenna Mallikārjuna*. Embarking on an amazing spiritual journey, Akka Mahādēvī put aside her clothing and, covered only by her hair, traveled through the regions of Karnataka and Andhra. She finally arrived at Basavanna's community of *Vīra-śaiva* saints.

While a younger contemporary of the *Vīraśaiva* saint Basavanna, Akka Mahādēvī was generally held to be fully advanced in her spiritual attainment, an achievement that earned for her the designation of "Akka" ("an elder sister"), which comprises part of her name. Akka Mahādēvī impressed the community's male leaders with her demonstration of faith and with her skill as a poet. They agreed that her devotion often proved to be the equal of, and sometimes even exceeded, that of her teachers.

Akka Mahādēvī soon recommenced her spiritual journey, leaving the community of *Vīraśaiva* saints and traveling north toward Śrīśaila, the Holy Mountain inhabited by her Lord. Once her destination had been reached, she surrendered herself to the contemplation and worship of her Lord.

While many *vachana* writers of Kannada exist, Akka Mahādēvī's work represents an exceptionally high level of poetic achievement. Kannada, a branch of the language family of India known as Dravidian, is distinguished for having one of India's oldest literary traditions. The *vachanas* of the medieval *Vīraśaiva* saints are regarded as constituting some of the most original literary works produced during this long history. The religious content of the *vachanas* has even suggested their comparison, as a type of wisdom literature, with the Hindu Upaniśads.

Attribution of lyrics to a specific poet–saint is fairly easy to assign since the poet includes in each poem an *ankita* ("a signature"), which is the form the poet uses to address the Lord. Akka Mahādēvī's *ankita*—*Chenna Mallikārjuna* (the name by which Śiva was known in

Akka Mahādēvī's hometown village temple)—is often translated as meaning "Lovely Lord White as Jasmine" (Ramanujan), although another rendering has recently been suggested: "Mallika's beautiful Arjuna," with "Cenna" meaning "beautiful" or "lovely" (Tharu and Lalita).

What is known about Akka Mahādēvī's experiences has been necessarily reconstructed from the circumstances surrounding her literary output and from the inferences scholars have drawn from her 350 *vachanas*, which provide insight into her incredible spiritual journey. In her *vachanas*, Akka Mahādēvī characterizes the struggles she personally faced and subsequently overcame. Her quest for ecstasy is both passionate and defiant. Akka Mahādēvī, a strong, unique personality, strove to live a liberated life as a firm believer in and steadfast devotee of Śiva.

Akka Mahādēvī charts her path of devotion in three conventional expressions of love: the agonies of forbidden love, the longings of separated lovers, and the ecstasies of love finally fulfilled. In her guise as wife/lover, Akka Mahādēvī addresses the husband/lover (God) with impassioned outpourings that range from anguish to ecstasy.

Above all, Akka Mahādēvī desired total union with the Divine. According to legend, she prayed for release from her body and from her earthly existence. While still a young girl of around twenty or so, amidst a brilliant flash of light, Akka Mahādēvī is reported as having suddenly vanished, presumably into her desired union with Śiva. Her complete devotion and total surrender to the Lord led her to undertake an incredible spiritual journey. The *Vīraśaiva* saint Akka Mahādēvī commands enormous respect for refusing to abandon her religious beliefs.

BIBLIOGRAPHY

Barnstone, Aliki, and Willis Barnstone, eds. *A Book of Women Poets from Antiquity to Now*. New York: Schocken, 1980.

Ghanananda, Swami, and Sir John Stewart-Wallace, eds. "Akka Mahādēvī." In *Women Saints: East and West*. Hollywood, CA: Vedanta, 1955. 30–40.

Hirshfield, Jane, ed. *Women in Praise of the Sacred: 43 Centuries of Spiritual Poetry by Women*. New York: HarperPerennial, 1994. 77–84.

Ramanujan, A. K., trans. *Speaking of Śiva*. New York: Penguin, 1973.

Tharu, Susie, and K. Lalita, eds. *Women Writing in India: 600 B.C. to the Present*. Vol. 1, *600 B.C. to the Early 20th Century*. New York: The Feminist Press, 1991.

Debra Barrett-Graves

SOFONISBA ANGUISSOLA
(ca. 1532/1535–1625)
Italy
Portrait Painter

Sofonisba Anguissola, the daughter of a provincial Italian nobleman in Cremona, a tributary for the duchy of Milan, achieved fame throughout Europe for her portrait paintings. Sofonisba's portraits, along with her original composition scenes drawn from ordinary life, received international acclaim, as much for their beauty as for their invention.

As a result of the superior education and training that Amilcare Anguissola (ca. 1494–1573) and his second wife, Bianca Ponzoni, provided, their daughters enjoyed a reputation as child marvels. The eldest, Sofonisba, along with her five talented sisters—Elena, Lucia, Minerva, Europa, and Anna Maria—learned to read Latin and to play musical instruments. Amilcare further arranged to provide Sofonisba and her sister Elena with professional painting lessons. Sofonisba's artistic training would eventually enable her to teach three of her younger sisters—Lucia, Europa, and Anna Maria—how to paint as well.

Sofonisba's unusual education isn't the only amazing event of her long life. Most women who gained recognition as artists had relatives who were successful male artists. Sofonisba's father, who was a provincial nobleman and not an artist, took the unusual step of sending two of his daughters to serve an apprenticeship under the instruction of Bernardino Campi (ca. 1522–1592), a local painter associated with the style of Italian art known as Mannerism, a style notable for its rendering of lengthened figures. With encouragement from their father, Sofonisba and Elena trained under Campi for approximately three years (ca. 1546–1549), until Campi moved to Milan in 1549. Sofonisba continued her artistic training with Bernardino Gatti (ca. 1495–1576) for a period of approximately three more years. Through her teachers, Sofonisba had exposure to two significant artistic trends: the controlled, ordered, and balanced compositions that had been

Sofonisba Anguissola, self-portrait. Credit: Alinari/Art Resource, NY. Reprinted with permission.

characteristic of the High Renaissance, and the distorted figures and uncontrolled, agitated, and unbalanced compositions characteristic of Mannerism.

A letter written by Amilcare Anguissola, dated 7 May 1557, establishes an important connection between Sofonisba and *Il divino* Michelangelo di Lodovico Buonarroti Simoni (1475–1564), the famous sculptor, painter, and poet. Michelangelo's praise of Sofonisba's work is acknowledged in another surviving letter, dated 15 May 1558. When Sofonisba spent a two-year sojourn in Rome, she may have even had the opportunity to receive personal advice from the old master Michelangelo.

In response to a suggestion from Michelangelo after he had seen her drawing of a smiling girl, Sofonisba drew an early sketch of a boy being bitten by a crab, which was famous in her own lifetime. Michelangelo's comment that a weeping boy would present a more difficult challenge for the young artist had served as the inspiration for Sofonisba's finished drawing. Sofonisba's sketch earned widespread acclaim, circulating for nearly half a century before eventually providing inspiration for Michelangelo Merisi da Caravaggio's (1573–1610) oil painting entitled *Boy Being Bitten by a Lizard* (ca. 1597).

Sofonisba's contemporaries praised her portraits and her genrelike studies of family members. Sofonisba created numerous self-portraits, making her one of the first Italian artists to specialize in portrait paintings. When Sofonisba began producing her self-portraits, self-portraiture had only been around for about fifty years, after originating with Albrecht Dürer (1471–1528). Sofonisba's output rivals that of Dürer and of Rembrandt van Rijn (1606–1669), artists both famous for self-portrait studies. In her self-portraits, Sofonisba indicates a desire to express herself as a creative, intellectual woman of noble birth. Sofonisba's production of group portraits of her family members constitutes an equally noteworthy achievement. *The Chess Game* (ca. 1555), which depicts three of Sofonisba's sisters gathered at a chess table as their nurse looks on, constitutes an innovative contribution to the emerging category of genre painting.

Sofonisba's fame eventually earned her a prestigious appointment at the court of King Philip II of Spain (ruled 1556–1598). Philip invited Sofonisba to join his court in Madrid as a painter, which she did in 1560. Sofonisba's position as a court painter at the Spanish court holds particular historical significance, since her work may have helped to introduce northern Italian artistic trends into Spain.

An extremely capable portrait artist, Sofonisba earned an international reputation; her contemporaries report that the princes of Europe viewed her portraits with astonishment. During her stay at Philip's court, Pope Pius IV (ruled 1559–1565) asked for and received from Sofonisba a portrait of Philip's third wife, Queen Isabella of Valois. Even the great art historian Giorgio Vasari (1511–1574) paid a personal visit to the Anguissola home in 1566, and his written praise of Sofonisba's skill had the effect of contributing to her fame even further.

In addition to her role as a court painter, Sofonisba had served as a lady-in-waiting to Philip's wife, Queen Isabella, a role that indicates Sofonisba's noble status. The Spanish monarchs certainly regarded Sofonisba as more than a mere craftsman. They bestowed gifts upon the Cremonese artist, enabling Sofonisba to provide her family with financial support.

When Queen Isabella died in October 1568, Sofonisba transferred her former affection for her mistress, whom she had also taught to paint, to Isabella's two young daughters: Isabel Clara Eugenia (b. 1566) and Catalina Micaela (b. 1567). King Philip, in gratitude for Sofonisba's many services, arranged a suitable marriage for her and provided her with a dowry. Around 1570, Sofonisba married a Sicilian lord named Fabrizio de Moncada, and the match took her to Palermo. After Fabrizio unexpectedly died (ca. 1578), Sofonisba met and fell in love with Orazio Lomellini, a ship's captain, whom she married soon thereafter.

The Lomellinis are believed to have made their home in Genoa, where Sofonisba's house served as an active gathering place for artists. Peter Paul Rubens (1577–1640), the future court painter for the Princess Isabel Clara Eugenia, may have paid Sofonisba a visit during her residence in Genoa. The Lomellinis eventually moved their household to Palermo, Sicily, around 1615, where another noteworthy artist visited Sofonisba. Anthony van Dyck's (1599–1641) *Italian Sketchbook* commemorates his 1624 visit with the aged artist; to document his visit, van Dyck included in his sketchbook a drawing of Sofonisba and a written entry.

Sofonisba's remarkable career spanned approximately seven decades, during which time she earned the encouragement and advice of the Renaissance sculptor and architect Michelangelo Buonarroti (*Il divino*), the praise of the art critic Giorgio Vasari and the patronage of the King of Spain, Philip II. Her fame spread throughout Italy and abroad.

Sofonisba Anguissola was the first woman artist of the Renaissance to establish an international reputation, and she is the first female painter in Europe for whom a substantial body of work survives. Unfortunately, a number of the paintings produced by Sofonisba at the Spanish court remain either unsigned or undocumented. A seventeenth-century fire is believed to have destroyed other works Sofonisba executed during her residence at the Spanish court. Sofonisba Anguissola's spectacular career and amazing success as an artist must have certainly proved inspirational for other young Italian women, such as **Lavinia Fontana** (1552–1614).

BIBLIOGRAPHY

Ferino-Pagden, Sylvia, and Maria Kusche. *Sofonisba Anguissola: Renaissance Woman*. Washington, DC: National Museum of Women in the Arts, 1995.

Greer, Germaine. *The Obstacle Race: The Fortunes of Women Painters and Their Work*. New York: Farrar, Straus and Giroux, 1979.

Harris, Ann Sutherland, and Linda Nochlin. *Women Artists: 1550–1950*. New York: Knopf, 1981.

Heller, Nancy G. *Women Artists: An Illustrated History.* New York: Abbeville, 1987.
Perlingieri, Ilya Sandra. *Sofonisba Anguissola: The First Great Woman Artist of the Renaissance.* New York: Rizzoli, 1992.

Debra Barrett-Graves

ANNE ASKEW
(1521–1546)
Britain
Protestant Martyr

Anne Askew, burned as a heretic in the reign of the English king Henry VIII, was a woman of exceptional bravery. She was also forthright and articulate and had the foresight to keep a record of her travails as a testament to her faith, although today we do not know how much of what was posthumously published were Anne's actual words. Anne was well born and well educated; she was the daughter of Sir William Askew of Stallingborough, near Grimsby in Lincolnshire. Anne had two sisters as well as several brothers. Sir William insisted that his daughters be educated as well as his sons. He possibly brought a tutor into the house for his daughters, and they could read and write English and perhaps also Latin. Anne spent her early years studying the Bible, particularly William Tyndale's translation of the New Testament, and she had clearly defined Protestant beliefs.

Henry had been a conventional Catholic and England a Catholic realm until the Pope had refused to grant Henry a divorce from his first wife, Catherine of Aragon. In 1533 Parliament had declared the English Church separate and Henry the Supreme Head of the Church. By the late 1530s there had been a redistribution of Church land and the printing of 8,500 English Bibles so that every parish church could be so equipped. But the resistance of many of the English people to the Protestant Reformation, and Henry VIII's natural religious conservatism, led to the Act of the Six Articles in 1539, which halted the legal spread of Protestant teachings. Although the Church of England was independent from the Catholic Church with Henry VIII as Supreme Head, the 1539 act made Roman Catholic doctrine, such as transubstantiation, the legal law of the land. But by 1539 Anne Askew was already a committed Protestant who passionately believed that one took the Eucharist as a remembrance of Christ's death, that the bread remained bread, a denial of transubstantiation. Anne was also convinced as a good Protestant that Scrip-

The burning of Anne Askew. From John Foxe, *Acts and Monuments* (London: Company of Stationers, 1684). Reprinted by permission of the University Libraries of the University of Nebraska-Lincoln.

tures, not church councils, were the only real authority on any matters of faith, including the Sacraments. The 1543 Act for the Advancement of True Religion, making vivid distinctions of class and gender, forbade all women and men below the class of yeomen from reading the Bible publicly and allowed only upper-class men and noblewomen and gentlewomen to read it privately to themselves only—not aloud to others. Askew's public reading of the Bible was in defiance of what she would perceive as an unjust and unchristian law.

Anne's older sister Martha was betrothed to a local farmer, Thomas Kyme, whose father owned extensive lands, and on her sister's death in 1539, Anne's father insisted that she marry Kyme instead. It was a disastrously unhappy marriage. Kyme was appalled by his wife's beliefs, her conflicts with priests, and her refusal to be silenced. The priests were outraged that Kyme could not keep his wife from going about the community reading the Bible and talking about her beliefs. Despite the couple having two children, Kyme finally threw Anne out, and she went back to her brother's house. Eventually Kyme reconsidered and asked his brother-in-law to send Anne back. She, however, had other ideas. She argued that St. Paul (First Epistle to the Corinthians) stated that a woman had the right to depart from an unbelieving husband if he refused to live with her. According to Askew, Kyme was not a true Christian, and thus her marriage was invalid. Anne never referred to herself by the name of Kyme but always signed any documents "Anne Askew," which was unusual enough to draw the attention of both detractors and sympathizers. In 1544 Anne sought a divorce from Kyme at the bishop's court in Lincoln. When she lost her case there, Anne left Lincolnshire to seek an annulment from her marriage from the Court of Chancery and a community of the faithful in London. Anne found her community, and through John Lascelles, a lawyer and reformer who had ties at court and who would later be burned with her, she gained introduction to some of the women who surrounded Henry VIII's sixth wife, Katherine Parr, who was also sympathetic to reformed ideas.

In 1545 her outspoken denial of transubstantiation led to her arrest and an examination for heresy, but her elusive answers to the questions placed made it difficult to condemn her. Edmund Bonner, Bishop of London, attempted to force her to sign a confession and recantation, and he was infuriated by her refusal. The intervention of several influential friends finally led to her freedom. Anne apparently began to keep records of her examinations as a way to bear witness to her faith; these were eventually to be published after her death. In her examinations the Bishop of London's Chancellor challenged Anne about speaking out about her beliefs. Didn't St. Paul forbid women to speak, she was asked? Anne replied that Paul had meant women could not preach and asked in turn how many women he had seen go into the pulpit and preach. When he admitted he had never seen one, Anne scolded him that he should find no fault in women who had not broken the law. Anne was rearrested the following year and examined by the King's Council at Greenwich and subsequently at the London Guildhall. When she refused to recant, she was convicted of heresy and condemned to death. She was then moved from Newgate prison to the Tower of London for further questioning.

In 1546 it was clear to those at court that King Henry's health was failing, and the conservative faction at court was in a desperate power struggle with those of reformed leanings. Lord Chancellor Thomas Wriothesley, Bishop of Winchester Stephen Gardiner, and Solicitor

General Richard Rich attempted to force Anne to incriminate Protestant ladies at court, such as **Catherine, Duchess of Suffolk**; Anne,
Countess of Hereford, wife of Edward Seymour and head of the reformed faction; and Lady Joan Denny, wife of Sir Anthony Denny,
an ally of Seymour. Also at risk was Henry VIII's wife, Katherine
Parr, since she was a supporter of reformed beliefs. To try and force
her to implicate others, Anne was placed on the rack, an instrument
of torture that pulled her limbs apart. When the Lieutenant of the
Tower refused to continuing racking her because of her weakness and
pain, and his horror in racking a woman of her status, Wriothesley
and Rich continued the torture themselves, but despite the pain,
Anne refused to incriminate others. While Wriothesley and Rich
hoped to use Anne to bring down the opposition, Anne brilliantly
defended her beliefs and frequently used her gender to frame her
responses. She called herself a "weak" woman to discomfort her in-
terrogators. Her later editor John Bale implies this was a rhetorical
tool. Although gentle with those of the true faith, to the enemies of
truth Anne was "scornful" and "high stomached" (Beilin 1996, 11,
12).

Anne absolutely refused to recant or to name anyone else. She was
also convinced that she was racked without the king's knowledge and
held to the belief that Henry was a just king but misled by his coun-
cillors. She was so badly injured by the torture that she had to be
carried to the stake at Smithfield, where heretics were executed. At
the order of Henry's Council, she was burned on 16 July 1546 with
John Lascelles, John Hemley, a priest, and John Hadlam, a tailor,
three men who had been arraigned with her. According to martyr-
ologist John Foxe, Askew's constancy was a bracing example for the
three men condemned to die with her (Beilin 1996, 192). Nicholas
Shaxton preached at the event, and even though she was about to be
burned, Anne criticized Shaxton's sermon. Also attending were the
Duke of Norfolk, Thomas Wriothesley, other nobles from the court,
members of the King's Council, the Lord Mayor, and aldermen of
the city of London. The king whom she had refused to blame was
to die in his bed only six months later.

Less than a year after her death, Anne's brilliant answers to her
examinations were publicized early in the reign of Henry's son Edward by the Protestant polemicist John Bale. He edited and published
her writings, which were Askew's chronological accounts of her examinations and imprisonments, together with supporting documents

and letters that had apparently been smuggled out of prison. Anne's words were available to an even wider audience in the Elizabethan period because of her place of honor as one of the martyrs in John Foxe's *Acts and Monuments*. She was a woman of undaunted courage and a great inspiration to other Protestants.

BIBLIOGRAPHY

Beilin, Elaine V. "Anne Askew's Self-Portrait in the *Examinations*." In Margaret P. Hannay, ed., *Silent But for the Word: Tudor Women as Patrons, Translators, and Writers of Religious Works*. Kent, OH: Kent State University Press, 1985. 77–91.

Beilin, Elaine V., ed. *The Examinations of Anne Askew*. Oxford: Oxford University Press, 1996.

Wilson, Derek. *A Tudor Tapestry: Men, Women and Society in Reformation England*. Pittsburgh: University of Pittsburgh Press, 1973.

Carole Levin

ELIZABETH BARTON

(ca. 1506–1534)

Britain
Visionary and Martyr

Elizabeth Barton was a servant in the household of Thomas Cobb, steward of estates near the village of Aldington owned by William Warham, Archbishop of Canterbury. When she was about sixteen years old, Elizabeth claimed to have experienced visions during an illness in which she communicated with the Virgin. Her pastor, Father Richard Masters, supported her claims and reported the events to the Archbishop. Warham established a commission of inquiry into the matter, and Benedictine monk Dr. Edward Bocking headed the commission and reported back favorably. As a result, Elizabeth entered the Benedictine convent at Saint Sepulchre convent near Canterbury. All of this occurred before the end of 1526, and Elizabeth spent the next eight years at the nunnery, experiencing mystical trances and special revelations. She was highly and respectfully regarded by eminent Renaissance figures such as Sir Thomas More, Bishop John Fisher of Rochester, and Warham.

England before the Reformation was a society where the popularity of religious cults, shrines, and holy men and women cannot be overestimated. As a nun at Saint Sepulchre's, Elizabeth Barton exercised what amounted to a female ministry, preaching and calling sinners to penance and, in some cases, recalling in detail the particular sins of those who approached her. Such visionary figures were not altogether unusual in sixteenth-century Europe, and their importance was not diminished during the early stages of the Protestant Reformation.

Elizabeth is recalled today because of her utterances on the subject of King Henry VIII's marital affairs; had her prophecies not turned to politics, there is little doubt that she would have been left in peace. When Henry first indicated doubts about the validity of his marriage to Catherine of Aragon in 1527, Elizabeth voiced her opposition to Henry's position. She was by no means alone in this respect; indeed, the king had consulted a number of public authorities and professed to have an open mind on the matter. A wide range of scholars in England and on the Continent had been actively solicited by the government for comment on the issue. Elizabeth's reputation as a "holy nun" with special access to divine intentions had grown enormously in the two years since her initial claims were made, and after a meeting with the king's chancellor, Cardinal Thomas Wolsey, Elizabeth was granted an audience with the monarch. Here she spoke against the effort to end the royal marriage to Queen Catherine and predicted ruin should Henry continue in his efforts to secure a papal annulment of his marriage. Not content simply to rebuke the monarch, Elizabeth also threatened Pope Clement VII with divine punishment if he acquiesced in the king's call for an annulment.

Elizabeth was not punished for her strident views until 1533. Indeed, the king's pursuit of a divorce was widely unpopular, and women in particular sympathized with the situation of Queen Catherine of Aragon, who had been a faithful wife for over twenty years. When two royal emissaries were sent to Oxford in 1530 in order to win support from academics for the king's position, they were pelted with rubbish by the women of the town. But by mid-1533 the king had already undertaken a full-scale assault upon the Roman Catholic Church in England and was now facing the prospect of excommunication by Pope Clement.

Elizabeth was moving in a bold and dangerous direction, prophesying that if the king married another woman, he would lose his throne in a matter of months and die a villain's death for his sin. It appears that Bocking was by this time using the popular visionary to forward his own and others' opposition to the king's divorce. Thomas Cromwell was now the king's principal adviser, and Thomas Cranmer was the new Archbishop of Canterbury. Both men were wary of anyone who dissented from what was accomplished fact by the summer of 1533: Henry's marriage to Anne Boleyn and England's separation from the Roman Catholic Church. Elizabeth was examined by agents of the Crown in July 1533, and in November, she was arrested and removed to the Tower of London. She was then examined by the King's Council together with a number of royal judges and bishops.

While held in the Tower, Elizabeth was subjected to repeated interrogation, bullying, and threats, and it was reported by supporters of the king that she "confessed" to the imaginary nature of her revelations. At this same time, all copies of an account of her early life, together with writings about her by her supporters, were seized and destroyed. The king wanted the nun and her supporters condemned as traitors and heretics, but for the moment, they were allowed to languish in prison. Sermons were preached pouring ridicule on Barton and those who had encouraged her, and on 23 November 1533 Elizabeth and a number of her closest supporters were brought to a scaffold at St. Paul's Cross, London, and subjected to public ridicule.

Finally, Elizabeth, Bocking, and five others were convicted of high treason—without trial at common law. Bishop Fisher and Thomas More were also implicated in the treason, although their fate hinged on additional charges. On 21 April 1534, Elizabeth Barton, aged twenty-eight, was hanged at Tyburn along with Dr. Bocking. They were the first victims of the Henrican Reformation, obvious targets of a government fearful lest charismatic figures rally popular and widespread opposition to the government on a highly controversial issue. The year after Barton's death Fisher and More were also executed. The example of the peasant visionary Joan of Arc could not have been lost on the government. With Elizabeth's "confession" that her prophecies were fraudulent, Henry's government could better secure the consent of the nation for the break with Rome.

BIBLIOGRAPHY

Knowles, David. *The Religious Orders in England*. Cambridge: Cambridge University Press, 1961.

Rex, Richard. *Henry VIII and the English Reformation*. New York: St. Martin's Press, 1993.

Scarisbrick, J. J. *Henry VIII*. Berkeley: University of California Press, 1968.

W. M. Spellman

BLANCHE OF CASTILE
(1188–1252)
Spain
Queen, Ruler, and Religious Activist

One of the most influential women in thirteenth-century Europe, and the de facto ruler of France from 1226 until her death in 1252, Blanche of Castile (in Spain) was the daughter of Alfonso of Castile and Eleanor of England. As granddaughter to Eleanor of Aquitaine and King Henry II of England, Blanche was an attractive prize in the complicated diplomatic relations between England and France at the close of the twelfth century. In the year 1200, Blanche's uncle, King John of England, entered into an agreement with the Capetian King Philip Augustus of France whereby Louis, the heir to the French throne, would marry the daughter of Alfonso and Eleanor. At the age of eighty, the indomitable Eleanor of Aquitaine was sent to the Castilian court in Spain to retrieve her twelve-year-old granddaughter and now bride-to-be. The two women traveled back to France together in what was to be the last public act of one of the most powerful women of the twelfth century. Blanche, destined to become an important political figure in her own right, married Louis of France (later Louis VIII) on 23 May 1200 in a church located just inside the boundaries of the English possessions in Normandy.

The arranged marriage between thirteen-year-old Prince Louis and twelve-year-old Blanche was by all accounts a happy one. There were a total of twelve children born to the royal couple during a twenty-six-year marriage, but seven were to precede their father to the grave. Included among the dead was the eldest son and heir apparent Philip. The line of succession thus passed to the future "Most Christian King of France" (St. Louis IX). With the sudden death in 1226 of her forty-year-old husband after a brief three-year reign, Blanche became regent for her young son. The elevation of a woman to the position of regent for twelve-year-old Louis IX was an unprecedented action but is testimony to the close relationship between Louis VIII and his wife. The king had named her in his will as guide and adviser to their

Blanche of Castile and Louis IX, King of France (top); author dictating to a scribe (bottom). Moralized Bible, France, ca. 1230, M.240, F.8. Credit: The Pierpont Morgan Library/Art Resource, NY. Reprinted with permission.

oldest surviving son, and Blanche was determined to secure the throne for the young king. For years she had instilled in her children a deep sense of piety and respect for the secular virtues of justice and peace. And while this intensely devout woman had not taken an active role in affairs of state during her husband's reign, she quickly emerged as the leading political figure at her son's court.

It was an unenviable assignment. The prerogatives of the monarch over the feudal aristocracy had only recently been asserted in France, and now an opportunity presented itself for the fractious barons to reassert their feudal rights. King Philip Augustus (1180–1222) had spent the bulk of his long reign attempting to curb the autonomy of his leading vassals while simultaneously extending the royal domain, and his work of royal centralization was now put into jeopardy by the emergence of a woman ruler. The penchant for aristocratic localism and independence was still very strong in France, and it was essential for the well-being of the monarchy that Blanche and her advisers successfully build upon the work of her husband and father-in-law. In addition to internal dangers, Blanche's cousin, King Henry III of England, was now eager to reclaim some of the lands in France lost by his father King John.

The queen quickly arranged for the coronation of her son at Rheims Cathedral before potential opposition could gain momentum. Once crowned and anointed with the holy oils, symbolic of divine approval, the king's mother set about preempting the nobles by making generous gifts of land and money to loyal supporters. Disgruntled opponents of the Crown absented themselves from the coronation and attempted to engender antiforeign sentiment against the regent, and accusations of an illicit relationship between Blanche and a young courtier were made. But the Spanish-born queen retained the support of the majority of the barons, and perhaps most important, she secured and held the endorsement of the papacy for her actions as regent. Plots and regional revolts against the boy king continued until 1231, but on each occasion, the queen was able to raise an army and rally the majority of the barons to the Capetian dynasty. During these years, the queen successfully organized military campaigns against internal rebels in the north, south, and west, and against an invasion by Henry III of England, and effectively reasserted the power of the Crown throughout most of the kingdom.

Although Queen Blanche received the blessing of the Church in her struggles against baronial opponents of the Crown, she did not relax any of the royal claims with respect to the power of ecclesiastical lords in France. In particular, Blanche refused to permit any intrusion by religious authorities into the affairs of state. The most troublesome way in which Church authorities attempted to influence Crown policy was through the spiritual weapons of excommunication and interdict. The first excluded a person from the sacraments and services of the Church (outside of which there was to be found no salvation), whereas the second denied Church services in particular localities. Church leaders insisted that the Crown enforce these ecclesiastical censures whenever they were imposed by religious authorities, but Queen Blanche was disturbed by their use against individuals in the employ and service of the Crown. In short, the queen opposed the use of temporal coercive power to enforce Church decisions, especially when excommunication was used as a weapon against royal officials. Intermittent conflict between Church and state over this issue continued throughout the queen's lifetime.

Blanche also engaged in a protracted struggle with the students and masters at the University of Paris. The university had been founded in the capital during the second half of the twelfth century, and by the 1220s, the institution had become an important part of the cultural, economic, and intellectual life of the city. University authorities were keen to preserve their autonomy from Crown interference, but when riotous students took to the streets in 1229 for a holiday celebration, the fighting and destruction of property in the suburb of St. Marcel triggered a swift and harsh response by the queen's government. Soldiers were sent in to end the rioting, and when some scholars were killed in the ensuing clashes, the masters of the university closed down all lectures and dispersed the students—and lecturers—to other cities. King Henry III of England even offered inducements to the students and masters if they would relocate to Oxford. It was not until 1231, after more than two years of mutual recriminations, that the masters and students returned to Paris. Although Blanche did not oppose the growth of the university at Paris, her first concern was always with religious foundations and especially the Cistercian monastic order, which was dedicated to reviving the original Benedictine rule. Her bequests to a new Cistercian foundation at Royaumont, for example, resulted in the construction of one of the largest religious houses in thirteenth-century France.

Blanche remained a virtual co-ruler of France even after King Louis married thirteen-year-old Marguerite of Provence in 1234. Although she had several houses in the capital city, she spent most of her time at court, where she maintained her own household staff. From the point of the king's marriage until 1248, the dowager queen remained a key adviser to her son, accompanying him on his travels and even serving another term as regent from 1248 until 1252 while Louis was on religious crusade. The dowager queen was now in her sixties. During these four years, she once again asserted Crown authority over the Church in France, quarreling with the religious authorities at Notre Dame Cathedral over their right to tax peasants who worked on Church-controlled lands and even expressing disappointment at Pope Innocent IV's lackluster support for the crusade that had engaged her son. Just before she died in 1252, and two years before her son the king returned from crusade, Blanche put on the habit of a nun and joined the Cistercian order. The Cistercians sought to revive the original ideals of the Benedictine rule, living far from centers of population and dedicating themselves to a life of work on behalf of the church and prayer. Never eager to assume political power for her own private ambitions, the queen had cultivated in her children the same virtues. The fact that one of her sons was canonized, another daughter beatified, and she herself held viewed as a strong defender of the royal prerogative enhanced the collective reputation of the Capetian dynasty in France. Although never monarch in her own right, her work assured the stability of the monarchical principle in France for centuries to come.

BIBLIOGRAPHY

Fawtier, Robert. *The Capetian Kings of France: Monarchy and Nation, 987–1328.* Trans. Lionel Butler. New York: St. Martin's Press, 1960. 28–29.

Gies, Frances, and Joseph Gies. *Women in the Middle Ages.* New York: Crowell, 1978. 97–119.

Labarge, Margaret Wade. *Saint Louis: Most Christian King of France.* Boston: Little, Brown, 1968. 22–60.

Pernoud, Regine. *Blanche of Castile.* Trans. Henry Noel. New York: Coward, McCann & Geoghegan, 1975.

W. M. Spellman

BRIDGET OF SWEDEN
(1303–1373)
Sweden
Visionary, Prophet, and Pilgrim

It is true that the ideas and writings of visionaries and prophets frequently endure well beyond the facts of these individuals' own lives. Often the visionary's voice tends to be all that remains. Therefore, it is also unique that many of the facts of Bridget's life are known. What survives today is a detailed record of the life of a visionary and the ideas that guided her.

Bridget was born in the Upland, Finsta, a province of Sweden, in 1303. Her parents were Birger Persson, governor of Upland, and his second wife, Ingeborg, both of whom were connected with the royal line in Sweden. After her mother's death in 1310, Bridget was raised by her aunt, and at the age of seven, she experienced her first vision; she saw herself crowned by the Virgin Mary, her commission to a prophetic life.

Bridget, however, did not live a solitary life behind the cloistered walls of a nunnery as did many mystics of her time. Despite Bridget's desire to live a chaste life, her parents convinced her to marry, and she consented. In 1316, at the age of thirteen, she married Ulf Gudmarson, a nobleman who was trained in the law. Little information survives about Bridget's own education, but because of her lineage, she was a member of the royal household and helped with the education of King Magnus of Sweden and his bride Queen Blanche. Throughout her life, she also assumed roles in addition to those of visionary and prophet: She was an educator, wife, mother, and ultimately widow. She devoted her life to combining these separate roles into one acceptable idea of womanhood. Being a visionary did not deny her any of these other identities. At Bridget's request, she and her husband took a two-year vow of chastity. After two years she rethought her role in the marriage, and they subsequently had eight children.

Gudmarson was devoted to his wife's beliefs and joined her on an early pilgrimage to Santiago de Compostela. During their life together, Bridget was committed to her marriage and her faith; however, after Gudmarson's death in 1344, she rededicated herself to her spiritual life by entering a religious house at Alvastra. In a vision, she received a mandate to found her own religious order that was to be named the Ordo Sanctissimi Salvatoris (The Order of the Holy Savior), also known as the Brigittine Order. Her connection with the Swedish monarchy now benefited Bridget because in 1346 Magnus and Blanche donated their castle at Vadstena for her nunnery. Bridget's philosophy behind establishing her convent was simple: "per mulieres primum et principaliter" (for women first and principally). According to Bridget's *Rule of the Order of the Holy Savior*, the nuns of her order were to be widows whose vows of extreme poverty prevented them from owning any possessions. Their lives were strictly cloistered within the walls of the convent.

Despite her *Rule*, Bridget's life was not to be cloistered: She traveled far more than most women during this period. Through her visionary experiences, she was often commanded to undertake pilgrimages and obediently obeyed Christ's command. She traveled to sacred sites throughout Spain, France, Germany, Holland, Denmark, Norway, Sweden, Italy, and the Holy Land. Pilgrims, in visiting the Holy Land, would "walk" where Christ had. For Bridget, the experience was much more visually intense and personal; she witnessed, in her visions, the Passion and Crucifixion of Christ while visiting the holy cities of Jerusalem and Bethlehem.

Bridget's visions went beyond a visual experience of biblical events; they eventually became prophetic. In 1346 she experienced a vision in which Christ commanded her to leave Sweden for Rome. Once there she acted as a conduit for Christ and had the ecclesiastics more available to her. Bridget's prophesies received an unusually large degree of acceptance. In 1345, she proclaimed that Christ in the years to come would inflict a disaster to punish the sins of his people. When the plague, also called the Black Death, struck two years later, many of her contemporaries argued that she had accurately predicted this disease. Yet some of her other visions were not fulfilled during her lifetime. Another vision of Christ instructed her to travel to Rome in 1350 with the mission of bringing together the Pope and the emperor. She was not successful: Neither her many persistent letters to secular and religious leaders nor her visionary prophesies could return the Pope to Rome or bring about the end of the Hundred Years War.

Many of Bridget's visions confirmed her self-appointed role as Christ's voice in the world; she claimed that she could discern good and evil spirits. During this period, a woman acting as a visionary risked serious accusations and even death if it was believed that she spoke for the devil and not Christ. Bridget, in her early visions, clearly defined her visionary experience as sanctioned by Christ. This authority, complemented by the fact that her views supported the Church hierarchy, gave her more freedom to express her beliefs. Although she held no recognized authority from the Pope, her beliefs were popular not only with the ecclesiastics but with the lay people as well. Bridget, while advocating Pope Clement VI's return from Avignon to Rome, still recognized the supreme authority of the Pope and the Church. She also worked to have her Order officially recognized by the Church. The Church denied her request because the Lateran Council of 1215, a Church Council called by Pope Innocent III, strictly forbade the founding of new orders. Neither the Pope's return to Rome nor the Church's approval of her Order were realized until after her death in 1373.

However, Bridget was successful in her promotion of Church indulgences. At a time when the Church needed more money to sustain itself, she was a strong proponent of indulgences, a freedom from penance for the sins committed by laypeople as well as souls in purgatory. These indulgences came with a price that the Church could exact from anyone willing to pay. Because Bridget witnessed tormented souls begging for salvation in many of her visions, she believed indulgences shortened the time of the souls' torment in purgatory.

Bridget's visions were recorded in her eight-volume book *Revelations*. These revelations were most often messages dictated to her by Christ and the Virgin Mary. Bridget either wrote or possibly dictated her visions in Swedish; subsequently, they were translated into Latin by several of her male confessors: Mathias, her tutor and a Dominican canon; Petrus Olai of Skenninge; Prior Petrus Olai of Alvastra; and Alfonso of Jaén, a bishop of Spain. In addition to her *Revelations*, Bridget also wrote the *Rule of the Order of the Holy Savior*, the doctrine of the Brigittines; the *Sermo Angelicus* (*Conversations with the Angel*), revelations that an angel dictated to her; and finally the *Cantus Sororum* (*The Sisters' Songs*), the offices to be sung by her nuns. With these texts, Bridget accomplished what many women were never able to do: She voiced her religious ideas through her writings.

With Bridget's death in 1373, her popularity seemed to increase. Her Order grew and developed to include both a male and female religious community. Bridget had lived the remainder of her life in Rome, but in the year following her death, Catherine, one of her daughters, along with Petrus Olai, returned her body to Vadstena. Because of her spiritual renown and the circulated stories about her mystical healings, Bridget's arm bone was given as a holy relic to the nuns at Panisperna. At this same time, her texts were widely distributed in manuscript, and eventually her works were translated into the vernacular.

Because of Bridget's orthodox visions and writings, the process of canonization began almost immediately after her death, and in 1391, she was recognized as a saint of the Catholic Church. As a visionary, prophet, pilgrim, wife, mother, widow, and writer, Bridget wielded a great deal of influence with ecclesiastics, laypersons, and secular leaders of her time. She stands today as a remarkable example of what it means to be "a woman, first and principally" and to succeed at a time when it was nearly impossible for a woman to be heard or remembered.

BIBLIOGRAPHY

Holloway, Julia Bolton. *Saint Bride and Her Book: Birgitta of Sweden's Revelations.* Newburyport, MA: Focus Text, 1992.

Shahar, Shulamith. *The Fourth Estate: A History of Women in the Middle Ages.* London: Methuen, 1983.

Voaden, Rosalynn. *God's Words, Women's Voices: The Discernment of Spirits in the Writings of Late Medieval Women Visionaries.* Suffolk, UK; Rochester, NY: York Medieval Press, 1999.

Wilson, Katharina M. *Medieval Women Writers.* Athens: University of Georgia Press, 1984.

Stephanie Witham

ELIZABETH CARY
Lady Falkland
(ca. 1585–1639)
Britain
Author

Elizabeth Tanfield Cary is associated with a number of "firsts" in the history of English women writers. She is perhaps best known for her play *The Tragedy of Mariam, the Fair Queen of Jewry* (1613), the earliest surviving female-authored drama published in England. She is the first woman to be the subject of a biography written by a woman: *Lady Falkland Her Life* was the work of one or more of Cary's daughters, composed after their mother's death. There is increasing agreement among scholars that Elizabeth Cary is the author of a history of King Edward II, and if so, *The Life, Reign, and Death of Edward II* (1627, pub. 1680) is the first prose history by an English woman. According to *Her Life*, Cary also wrote a work of religious controversy in reply to her son, Lucius; this is an extraordinary move on Cary's part, because early modern women were discouraged even from reading arguments about theological matters.

Thanks to *Her Life*, we know more details about Cary than about many early modern figures, including Shakespeare. Written by one or more of her daughters (perhaps in collaboration), who were nuns in a French convent together, the biography emphasizes Cary's spiritual life, particularly her 1626 conversion to Catholicism. This was a controversial decision in Protestant England where religious beliefs and political loyalty were inextricably connected, and the impact on Cary's domestic life was severe. *Her Life* does not mention, for instance, that Cary received public acclaim for her learning and writing, notably her two plays. The poet Michael Drayton praised Cary's intellectual talents when dedicating two poems to her, and Sir John Davies, another well-known literary figure, complimented her plays in his verse and urged her to print them. It is important to remember as well that *Her Life* is a biography of a mother by her daughter(s) and that

Elizabeth Cary, Lady Falkland, by T. Athow from a painting by Paul Van Somer. Sutherland Collection, Civ. 20. Copyright Ashmolean Museum, Oxford. Reproduced by permission of the Ashmolean.

this personal relationship also has shaped the narrative. That said, *Her Life* provides important information about Cary's life and a seventeenth-century view of an extraordinary mother. Modern readers can explore for themselves the fascinating, familial dynamics at work in the biography.

The portrait it draws of Elizabeth Cary is quite remarkable. An only child, she grew up at Burford Priory in Oxfordshire. *Her Life* states that she taught herself French, Spanish, Italian, Latin, and Hebrew at a young age, translating Seneca's epistles and Abraham Ortelius's geography from Latin before her marriage. An avid reader, she gained considerable knowledge of poetry in both classical and modern languages and read numerous histories by Greek, Roman, and English authors, as well as many works of moral and natural philosophy. Her father seems to have encouraged her reading, at one point giving her Protestant reformer John Calvin's *Institutes* to read; according to the biography, the twelve-year-old Cary made numerous objections to Calvin's arguments. Her mother, however, was not sympathetic to her daughter's intellectual interests, and, to prevent her reading at night, she forbade servants to give Cary candles. Cary read anyway, promising to pay for the candles they brought to her in secret. She

owed and paid several hundred pounds to these servants on her wedding day. True or not, such stories present Cary as a woman with an
exceptional facility with languages and an early, abiding interest in
questions of religion.

In 1602, she was married to Sir Henry Cary; this match, arranged
by the parents, was apparently neither happy nor affectionate. The
author of *Her Life* remarks that her father married Elizabeth because
she was an heiress, and indeed, both families benefited from the marriage. Lawrence Tanfield, Cary's father, was a wealthy judge; his
money enhanced the fortunes of Sir Henry and his family, whereas
the Tanfields gained an aristocratic connection. For the first few years
of marriage, Cary remained at her family's home, while her husband
stayed at court or abroad. Later, Henry's mother summoned Elizabeth to live with her, even though Henry was content to have his
wife remain where she wanted. The two women evidently did not get
along; *Her Life* describes Lady Paget as desiring to be served and
humored, and it claims that when Cary did not please her, she confined Cary to her room and took away her books. In 1606, Henry
returned from the Low Countries, where he had been captured while
fighting against Spain, and the couple established a residence together.

Although the early years of the marriage were childless, nine of
their children survived into adulthood. The second, Lucius, became
a prominent intellectual, known for his religious toleration and
broadmindedness; in 1643, he died in battle defending Charles I during the English civil war. Sometime between her marriage and the
birth of her first child, Catherine, in 1609, Cary probably wrote *The
Tragedy of Mariam* (not mentioned in the biography) as well as a
play about Tamburlaine, presently lost. The Mariam play circulated
in manuscript before its printing and may have influenced Shakespeare's *Othello*. Drawing on Josephus's historical account in *Antiquities of the Jews*, Cary's play depicts the execution of Mariam, Herod's
beautiful, outspoken wife, who is wrongly accused of adultery. Scholars and readers generally agree that the play seriously questions early
modern prescriptions to wives to conform their thoughts, emotions,
and desires to their husbands' wishes.

Elizabeth seems to have tried to be a model wife, though her interests ran more toward ideas than fashion. One memorable passage
in *Her Life* describes Cary's attempts to accommodate both her husband's desires and her own; as she walks around her room, deep in

thought, her servants trail after her, trying to dress her properly. She would read or write while they fixed her hair and clothes. Although terrified, Elizabeth rode horses to please Henry and practiced needlework because it was expected of her. The biography remarks that (like a dutiful wife) she bent her will to her husband's and put his desires first, except where religion and her duty to God were concerned.

From an early point in her marriage, Cary was interested in Catholicism. She read works by both Catholic church fathers and Protestant divines and discussed theology with several high-ranking Anglican clergymen. Although proper religious reading for women included works of piety and devotion, Cary read works of religious controversy, including all by the Catholic Thomas More and much by Protestants Martin Luther, John Calvin, Hugh Latimer, and John Jewell—in the words of the biography, "most that has been written" by English and French writers, both Catholic and Protestant. At times, she refused to attend Anglican church services, as required by law. Her last daughter, Mary, was named for the Virgin Mary.

Meanwhile, Henry Cary pursued a successful career at the court of James I, becoming a protégé of the influential Duke of Buckingham. In 1622, Henry Cary, now Lord Falkland, became Lord Deputy of Ireland, charged with ensuring the political and religious conformity of Irish Catholics to English Anglican rule. Elizabeth accompanied her husband to Ireland, where she attempted to learn Gaelic to read the Irish Bible and set up a program to teach Irish children useful trades, which unfortunately was not a success. Some critics suggest that Elizabeth's experiences in Ireland, particularly her exposure to Catholic residents and their severe persecution, may have accelerated the breakdown of the Cary marriage. They probably increased her Catholic sympathies, if not her resolution to convert. She returned to England in 1625, while her husband remained in Ireland.

In 1626, Cary did convert to Catholicism. When her conversion became public, prominent courtiers and even Charles I pressured her to recant. The king ordered her confined to her residence for six weeks. During this time, her mother refused to assist her in any way or to allow Cary to live with her, as Henry desired his wife to do. He wrote scathing letters from Ireland that denounced his wife to the king and influential court figures. Furious, Henry cut off all financial support to Elizabeth, had the contents of the house removed, and the children taken away from her. Cary, in turn, wrote letters that defended her decision and asked not to be sent to her mother but to receive some allowance from Henry to cover food, clothes, and other necessary expenses. Destitute, Cary and her only remaining servant, Bessie Poulter (who also converted), survived with the help of friends and fellow Catholics. After months of lobbying by Elizabeth's supporters, including the Duke of Buckingham's wife and other powerful women, the Privy Council ordered Henry to pay his wife an annual allowance, but Elizabeth never enforced the order. Instead, she occupied a series of small houses where she lived without a stable income for the rest of her life, in conditions exacerbated by her apparent inability to handle money. In the years following her conversion, Cary wrote her history of Edward II, an elegy on the Duke of Buckingham, many lives of female saints in verse, and other religious poems. She also translated a work of religious controversy by the French Cardinal du Perron, which she dedicated to Charles I's wife, Queen Henrietta Maria, herself a Catholic. Cary's preface comments ironically on the need of university students (all of whom were men) for an English translation. Printed on the Continent by a Catholic press in 1630, most copies of Cary's translation were burned upon arrival in England.

Henry and Elizabeth may have reconciled shortly before his death in 1633. Afterwards, she was able to have some of her children live with her, at least for brief periods of time when she had sufficient resources to support them. Cary's home was frequented by Anglican clergy, Catholic priests, university students, and others who valued intellectual discussions of religious issues. Four of her daughters (Mary, Anne, Elizabeth, and Lucy) eventually converted to Catholicism and joined a convent in Lille, France. Another daughter, Victoria, served as a maid of honor to Queen Henrietta Maria. Her two youngest sons (Patrick and Placid) lived for a time with their brother Lucius, who was a friend of Protestant writer William Chillingworth. Deeply distrustful of Chillingworth and concerned for her sons' spiritual welfare, Cary engineered their abduction from Lucius's home and sent them abroad, illegally, for Catholic training. As he had for many years, Lucius provided for his mother and siblings, although relations between them were strained by this last episode. Near the end of her life, she began to translate the works of the Flemish mystic Louis de Blois; a manuscript copy was discovered recently. Cary died in 1639 of a respiratory illness and was buried in Queen Henrietta Maria's chapel. Her spiritual devotion and integrity led her to act in ways contrary to those prescribed for women of her time and to write works that weigh the competing demands of obedience and personal freedom.

BIBLIOGRAPHY

Cerasano, S. P., and Marion Wynne-Davies, eds. *Renaissance Drama by Women: Texts and Documents*. London: Routledge, 1996.
Weller, Barry, and Margaret Ferguson, eds. *The Tragedy of Mariam, the Fair Queen of Jewry with The Lady Falkland Her Life*. Berkeley: University of California Press, 1995.

Gwynne Kennedy

CATHERINE OF SIENA
(ca. 1347–1380)
Italy
Visionary and Religious Activist

Catherine was a visionary who convinced the Pope to leave Avignon and return the papacy to Rome. She was the twenty-third and youngest child of a Sienese dye-maker. Despite the size of her family, she felt loved by both of her parents. Because of the frequency of her mother's earlier pregnancies, Catherine had been the only child her mother had been able to nurse, and this may have created a special bond, at least according to some historians. Others talk about Catherine feeling deprived since there were so many siblings. Her father also showed a remarkable degree of understanding in his dealings with his daughter.

Catherine had her first vision of Christ when she was six. At about the same time she began to abstain from food as much as possible. Given the large size of the household in which she was living, she was able to do this fairly unobserved. For the rest of her life, Catherine used refusal to eat as others did as a way of obtaining inner grace. She consumed only bread, water, and greens; such a diet would have made it much easier for her to go into trances and have visions. Later in her life, some people would criticize her for ostentatious piety in fasting, and Catherine would sometimes respond by trying to eat; her body, however, had become so used to its regimen that much intake of food would make her severely ill.

At an equally young age, Catherine also took a vow of virginity, although she kept this secret from her parents. When she was about twelve her parents began to arrange a marriage for Catherine. To lessen her good looks so that she would be a less attractive prize (and also probably to deny her sexuality), Catherine cut off her hair. Catherine's parents, responding to what they thought was simply bad behavior, punished Catherine. Catherine, with her strong sense of sin and the need to expiate it, seems to have encouraged these punishments. Finally, however, Catherine told her parents of her vow, and

Saint Catherine of Siena by Giovanni di Paolo di Grazia. Courtesy of the Fogg Art Museum, Harvard University Art Museums, Gift of Sir Joseph Duveen. Photo credit: Photographic Service. © President and Fellows of Harvard College. Reprinted with permission.

her father, with remarkable understanding and sympathy, agreed to cancel the plans for the marriage. Yet this did not stop Catherine from continuing her own expiation. She wore an iron chain around her waist, slept on boards, often stayed up all night praying, and scourged herself three times a day.

Catherine joined the Sisters of Penance of St. Dominic, an order usually reserved for widows. This was not an enclosed order, and for the next three years, Catherine stayed in her room, speaking only with her confessor. During this period, Catherine had frequent visions of Christ and the Virgin Mary and conversed with them. Catherine considered herself a bride of Christ and had a ring she wore given by him that only she could see. Catherine also had, visible only to her, the stigmata of Christ as well. After three years of intense isolation in which she developed her mystical theology, Christ told Catherine it was his wish that she go out into the world and save souls. Catherine felt bound to obey this divine command but would have preferred to continue her mystical life. After such intense isolation, Catherine now spent her time with the poor and ill of the town, doing all she could to relieve suffering. She even went so far as to give away her family's possessions to the needy. There were many plague victims in Siena, and Catherine's courage and compassion in caring for them brought her great fame.

Word spread of her visions and fastings. People came to see her in her trances. Between trances, she settled quarrels and converted people. Catherine learned to read at twenty. From 1370 on, she took an increasing part in public life, exhorting rulers and prelates about how they should live their lives. Her influence lay in her absolute conviction that God's will and hers were one.

Through such grueling work, what comforted Catherine most was to take Holy Communion as often as she could. This frequently caused consternation with the priests since Catherine would often go into trances in the midst of the service and thus prolong it. People less spiritually minded than Catherine often complained that when entranced, Catherine had no sense of time. Catherine also continued to fast and punish her body in other ways in attempts to purify it. Word of Catherine's visions spread, and more and more people came to Siena to see her and hear her speak. She responded to everyone with great generosity and presence and sent many letters to those who had been to visit her or were too far away to come.

Catherine was living when the papacy was in great disrepute. Since 1309 the Popes had resided not in Rome but in Avignon and had been thoroughly dominated by the French kings. Avignon was a city of great cultural attraction but also deep corruption. With the Pope out of Rome, the Italian city–states were more and more involved with infighting. Clearly, the Church was in crisis. Catherine gained such a powerful reputation that the city of Florence asked her to go to Avignon and convince the Pope to return to Rome. She had an ardent following, especially in Florence. She was revered for her trances and raptures. At this time she was twenty-nine years old. Catherine believed her authority was the voice of God speaking directly to her while she was in a trance. It is perhaps amazing that a woman would take this role. Catherine was convinced that God had sent her to preach and teach as a woman so that immoral men might be shamed.

The Church had become more and more corrupt during the seventy years the papacy had been in Avignon, and the Pope was losing power. The wars in the Italian states and the Holy Roman Empire engulfed Rome and the papal states themselves. For the papacy to maintain control of the papal states from Avignon was impossible. Pope Gregory XI realized that it was necessary for the papacy to return home to Rome, but the pressure to stay in Avignon was intense.

In June 1376 Catherine arrived in Avignon and began to exhort Gregory. Catherine hated the stench and corruption of the city, but she passionately pleaded with him to return to Rome and revitalize the Church. Some of the ladies of Avignon so doubted Catherine's visions that they stuck pins into her to see if her trances were real. In both public and private audiences and in endless letters, Catherine poured out her heart to the Pope. She begged him to begin reform of the Church, to pacify Italy not with arms but through mercy and pardon. Catherine begged Gregory to return to Rome and passionately assured him that God was speaking to him directly through her. Catherine's stirring command that Gregory do "God's will and mine" persuaded him to return to Rome despite the pressure of the French king to remain in Avignon.

Catherine's appeals gave Gregory XI the strength to resist the pressures exerted by the French king and cardinals against return of the papacy to Rome. Gregory XI realized that only his presence could hold Rome for the papacy, and when Rome promised submission if he would return, he could postpone his return no longer. Despite his poor health, he left Avignon and finally entered Rome in January 1377. Gregory died only a year later. He probably wanted to die in Rome in order that the election of a new Pope should take place there and keep the papacy where it belonged.

On the death of Gregory the citizens of Rome saw a chance to finally end the reign of the French Popes. As the College of Cardinals met, crowds of Romans chanted outside that they wanted an Italian Pope who would stay in Rome. Urban VI, the Pope elected, promised to do just that. But Urban also almost immediately alienated a number of the high churchmen. A group of cardinals assembled and declared the election void since they had been pressured by the Italian mob, declared the papal throne vacant, and elected a new Pope, Clement VII. These cardinals thought this would force Urban to resign. But instead of resigning, Urban excommunicated the dissident cardinals, created an entirely new College of Cardinals, and hired a company of mercenaries to maintain his See by force of arms. Italy was clearly unsafe for Clement, and he and his College of Cardinals returned to Avignon. The Catholic Church was divided by what was known as the Great Schism, where each Pope was to declare he was the one and only Pope and the other was an anti-Christ. It was a terrible time for Christian Europe. When each Pope had excommunicated the followers of the other, who could be sure of salvation? According to a popular saying toward the end of the century, no one had entered Paradise since the Schism began. Although people could soon see all the problems caused by the Schism, the difficulty was how to end it. The Schism was to last for forty years and was not resolved until the Council of Constance, called in 1414.

By 1380, seeing the Church in decline, Catherine, in despair, fasted from both food and water in an attempt to expiate the sin from herself and society. This final self-punishment proved too much for her frail body. Despite finally ending her fast, Catherine died within a few months. Within a century, she was canonized a saint of the Catholic Church.

BIBLIOGRAPHY

Bynum, Caroline. *Holy Feast and Holy Fast: The Religious Significance of Food to Medieval Women*. Berkeley: University of California Press, 1987.

Noffke, Suzanne. *Catherine of Siena: Through a Distant Eye*. Collegeville, MN: Liturgical Press, 1996.

Undset, Sigrid. *Catherine of Siena*. London, New York: Sheed and Ward, 1954.

Carole Levin

CHRISTINA OF DENMARK
(1521–1590)
Denmark
Leader in Exile

Christina was the niece of the powerful Holy Roman Emperor and King of Spain Charles V. Her mother Isabella married King Christian II of Denmark in June 1514, part of an alliance that was initiated by the young woman's grandfather, the Emperor Maximilian. By 1520 King Christian had failed to check the growing Lutheran reform movement in his kingdom, whereas his numerous affronts against the aristocracy in Denmark led to great discontent among both clergy and nobility. After a series of clashes with his most powerful subjects, the king was deposed in 1523, and he and his family fled to Holland. The infant Christina of Denmark was never again to set foot in the land of her birth.

Christina's mother Isabella died in 1528 at the age of twenty-five, and the exiled king handed his children over to the care of their aunt **Margaret of Austria**, Regent of the Netherlands. For the next four years, until Margaret's death in 1531, Christina, together with her brother and sister, lived in Flanders under the direction of tutors and supportive relatives. Their father was later captured and imprisoned by his rebellious subjects, and his only male heir, Prince John, died of a fever in 1532 while traveling with his uncle, Holy Roman Emperor Charles V. The next year Christina's powerful uncle entered into an agreement with Francesco Sforza, Duke of Milan, whereby eleven-year-old Christina would be wed to the duke. Like so many arranged marriages within the ranks of royalty, this one was motivated by the emperor's larger strategic concerns in the Italian penninsula, in particular, an eagerness to preempt French ambitions in Northern Italy. The marriage between the forty-year-old Sforza and his child–wife lasted only eighteen months, however, when after a brief illness the duke died in November 1535.

Christina returned to Flanders in 1537, and almost immediately upon her arrival at her childhood home in Brussels, rumors began circulating of a proposed marriage alliance between the widowed Duchess of Milan and King Henry VIII of England. Henry's third wife, Jane Seymour, had died giving birth to the king's only son, the future Edward VI, and now the Protestant monarch was in search of a new queen. Henry hoped to forge an alliance with Emperor Charles V with such a marriage. Had he been successful, it would have represented a remarkable transformation of relations between the two monarchs, for Henry had precipitated the Protestant Reformation in England by seeking an annulment of his first marriage from Charles's aunt, Queen Catherine of Aragon. Needless to say, Henry's abandonment of his first wife and break with the Church of Rome infuriated the Holy Roman Emperor. The German Protestant reformer Philip Melanchthon wrote to a friend of his fears should such a marriage and subsequent alliance take place. Melanchthon and other Protestants feared for the worst out of such a marital and diplomatic union, but Henry's proposal required a papal dispensation due to the king's first marriage with Catherine of Aragon. Henry would never recognize the jurisdiction of the papacy in these matters, and the proposal was abandoned in 1538.

Christina's future remained in the hands of her uncle the emperor, and over the next few years a wide range of possible marriage partners were suggested, each time the strength of the match being evaluated in terms of its political repercussions for the Holy Roman Empire. Finally, in 1541, Christina married Francis I, Duke of Lorraine and nominal subject of the King of France. While initially designed to improve relations between the French and Charles V, chronic warfare between the emperor and the French monarch made life difficult at times for Christina. But in large measure the Duke of Lorraine was able to maintain a neutrality while attempting repeatedly to mediate between the two enemies. A child was born to the couple in 1543, named Charles after Christina's uncle, and the following year a daughter, named Renée after the Duke's mother, completed the family. For the next three years Christina enjoyed relative tranquility and happiness, until in June 1545 her second husband died, leaving her regent of the Lorraine at age twenty-three.

In 1552 troops of the new French king Henry II invaded Lorraine and removed Christina from her office as regent for her young son, Duke Charles III. France was again at war with Emperor Charles V, and Christina was obliged to return to her childhood home in Brussels. Here she remained for the next six years, with her only son left behind at the French royal court, until peace was again concluded in 1559. When her son Charles, now fifteen years old, returned to Lorraine as duke, his mother left the Netherlands for the last time. Once again she took up her old functions in an effort to rebuild after years of incursions by foreign troops. It was a time of enormous religious strife in France and in the Low Countries, as Catholics and Protestants engaged in the most indiscriminate sorts of terror and persecution.

In 1578 the duchess relocated to her dower lands—property she inherited as the widow of Francis I—in Italy and the northern city of Turdinae. She took an active role in the government of the city, and these final years were marked by a level of peace and stability never before experienced by Christina during her tumultuous life. At the time of her death in 1590, the long religious wars in France were at last coming to an end. Christina's entire life had been buffeted by dynastic conflict and religious intolerance, and she was a skilled survivor in an environment, and in life choices, largely outside her own control.

BIBLIOGRAPHY

Cartwright, Julia. *Christina of Denmark, Duchess of Milan and Lorraine.* New York: E. P. Dutton, 1913.

W. M. Spellman

CHRISTINA OF MARKYATE
(ca. 1096/1098–1160)
Britain
Anchoress and Visionary

Young women in the Middle Ages were generally powerless in determining their own future, but Christina of Markyate courageously resisted the life her parents chose for her and instead decided to devote herself to her spiritual calling by becoming an anchoress, or religious recluse, and later, a Benedictine nun.

Although we have little information about Christina's life, we do have an extant narrative chronicling her early years. Like most women of the twelfth century, Christina was probably unable to write; it appears that the memoir was transcribed by a close friend or companion. She was born at the end of the eleventh century to a prosperous Anglo-Saxon family; her given name was Theodora, but she is known by her spiritual name Christina, which she chose to indicate her closeness to Christ. When she was thirteen, she and her family visited St. Alban's Abbey, where she was so impressed by the monastic way of life she witnessed that she promised God she would become a nun. Her parents ignored her vow and insisted that she accept one of her many suitors. A battle of wills ensued between Christina and her parents. Her mother, Beatrix, attempted various strategies to force Christina to yield: purchasing herbal remedies with alleged aphrodisiac effects to tempt her daughter away from her vow of chastity, procuring a local fortune-teller to persuade her to marry, and ultimately beating and publicly humiliating her. Throughout all of this torment, Christina was sustained by her strong faith and her comforting visions of the Virgin Mary. Her parents prevailed, however, and eventually arranged for her to marry a man named Burthred.

Although the marriage took place, it was never consummated, in spite of the extreme measures Christina's parents took to force their daughter's submission to her husband. Christina insisted on her desire for a life of chaste devotion to God, and with the help of some of her spiritual allies, she escaped from the tyranny of her family. One day when her parents were away from home, Christina donned male clothes and made her way to the cell of an anchoress named Alfwen, about thirty miles away. Christina also adopted the anchoress's way of life, living in seclusion in a small cell. She managed to elude the furious search parties of her parents and husband, and she stayed with Alfwen for about two years. She was then taken to live with another hermit, an old man named Roger who served as an unofficial leader of five other hermits in the Markyate area near St. Alban's. There, Christina continued to live the solitary life of an anchoress, but this time the conditions were even more severe. Her cell was barely large enough to contain her; she had nothing but a hard stone to sit upon, and she endured great discomfort from the confined space and severe temperatures. Anchoresses generally lived in very small cells, but the particularly limited size of this cell ensured secrecy; it also offered Christina an opportunity to demonstrate her spiritual commitment through her physical and mental suffering. In her cell, her life of fasting, constant prayer, and visions continued under the tutelage of Roger, who had become a close friend and spiritual mentor.

Eventually her refuge was discovered by her husband, Burthred, who, prompted by a vision of his own, came to release her from her marital vows; the marriage was eventually declared annulled, and Burthred was free to remarry. Christina had lived in Roger's hermitage for four years when he died, and she was forced to leave the Markyate area. Although her commitment to the religious life was evident, she was not protected by any sanctioned ecclesiastical body; she had never taken the official vows necessary to become a nun or anchoress. After Roger's death, Christina came under the protection of Thurstan, the Archbishop of York, who offered her positions as abbess at Marcigny or Fontrevault, but she decided to return to Roger's hermitage near St. Alban's, where she had first vowed to devote her life to God. Her reputation as a woman of great piety grew; people came from all over the country to seek her advice and guidance.

In 1131 she made her official professional vows at St. Alban's, and with the support of Geoffrey, the abbot of St. Alban's, she established a community of nuns. Geoffrey, the leader of one of the richest abbeys in England, was initially far more concerned with wordly concerns than sacred matters, but through his acquaintance with Christina, he underwent a conversion and became far more interested in spiritual matters. Around 1145 a priory (a religious house) was built at Markyate, and Christina became the head of a larger community of religious women, serving as a spiritual adviser and healer for the next several years, until her death in 1160. Although several visions and at least one incident of a miraculous cure are recorded, Christina's success as a spiritual adviser resulted from the strength of character and the wisdom and piety she demonstrated for those who looked to her for guidance.

The wide respect in which she was held is indicated by the fact that King Henry II granted her a payment of fifty shillings for 1155–1156; it was not unusual for monarchs to make donations to the religious, but the gift was a mark of her reputation as a holy woman. Another example of her status is the extant St. Alban's Psalter, made for her use, a beautiful and costly illustrated prayerbook that suggests its owner was held in high esteem. The community of religious women Christina established lasted for the next several centuries after her death, until the dissolution of the monasteries in the early sixteenth century when King Henry VIII broke with the Catholic Church.

BIBLIOGRAPHY

Holdsworth, Christopher J. "Christina of Markyate." In Derek Baker, ed., *Medieval Women*. Oxford: Basil Blackwell, 1978. 185–204.

Talbot, Charles H., ed. and trans. *The Life of Christina Markyate, a Twelfth Century Recluse*. Oxford: Clarendon Press, 1959.

Jo Eldridge Carney

MARGARET GIGGS CLEMENT
(1505–1570)
Britain
Classical Scholar

Margaret Giggs Clement, regarded as an exceptionally knowledgeable woman, clearly profited from the training in humanist studies that her legal guardian, Sir Thomas More (1478–1535), had provided for her. Giggs's special talents lay in the fields of mathematics and medicine. Her unusual choice to devote herself to the study of medicine has earned Giggs an important place in the history of women. Giggs also demonstrated such an astonishing command of Greek that the humanist Juan Luis Vivés (1492–1540) praised her skill.

More's decision to provide training in humanist studies for all his children—**Margaret More Roper**, her sisters Elizabeth and Cecily, her brother John, and others attached to the More household, such as More's adopted daughter Margaret Giggs Clement—was truly unique. The students' classical education included instruction in grammar, rhetoric, and logic. The children learned to master Greek and Latin. Other subjects included theology, philosophy, astronomy, and medicine. To achieve his educational aim, More employed numerous tutors, including John Clement, the Greek scholar and physician, and Nicholas Kratzer, the astronomer, both of whom served at the Tudor court of King Henry VIII of England (ruled 1509–1547).

Whether or not women should receive such training was frequently debated at the time More chose to provide his children, irrespective of gender, with a humanist education. In a letter written to William Gonnell, one of his children's tutors, More states his reasons for extending instruction on "humane letters and liberal studies" to his daughters. More argued for the practical uses of such an education. An educated woman would be pious, charitable, and humble. In the ideal union More envisioned, her husband would profit from her company, whereas her children would benefit from the learned guidance and instruction provided by their mother. Through his daughters' education, Sir Thomas More hoped to effect these goals. In her

Margaret Giggs Clement (Mother Iak). Drawing by Hans Holbein the Younger. Cat. no. RL 12229 P 8. The Royal Collection © 1999, Her Majesty Queen Elizabeth II. Reprinted by permission of the Royal Collection Picture Library.

conduct—as a compassionate woman sympathetic to the sufferings of others and as a caring wife and mother—Giggs amply fulfills the goals of More's educational philosophy.

While Giggs's parentage remains obscure, More treated her as a beloved daughter, and she frequently represented More, as other members of his family did, by serving in his place to distribute food and money to the poor of Chelsea. A particularly striking account of her display of charity, which Giggs carried through at great personal risk, has survived; and while some scholars dismiss the account of Giggs's courageous act of charity as being unreliable, some accept it as being true. The charitable display of compassion for fellow human beings certainly seems consistent with Giggs's role as More's almoner.

According to various sources, King Henry VIII of England imprisoned a group of Carthusian monks and subjected them to inhumane treatment. Exactly where the monks' imprisonment occurred varies, with some placing the monks in the Tower of London and others in Marshalsea, a notorious prison reserved for common felons. With their necks bound by iron collars to wooden posts, the monks found themselves forced to stand upright for a period of approximately seventeen days. Giggs supposedly undertook the care of the unfortunate monks. The story runs that Giggs disguised herself, bribed the guards to gain admittance to the monks' cell, and proceeded to feed them with the food she had managed to smuggle in. Before leaving, Giggs did her best to relieve the monks' other bodily needs, by washing them and by removing their foul matter, in which the monks had had no other choice but to stand. When the guards refused her further admittance, Giggs is alleged to have tried to continue feeding the monks by lowering food to them through a hole in the roof.

Scholarly consensus remains divided over whether the story of Giggs's charity to the Carthusian monks is true or not; however, accounts do verify that Margaret Giggs alone saw More's beheading in 1535. Giggs also helped Margaret More Roper inter More's headless corpse at the Chapel of St. Peter Vincula in the Tower. These two brave women and devoted daughters remained loyal to More's memory even after his execution for treason, and both of them heroically endured interrogation by Henry VIII's ministers. Throughout her life, Giggs remained More's devoted daughter.

Both Giggs and her former tutor and future husband John Clement shared a special interest in and aptitude for mathematics and medicine. Toward the end of the 1520s, Giggs and Clement had married. Clement, who devoted himself to the study of medicine, earned general acclaim for his skills as a Doctor of Medicine. He even served as a physician at the court of Henry VIII, an appointment he received in 1528. Admitted to the London College of Physicians in the same year that he received his court appointment, Clement would eventually accept a position as its president in 1544. Clement and Giggs also demonstrated a unique talent for mastering foreign languages, especially Greek. Giggs's fluency in Greek is said to have enabled her to help Clement fully grasp the precise meaning of Greek passages he found particularly challenging.

Clement's contemporaries held him in high regard, both as a physician and as a classical scholar; however, the scholarship of Clement's wife, Margaret Giggs, rivaled his own. Giggs's study of medicine enabled her to assist her husband in his medical practice. In an indirect reference that appears in a passage from More's *Dialogue of Comfort* (one of the two major texts More wrote while in prison for treason), a knowledgeable young girl consults Galen's medical treatise to identify a fever. That young girl is traditionally viewed as being More's adopted daughter, Margaret Giggs.

As did Margaret More Roper, Giggs provided her daughters—Winifred, Margaret, Dorothy, Bridget, and Helen—with training in humanist studies, including instruction in Greek and Latin. Giggs's daughter Winifred (d. 1553) married William Rastell, who oversaw the publication of More's *English Works* (1557), another tribute to the memory of Sir Thomas More. Giggs's daughter Helen married Thomas Pridieux of Devonshire, and she provided, in her turn, the same training to her daughter, Magdalen Pridieux, with the result that More's educational theories were transmitted through three generations of women in Margaret Giggs Clement's family.

In the troubled years that followed More's death, the religious tensions that tore England apart forced Giggs and her family into exile to escape persecution for their faith. Many Catholics fled England to live in the Spanish Netherlands under the protection of King Philip II of Spain (ruled 1556–1598). Clement and Giggs returned from exile for a brief time during the reign of the Catholic Queen Mary I of England (ruled 1553–1558), but they returned to permanent exile in 1563 during the reign of the Protestant Queen Elizabeth I (ruled 1558–1603).

Margaret Giggs Clement and her husband, John Clement, both died while still in exile, Giggs in 1570 and Clement two years later. Many believe that Giggs died on the anniversary (July 6) of More's death. A manuscript account of her death, written by one of her daughters, has been preserved in an English convent at Bruges. The account describes how Giggs told her husband that she knew her end had come because the monks she had relieved in England were at her bedside and were calling for her to join them. Two of Giggs's daughters—Margaret and Dorothy—chose to enter nunneries rather than return to England.

A pious and charitable woman of deep faith, a devoted daughter, wife, and mother, and an eminent classical scholar, Margaret Giggs Clement clearly fulfills the role of the ideal female humanist once envisioned by Sir Thomas More.

BIBLIOGRAPHY

Marius, Richard. *Thomas More: A Biography.* New York: Knopf, 1984.

Murray, Francis G. "Feminine Spirituality in the More Household." *Moreana* 27–28 (1970): 92–102.

Reynolds, E. E. *The Field Is Won: The Life and Death of Saint Thomas More.* Milwaukee, WI: Bruce, 1968.

Reynolds, E. E. *Margaret Roper: Eldest Daughter of St. Thomas More.* New York: Kennedy, 1960.

Warnicke, Retha M. *Women of the English Renaissance and Reformation.* Contributions in Women's Studies, No. 38. Westport, CT: Greenwood, 1983.

Debra Barrett-Graves

LADY ANNE CLIFFORD
(1590–1676)
Britain
Artistic and Literary Patron, Builder, and Diarist

"Preserve your Loyalties, Defend your Rights" was Lady Anne Clifford's personal motto, and she dedicated her life to fulfilling it. As the daughter of George, the 3rd Earl of Cumberland, and Margaret Russell, daughter of the Earl of Bedford, Anne Clifford stood to inherit her father's entire estate. Centuries earlier, an entail by King Edward II decreed that the Clifford estate should pass to the direct heir regardless of gender. Therefore, Anne, their only surviving child after the deaths of her brothers Robert and Francis, should have received title to the nearly 90,000 acres of land in the counties of Westmoreland and North Yorkshire. However, George willed Anne £ 15,000 and left all his lands to his brother Francis, disinheriting his daughter who at the time was only sixteen years old.

Without delay, Margaret initiated a case on Anne's behalf to regain the Clifford estates. Anne obviously inherited her mother's determination and iron will because she, upon the death of her mother in 1616, assumed the fight to reclaim her inheritance, which continued for many years. Anne was undoubtedly an intelligent and well-educated woman; Samuel Daniel, poet, writer, and historian, was her childhood tutor and lifelong friend. Anne gathered documents and recorded her family's history to strengthen her case. To prove herself the rightful heir to the Clifford estates, Anne kept a diary called the Great Book, which documented her family connections and personal life.

Anne took great pride in her family's history, even though her father had disinherited her. Despite her disenfranchisement, Anne secured herself a good marriage in 1609 to Richard Sackville, the 3rd Earl of Dorset, a nobleman with great political influence. He did not, however, completely support Anne's pursuit of her inheritance, claiming that her obsession made her "devoid of reason." Anne simply responded, "Be assured that I will stand as constantly to my birth-

The Great Picture, depicting Lady Anne Clifford at the ages of fifteen and fifty-six (left- and right-hand panels), and her brothers, Robert and Francis, and parents, Lady Margaret Russell and George, Earl of Cumberland (central panel). Attributed to Jan van Belcamp (1646). Reproduced by courtesy of Abbot Hall Art Gallery, Kendal, Cumbria, England. Reprinted with permission.

right as is possible for me" (qtd. in Lewalski, 135–36). She was undaunted because she now had two daughters, Margaret and Isabella, for whom she undoubtedly continued her fight. Anne now had heirs to whom she could bequeath her estates if she could only reclaim them.

Even James I could not deter Anne from her mission. James, despite his own wife's urgings on Anne's behalf, tried to convince her to part with Westmoreland, the larger estate. Her husband tried the same. Although she did not wish to show disrespect for her husband or the king, she vowed never to part with any of her inheritance. The courts proved to be no more understanding, and in 1617, her cases to reclaim Westmoreland and Craven, respectively, were denied. Anne refused to acquiesce and again took her case to court until conflicts leading to the English Civil War between the king and Parliament broke out in the north. No more claims could be made on the land during this time.

In 1624, Anne's life became increasingly more difficult because of the death of her husband, leaving her a widow with two young children. Six years later, she married Philip Herbert, Earl of Pembroke and Montgomery, and found her social status greatly improved, but her efforts to reclaim her estates had produced no results after years of court battles. Her life, regarding her inheritance, changed dramatically with the deaths of her Uncle Francis, Earl of Cumberland, in 1641 and his son Henry two years later. In accordance with the will, Anne now became the indisputable heir to her father's estates; however, she had to wait another seven years before she could return to Westmoreland and Craven. The Civil War raged between the parliamentary forces and the royal forces of King Charles I, thus delaying her return since it was too unsafe to travel.

In 1650, at the age of sixty, Anne reclaimed her inheritance, although her friends still believed it was unsafe to travel. Anne felt that she had waited long enough. She now faced the monumental task of repairing thirty years of neglect and the damages of war. A genuine fear existed because her land could come under renewed attack by Oliver Cromwell, leader of the parliamentary army. Anne responded, "Let him [Cromwell] destroy my Castles if he will, as often as he levels them I will rebuild them, so long as he leaves me a shilling in my pocket" (Clifford, 101). Now that she finally possessed the lands that she had lost thirty-eight years earlier, she intended to waste no time in repairing them. She restored her six estate castles, seven churches, and Barden Tower and built two almshouses, a mill at Barden Tower, and a bridge over the River Eden. She also erected a pillar to commemorate the place where she last saw her mother; in addition, she commissioned monuments for the graves of her mother and father as well as her own tomb.

Anne's familial alliances never wavered. Anne firmly established her identity through the Clifford line, never through her husbands'. Shortly after regaining the title to her father's estates, she commissioned two copies of *The Great Picture* in 1646. This triptych (a picture in three panels side by side), which still hangs in Appleby Hall, depicts Anne, in the first panel, at the age when she was disinherited. The second shows Anne's parents along with her brothers Robert and Francis; the third panel shows Anne as she most likely appeared in 1646—the restored heir to the Clifford estates. In smaller versions within the large painting appear Samuel Daniel, Mrs. Taylor, her governess, and her two husbands, George Sackville and Philip Herbert. Anne is also surrounded by volumes of literary works such as the Bible, Spenser's *Faerie Queen*, and Sidney's *Arcadia*.

Anne apparently liked to be surrounded by words. She had the Bible along with Ovid's *Metamorphoses*, Leicester's *Commonwealth*, Knolles's *The Generall Historie of the Turks*, Chaucer's works, Sidney's *Arcadia*, and *In Praise of a Solitary Life* read to her, and she had her favorite passages pinned to the curtain of her bed so that she was constantly surrounded by them.

Her love of literature also manifested itself in her artistic patronage. In addition to the costly renovations that her estates demanded, Anne used her own money to erect monuments to honor her tutor and friend Samuel Daniel and the author Edmund Spenser at Westminster Abbey. Anne did a great deal to refurbish and perpetuate the Poet's Corner in Westminster Abbey.

Anne spent a lifetime documenting her family's history and rebuilding her estates. Anne also did what no other Clifford had done: She inhabited all six houses. In the latter entries of her diary, Clifford detailed the visits of her children and grandchildren whom she entertained at the various Clifford castles; she was the first Clifford to do so in many generations. At her funeral, Edward Rainbowe, Bishop of Carlisle, adopted Proverbs 14:1 as the verse best summarizing Lady Anne Clifford's life: "Every wise woman buildeth her house." Seemingly he understood Anne's life and mission. All of Anne's accomplishments worked, according to Rainbowe, to the glory of her gender. She had built her own mansions with many rooms for all her children. Anne was indeed a noble, wise woman whose determination and iron will returned the Clifford estates to her own family line: "Thus died this great wise Woman; who while she lived was the Honor of her Sex and Age, fitter for an History than a Sermon" (Rainbowe, 67). This is how she should be remembered.

BIBLIOGRAPHY

Clifford, Lady Anne. *The Diaries of Lady Anne Clifford*. Ed. D.J.H. Clifford. Wolfeboro Falls, NH: Alan Sutton Publishing, 1992.

Lewalski, Barbara Kiefer. *Writing Women in Jacobean England*. Cambridge, MA: Harvard University Press, 1993.

Rainbowe, Edward, Bishop of Carlisle. *A Sermon Preached at the Funeral of the Right Honorable Anne Countess of Pembroke, Dorset and Montgomery*. London: R. Royston, Bookseller, 1677.

Spence, Richard T. *Lady Anne Clifford, Countess of Pembroke, Dorset and Montgomery (1590–1676)*. Stroud, Gloucestershire: Alan Sutton Publishing, 1997.

Stephanie Witham

VITTORIA COLONNA
(1492–1547)
Italy
Poet and Patron of the Arts

When Vittoria Colonna died in 1547, her great friend Michelangelo was at her side. Upon her death, he wrote, "Heaven has taken from me the splendor of the great fire that burned and nourished me," but he acknowledged that some solace could be found in the "sweet, graceful, sacred verses" that Colonna left behind (Gibaldi, 28). A friend and inspiration to Michelangelo and many other artists and writers of the Italian Renaissance, Colonna was even more well known in her day as a poet in her own right.

Vittoria Colonna was born in 1492 into the celebrated Colonna family of Rome. Her father, Fabrizio Colonna, was a famous military general; he is one of the spokesmen on military matters in Machiavelli's *The Art of War*. Her mother, Agnese de Montefeltro, was equally interesting: she was the daughter of Duke Federigo of Urbino and Battista Sforza, whose court would later provide the setting for Baldassare Castiglione's *Book of the Courtier*, a famous work on courtly manners and behavior. Like many of the aristocratic women of the Italian Renaissance, Vittoria received a fine classical education.

When Vittoria was three years old, she was betrothed to Francesco de Avalos, the son of the Marquis of Pescara. This alliance was made in order to unite the Colonna family to the powerful Neapolitan Avalos family. The actual wedding contract was signed in 1507, and in 1509, when Vittoria was seventeen and Pescara was nineteen, they were married near Naples.

Vittoria claimed that the marriage was a happy one, but there is evidence that this may not have been the case. Pescara was a military man, just as Vittoria's father was. In 1510, after he had been married one year, Vittoria's husband left with her father to fight against the French in northern Italy on the side of Pope Julius II and Spain. From then on, Pescara spent most of his time away from home on military excursions.

Portrait of Vittoria Colonna by Girolamo Muziano. Credit: Alinari/Art Resource, NY. Reprinted with permission.

Colonna was left at home in southern Italy; they had no children, but she did help raise her husband's orphaned cousin, Alfonso d'Avalos, who became a successful military figure himself. An enthusiastic traveller all of her life, Vittoria spent a good deal of time visiting her parents' various estates. She also began writing, and her work gradually became known in literary circles.

It was during this period that she formed friendships with some of the most important literary figures of the Italian Renaissance: the humanist and poet Pietro Bembo; Baldassare Castiglione; and the epic poet Ludovico Ariosto. Of particular importance was her friendship with Pietro Bembo, who encouraged Vittoria's writing; she wrote a sonnet for him, "Spirito Felice," and it was partly through Vittoria's later intervention that Bembo became a cardinal. It was most likely Bembo who introduced Colonna to Castiglione; Bembo himself figures largely in Castiglione's *Book of the Courtier*. In 1524, Castiglione sent Colonna the manuscript of that work for her opinion; she so admired it that she began to share it with others, much to Castiglione's dismay. Castiglione was afraid that a corrupt edition might be published, so he himself had the book published in 1528. During this time she also met Ariosto, who was frequently in Rome on diplomatic business. Ariosto would later pay tribute to Colonna's poetic talent in his own epic poem *Orlando Furioso*.

Meanwhile, Vittoria and her husband lived mostly apart, for he was always away at war. He was a very successful soldier, but in 1525 he was seriously wounded in battle and died in Milan on 25 November 1525 at the age of thirty-five.

Vittoria, widowed at thirty-three, went to live in the Convent of San Silvestro near Rome. She chose not to remarry; she spent the rest of her life traveling extensively throughout Italy and living in various convents, though she never became a nun herself. In addition to her continued interest in the arts, she became involved in political, intellectual, and religious issues of the day and offered support to various charitable organizations.

Vittoria became associated with important Catholic reformists, including Cardinals Contarini and Reginald Pole, as well as with the more unorthodox reformists Juan de Valdes and Bernardino Ochino, a popular and charismatic preacher and leader of the Franciscan order of the Capuchins. Colonna was particularly moved by the preachings of Ochino, and she became a vigorous advocate for the Capuchin order. For several years, Colonna adopted the Capuchin ascetic practice of extreme fasting and wearing coarse hairshirts, but she later became more moderate in her expressions of faith and her beliefs.

The teachings of Ochino and his followers became increasingly dangerous and controversial, and in 1542, Ochino was summoned to Rome by the Inquisition, a Catholic tribunal that punished religious heresy. Rather than face certain persecution, Ochino fled to Geneva and spent the remaining years of his life in exile. Colonna's own beliefs were not as radical as the Ochino circle's and she eventually broke off communication with them, but she still remained under suspicion from the Vatican for her religious views. Like her close friend and countrywoman **Giulia Gonzaga**, a noblewoman also interested in reformist ideas, Vittoria ultimately escaped investigation for heresy only through her own death.

In addition to her profound interest in matters of religious reform, Colonna also continued to write her own poetry and to be an admired friend of many writers and artists. Her portrait was painted by several Renaissance artists, including Sebastiano del Piombo and Girolamo Muziano; many scholars also believe that Veronese's depiction of the Virgin in his *Marriage at Cana* is based on Colonna. In addition to her friendships with Bembo, Castiglione, Ariosto, Annibale Caro, and numerous other poets of the day, Colonna's greatest friendship, one of the most celebrated of the Renaissance, was with Michelangelo.

Theirs was a very close platonic friendship that began in the mid-1530s and lasted until her death in 1547. For over a decade, they wrote poems for each other, corresponded, and exchanged visits. Michelangelo often drew sketches for Colonna. Many art historians believe that one of Michelangelo's drawings now in the British Museum is of Colonna as is the figure at the feet of the Virgin Mary in his painting *The Last Judgment.*

Colonna was renowned for the inspiration she gave to painters and poets, but she was also recognized as an impressive poet in her own right. Her book of poems *Rime Spirituali* was published in 1538. When she first began writing, she did not publish her work, but copies of the manuscript were in circulation and she frequently sent individual poems to various friends. She also sent manuscripts to Marguerite de Navarre, Michelangelo, and other famous artists and writers. Four of her poems appeared in print in anthologies, and then in 1538, a complete volume of her work was published; four editions were printed between 1538 and 1544; twenty more editions would appear in subsequent decades.

Rime Spirituali contains almost 400 poems, mostly in the form of the sonnet, about both human love and spiritual love. The love poems, written after her husband's death, show the clear influence of the fourteenth-century Italian lyric poet Petrarch, not only in form but in tone. She praises her husband as my "beautiful sun" and writes about her desire to join him in the afterlife. Many of the poems focus very specifically on her grieving and misery in widowhood.

The spiritual sonnets focus on eternal love; these poems are positive avowals of her love of Jesus Christ and reflect Colonna's increasing interest in religious matters. Her spiritual poems resulted in the *Triumph of Christ's Cross,* a long poem about Christ, the Virgin Mary, and Saint Mary Magdalene. Colonna had long been interested in Mary Magdalene; she admired her as the first witness to Christ's Resurrection and as a woman who moved from earthly love to spiritual love. It may have been Colonna's interest in Mary Magdalene that led her to join some other aristocratic women in Rome in establishing a shelter for women who wanted to abandon prostitution.

In his epic poem *Orlando Furioso,* Ariosto comments on the many excellent women writers of his time, but, he says, he will single out one for praise: Vittoria Colonna: "This woman has not only made herself immortal with a sweet style that has not been surpassed; but whomever she speaks or writes about she can draw from the tomb and give eternal life."

BIBLIOGRAPHY

Bainton, Roland. *Women of the Reformation in Germany and Italy.* Minneapolis: Augsburg Publishing House, 1971.

Bullock, Alan, ed. *Rime.* Rome and Bari: Laterza, 1982.

Gibaldi, Joseph. "Vittoria Colonna." In Katherina Wilson, ed., *Women Writers of the Renaissance and Reformation.* Athens: University of Georgia Press, 1987.

Jerrold, Maud. *Vittoria Colonna with Some Account of Her Friends and Her Times.* New York: E. P. Dutton, 1906.

Jo Eldridge Carney

THE COOKE SISTERS
Mildred (1526–1589), Anne (1528–1610), Elizabeth (1528–1609), Katherine (d. 1583), Margaret (d. 1558)
Britain
Writers

Anthony Cooke, former tutor to Edward VI and a member of Parliament under Queen Elizabeth I, and his wife Ann Fitzwilliam had five daughters at a time when girls were more of a financial curse than a familial blessing. During the early sixteenth century, humanists encouraged female education, and Cooke had his daughters Mildred, Anne, Elizabeth, Katherine, and Margaret study Greek, Hebrew, Italian, and Latin. Their father, a devout Protestant, insisted their education also have a religious focus. Margaret died young, and her writings did not survive her; the other sisters were all known for their education and as translators of religious works. Such translations, as opposed to original works, were more acceptable for women scholars of the period.

Mildred Cooke, the oldest of Anthony's daughters, was tutored by Giles Lawrence, a prominent Greek professor. Although Roger Ascham, Elizabeth I's tutor, claimed that Mildred and Lady Jane Grey, Elizabeth I's cousin, were the two most learned women in England, we have only Mildred's contemporaries to rely upon regarding her reputation as an exemplary author, as her work has not survived. None of her works ever saw publication even though she was probably the most famous of the Cooke women, possibly due to her marriage to William Cecil, Lord Burghley, principal secretary to Queen Elizabeth I. Credited with being a devout reader, Mildred translated the work of Chrysostom, a Greek author and early church father. Her translation, which most likely received a wide circulation, was considered by her contemporaries as an impressive accomplishment. In addition to her writing, Mildred also cared for her own children and her husband's many wards.

Anne became the second wife of Sir Nicholas Bacon and as one of the Catholic Queen Mary I's attendants may have used her influence to help protect her brother-in-law Sir William Cecil, who had been involved in an unsuccessful plot in 1553 to keep Mary off the throne. In the reign of Mary's sister, the Protestant Elizabeth I, Anne's husband gained more power and Anne a greater reputation as a scholar. Her works were widely published and acknowledged. She translated fourteen sermons by Bernadino Ochino, a Calvinist, from Italian into English. In addition to this work, Anne published her English translation of Bishop John Jewell's *The Apology of the Church of England* (*Apologia Ecclesiae Anglicanae*) in 1564, a document advocating the unity of the church. Interestingly, Anne chose a text that by the decree of the Convocation of 1563 was to be placed in all churches as an official document of the Church of England. Matthew Parker, the Archbishop of Canterbury, praised Anne not only for the faithfulness of her translation but also for her modesty and intelligence. Women who dared to publish and even write independently were often attacked for having loose morals, and it was reported that Parker published her work without her knowledge so as to avoid calling her character into question. He considered her a model example to all women and believed that she bestowed honor on her gender.

Despite her modesty, Anne also defended her work as a woman writer. She dedicated her translation of Ochino's sermons to her mother. In the dedication, Anne defends her right to an education and how she put that education to use as a translator. She also educated her two sons, Anthony and Francis, before they went to study at Cambridge. Later in her life as a widow she supported radical Protestants and gave them haven at her home at Gorhamby.

Anthony's third daughter, Elizabeth, followed a path similar to her sisters'. She, too, chose to translate religious texts and married well. Her first husband was Sir Thomas Hoby, translator of Castiglione's *Courtier*. Her second husband was Lord John Russell, heir to the Earl of Bedford. Elizabeth translated into English John Poynet's Latin work *A Way of Reconciliation of a Good and Learned Man, Touching the Truth, Nature, and Substance of the Body and Blood of Christ in the Sacrament*. The text treated the topic of transubstantiation, the sacrament, and salvation. Elizabeth dedicated her careful translation to her daughter Anne, and here one reads Elizabeth's own words, where she justified her translation and the importance of education for women. She considered this book her last legacy to her daughter, and she wanted it to encourage her Protestant faith. Elizabeth wrote that she translated the text as a means of more fully learning the matter and to provide writing that would benefit her daughter's learning. In this manner, Elizabeth found the means, just as her sister Anne had done, to make her writing more accepted.

Katherine was the last daughter to leave a record of her writings. She was the wife of Sir Henry Killigrew, a man who performed diplomatic missions for Queen Elizabeth. Katherine was not as socially well connected as her sisters, and her collection of writings is substantially smaller. An epitaph and a Latin verse written to Mildred requesting Cecil's help to change one of Killigrew's diplomatic assignments are all that survive. Although she herself did not enjoy an influential lifestyle, she clearly understood Mildred's when seeking assistance for her husband. Katherine was the mother of four daughters. She died in childbirth in 1583; her son also did not survive. Her sisters mourned her; Anne's Puritan ministers wrote verses for her monument as did Elizabeth.

How were these women able to be successful authors during the Tudor period? They were writing at a time when it was considered unwomanly to write. It was even more certain that women were not allowed to preach publicly, yet the Cooke sisters produced religious texts that were either published or well circulated. Remarkably, these women found their voices in the ancient church texts and were able to avoid attacks on their character because of their pious literary selections. These women were undoubtedly some of the most educated and intelligent women of their time, and they found the means to exercise their learning and establish a genre in which a woman could write. This option may seem limiting in that they perhaps lacked the freedom to express their own religious thoughts and ideas, but they are to be admired for their enduring literary legacy.

BIBLIOGRAPHY

Lamb, Mary Ellen. "The Cooke Sisters: Attitudes toward Learned Women in the Renaissance." In Margaret Hannay, ed., *Silent But for the Word: Tudor Women as Patrons, Translators and Writers of Religious Works.* Kent, OH: Kent State University Press, 1985. 107–125.

Warnicke, Retha. *Women of the English Renaissance and Reformation.* Westport, CT: Greenwood, 1983.

Stephanie Witham

MARGHERITA DATINI
(ca. 1360–1423)
Italy
Merchant's Wife

In the late Middle Ages and Renaissance, women were supposed to marry and provide their husbands with heirs. In their marriages they were expected to be silent and obedient. The model that was told to women was to obey whether the request was reasonable or unreasonable, something that could be accomplished or was utterly futile. Many women, except those at the top of the social scale and those in nunneries, were illiterate. Most of all, wives were expected not to demand equality with their husbands. Although Margherita di Domenico Bandini was only sixteen when she married the Italian merchant Francesco Datini in 1376, and he was over forty, in this marriage Margherita demonstrated courage and compassion and an insistence on equality rare for her time period. Over a hundred of her letters to him have survived, which give a rare glimpse into the marriage of an extraordinary woman.

Margherita's new husband had built up a thriving career as a merchant. Although they were both from Italy, they married in Avignon, where Francesco had been engaged in trade for many years, since that was in the fourteenth century the seat of the papacy. Francesco's family had been pressuring him for years to marry and had feared because of his traveling he would not marry a hometown girl. They were delighted when he settled on Margherita, even though she was an orphan and did not bring her husband a dowry; she was, however, young, attractive, and on her mother's side connected with Florentine nobility, making her a good catch for a merchant.

Soon after the marriage, the Pope left Avignon to return to Rome; soon Francesco Datini and Margherita returned to Tuscany. As a merchant, Francesco traveled frequently. When he was away, he would write at least twice a week to Margherita. Even though Margherita was young and wives at the time were told to be silent and obedient, Margherita was frequently outspoken in her responses.

In the first years of her marriage, Francesco's letters were read to Margherita, and she dictated her letters back to him. Like many women of her time, Margherita had not been taught to read as a child. But Margherita tired of having letters read to her and dictating responses. At the age of thirty, she decided to learn to read and write and asked a family friend to teach her. She persevered until she could do so fluently.

Margherita's time was filled with domestic duties. These increased with each year, together with Francesco's fortune and the size of his household. Margherita supervised the house, the cellar, the kitchen-garden, the stable, and the mill. She was up in the morning before the front door was opened and was the last of the household to retire to her bedchamber. She supervised both free servants and slaves.

In the early years of their marriage, Margherita was upset by how often Francesco was away, as we can see in her letters to him. Francesco was irritable, restless, and often unfaithful. Margherita and Francesco were both deeply unhappy that Margherita could not get pregnant. She was all too aware that the problem lay with her, as Francesco had several illegitimate children. She tried all the prescribed remedies concerned friends and family members sent her, but none of them worked; Margherita failed to conceive. Margherita was as disappointed in not being able to give her husband a household of children as he was. She adopted Tina, the daughter of Francesco's sister, when the sister's family had gone bankrupt. Later, when she had given up hope of having a child of her own, she eventually agreed to raise Francesco's illegitimate daughter. Ginevra was born in 1392 to Francesco's twenty-year-old slave girl Lucia. Apparently at first Margherita refused to bring the child up in her home, and Francesco sent Ginevra off to be nursed and later kept by a foster mother. But when Ginevra was six, Margherita relented, and the child was brought into the household to be raised as their own daughter. Margherita made the decision to adopt the child as her own and grew to love her dearly. While wives may well have been pressured to take an illegitimate child into the household, Margherita is unusual in the love and care she gave Ginevra; she felt great pride in the girl she came to regard as her own daughter. Her letters to Francesco are filled with her love for Ginevra, and she was very proud that she was the only one who could control the child, telling her husband that Ginevra was the best child possible when in her presence, but when she was with others, she refused to do what she was told.

When Ginevra was ill and Francesco, away from home, was worried, Margherita assured him that she was looking after her as if she were her own daughter; that was how she now considered her. She bought Ginevra fine clothes and toys and made sure that she—unlike Margherita—learned to read as a child. As Ginevra grew up, Francesco was very concerned that he find his daughter a good husband, someone who would not be ashamed of her since she was a slave's daughter. He provided her with a large dowry, a lavish trousseau, and an extravagant wedding. He had also provided well for Ginevra's natural mother, marrying her off to one of his servants and remembering her in his will.

The last decade of his life Francesco spent in Prato with his wife, and thus we have few letters between them. In a letter we do have we find Margherita promising him that if he spent his last years peacefully with her, they could live in a way that would fill him with joy. Francesco died in August 1410. In his final will, he freed all his slaves. After her husband's death, Margherita went to live with Ginevra and her husband. She died in 1423.

Despite the difficulties in their marriage, it seems at the end to have been a successful one. Although they had no children, Margherita raised Ginevra as if she were her own. And she refused to be passive and submissive to Francesco, even learning to read and write so that she could communicate with him more directly. Their letters give us special insight into an Italian merchant marriage where we find a core of affection and mutual respect. Margherita Datini took a marriage to a much older man who traveled frequently and the disappointment of not being able to bear children and carved out a life of satisfaction and equality.

BIBLIOGRAPHY

Gies, Frances, and Joseph Gies. *Women in the Middle Ages.* New York: Crowell, 1978.
Origo, Iris. *The Merchant of Prato: Francesco di Marco Datini.* London: Jonathan Cape, 1957.

Carole Levin

MARIE DENTIÈRE

(fl. 1530s)
Switzerland
Reformist, Defender of Women, and Writer

Marie Dentière was the abbess at a convent of Augustinians in Tournai in the 1520s, but she left the convent and married former priest Simon Robert. Shortly after their marriage, they met Guillaume Farel, a well-known Protestant reformer; they moved to Aigle with him, then to Strasbourg, where they grew increasingly involved in reformist activity. After Robert's death in 1533, Marie married another reformist, the shopkeeper Antoine Froment.

Marie, Froment, and their five children moved to Geneva to be near their friend, Guillaume Farel, who was especially instrumental in fanning the flames of political and religious rebellion in the city that played such an important role in the history of the Reformation. Farel, Froment, Dentière, and other activists helped galvanize the Protestant reformists' opposition to the Catholic clergy in Geneva. Several years of dissent followed, and by May 1536, Geneva had successfully overthrown the clergy and become an independent Protestant city. The transition to a Protestant city was not, however, a smooth one, given the various religious and political factions all vying for power. In 1536 the religious leader John Calvin arrived: He and Farel were influential for awhile in Geneva, but their reformist practices were ultimately considered too radical, and they were exiled from the city for several years. Calvin did not return to Geneva until 1541 when he was eventually successful in establishing himself as the powerful leader of the city's reform movement.

Marie Dentière was active in this Protestant reform movement as a speaker and as a writer of religious tracts. She published two works: The first was an account of the reform movement in Geneva in the 1520s and 1530s, *The War for and Deliverance of the City of Geneva*. Dentière's version of these events makes no attempt to be impartial; her chronicle is a celebration of reformist achievement, filled with biblical allusions and colorful, contemporary language. It is no surprise that in spite of her active role in the reform movement, Marie still felt compelled to publish this work as written by "a merchant living in that city." She must have felt that her writing would be taken more seriously if its readers thought the author was male. It was not until the nineteenth century that this work was fully proven to be Dentière's.

Dentière's second work was more outspoken in defense of women. This publication was addressed to Marguerite de Navarre, sister of the French king Francis I and wife of Henri de Navarre, ruler of the small French territory in southern France; this publication also included a letter to Marguerite de Navarre, "A Most Beneficial Letter Prepared and Written Down by a Christian Woman of Tournai," and a tract in defense of women's involvement in religious reform. Marguerite would have been an appropriate recipient since she herself was a woman of power and sympathetic to reform.

This time Dentière fully acknowledged her identity as the female author of the work. She begins her letter with a defense of women and an argument in favor of women's right to interpret and discuss Scripture on their own. She is also extremely critical of some of the Genevan ministers who were not, in her view, sufficiently supportive of reformist ideals, and she spoke out in defense of some of the exiled leaders, especially Guillaume Farel. Her criticism of some of the leading officials of the city resulted in a scandal: Although the printer, Jean Gerard, published 1,500 copies of this work under another name, his identity was discovered, he was imprisoned, and the remaining copies were confiscated. Gerard was eventually set free, but the work was censored for years. Dentière's husband tried repeatedly but unsuccessfully to obtain some of the confiscated copies of the work. Dentière passionately believed in the need to include women in the mission of Christianity. She wrote to Marguerite de Navarre: "Didn't Jesus die just as much for the poor illiterates and the idiots as for the shaven, tonsured, and mitred lords? . . . Did he not say, 'To all?' Do we have two Gospels, one for men and one for women?" She makes many allusions to the many good women named in the Bible and argues that it would be wrong for women to hide the talents God has given them.

According to another memoir written by a woman at the time, *The Germ of Calvinism*, by Sister Jean de Jussie, a nun, Dentière came to visit the sisters of de Jussie's convent. Dentière repudiated the ideals of chastity and celibacy, and she spoke of her own happiness as a wife and a mother. She also vigorously defended the right of women to discuss and interpret Scripture.

In spite of Dentière's defense of Farel in this work, he eventually repudiated both her and her husband Froment. Dentière's work on behalf of the reform movement and for women's role within that movement was powerful and influential, but ultimately, the extremity of her views caused their suppression. Even the reformists themselves were not willing to concede positions of power to women. Women were excluded from public discourse on matters of religion, and important writings like Dentière's were censored or ignored. It is only now, centuries later, that those works are being discovered again. We do not know what happened to Dentière in the later years of her life, but we know that her courageous and vigorous activism was important in the early years of reform even though her powerful voice was suppressed once the reform movement became more established.

BIBLIOGRAPHY

Douglass, Jane Dempsey. *Women, Freedom, and Calvin*. Philadelphia: Westminster Press, 1985.

Head, Thomas. "Marie Dentière: A Propagandist for the Reform." In Katharina Wilson, ed., *Women Writers of the Renaissance and Reformation*. Athens: University of Georgia Press, 1987.

Jo Eldridge Carney

JANE DORMER
(1538–1612)
Britain
Catholic Loyalist

The sixteenth-century Catholic English exile Jane Dormer knew personally many of the players on the international stage. Jane was a woman who both kept her faith and followed her heart. She was a loyal and loving wife and mother and a great supporter to those of her religion. Jane was the older of two daughters of Sir William Dormer and his first wife Mary Sidney. Jane was the first cousin to Philip Sidney, one of the great writers and heroes of the age. But Jane's mother died when Jane was only four years old, and her connections with her mother's relations, who supported the Protestant Church in England after Henry VIII's break with Rome, were never emphasized.

Jane was brought up by her grandmother, a devout Catholic, who insisted that Jane be thoroughly educated; by the time she was seven she was reading both English and Latin. In the reign of Henry VIII's young son Edward VI, at her grandmother's urging, she joined the household of Mary, Henry's daughter by his first wife Catherine of Aragon. Jane was very loyal to the Catholic Mary and cared about her deeply. In July 1553 Edward VI died. John Dudley, Duke of Northumberland and close adviser to the young Edward, unsuccessfully attempted a coup to put Mary's cousin Jane Grey, whom he had just married to his youngest son, on the throne. Jane Dormer's father William was one of the knights who gathered followers to support Mary instead of Northumberland. When Mary became queen, Jane was made a lady-in-waiting at court.

Jane was Mary I's most intimate companion. Mary kept Jane with her during most of her waking hours and often had her sleep with her at night. When Mary visited families living near her palaces, she brought Jane with her and asked Jane to take notes so that she could help all the children in the families. She had Jane keep a record of any complaints about bailiffs on the royal estates or about ill-

Lady Jane Dormer (unknown lady supposed to be Jane Dormer by Antonis Mor Van Dashort).

treatment by any local officials. Jane read prayers with Mary, took care of Mary's jewels, and cut Mary's meat for her at meals. Jane was with Mary during the rebellion against the queen's proposed marriage to Philip of Spain led by Thomas Wyatt in early 1554. In part due to Mary's courage rousing the London citizens, the rebellion failed, and the unpopular marriage took place. Philip's arrival with his entourage was to have a decisive impact on Jane's own life. Mary was deeply shaken by the rebellion. She had been extremely merciful in 1553, but after the Wyatt rebellion, she ordered the execution of Jane Grey and her husband Guildford Dudley and the arrest and examination of her own sister Elizabeth. For some months Elizabeth, Henry VIII's daughter by his second wife, Protestant Anne Boleyn, was lodged in the Tower, wondering if she would follow her cousin Jane Grey to the block.

Jane Dormer was beautiful and a favorite of the queen. It is hardly surprising that she had many suitors among the nobility who were eager to marry her. But Mary did not think any of them was deserving of her great friend. Jane realized the queen wanted her to stay at court with her and took her time in choosing her own husband, a bold step of autonomy for a woman of her class and time. Mary's reign, with the burning of heretics, was a disaster for England. It was also a personal tragedy for her. Although convinced that she was pregnant, Mary never had a child, and Philip, once he realized the unlikelihood of an heir with her, was infrequently in England. Mary recognized that the Catholicism she had tried to restore to England would die with her.

In 1558, with her beloved queen in ill health, Jane finally chose the man she wished to marry: Don Gomez de Figueroa, Count of Feria from Cordova, Spain. At thirty-eight, he was a member of Philip II's entourage and briefly served as ambassador to England. It was clearly a match based on love; Feria's mother opposed it, as did some of Jane's relatives. Jane realized that once she married Feria, she would be leaving her homeland. Mary realized that too, and though she was delighted with the match, the queen requested that they wait for Philip II to come back to England before she saw Jane married. Jane agreed to wait, but Philip was never to return. When she knew she was dying, Mary was deeply sad she would not live to see the couple married.

Jane was at the bedside of the dying queen. Mary showed her complete trust in Jane by asking her to deliver Mary's jewels to her successor, Elizabeth, in Hatfield in mid-November. At Mary's behest, Jane also asked Elizabeth to promise three things: that she would keep England Catholic, that she would take good care of Mary's servants, and that she would pay Mary's debts. If Elizabeth assented, it was a promise she certainly did not keep. Jane, her mission accomplished, returned to her queen and was with Mary when she died peacefully on 17 November 1558.

After Mary's death and funeral, Jane went to live with her grandmother at her town house. It was there she married Feria on 29 December 1558. Soon after the wedding, Feria left England to join Philip II in Flanders. Jane remained in England until he sent for her the next summer. Jane knew she was preparing to leave her homeland forever. On July 23 she took her leave of Elizabeth. Jane was at that time about seven months pregnant. Jane's grandmother accompanied her to Flanders and stayed with her when her son Don Lorenzo was born in September. Her grandmother then settled in Louvain, where she lived in a community of English Catholic exiles until her death twelve years later.

The next spring Feria wanted to bring his wife and son to Spain, but they made a number of stops along the way. The day before

Easter they entered Paris and lodged in the house of the Duke of Guise, one of the leaders of the Catholics in France, for the holidays. Then they joined the new young French king Francis II, his wife Mary Stuart (later Mary Queen of Scots), and his mother Catherine de Medici. Jane and Mary became immediate friends. Mary was so taken with Jane that she decided to cease wearing mourning for her father-in-law, Henry II, and dressed in white to honor Jane. She also begged Jane to dress in the French manner and gave Jane a dress. Jane would keep it for the rest of her life. The two corresponded through all the changes in Mary's life: the death of her husband Francis; her move back to Scotland to rule as queen; her marriage to Lord Darnley and, after his mysterious murder, to Lord Bothwell; the rebellion against her and her forced abdication; her flight to England, where Elizabeth kept her in restraint until her execution nearly twenty years later in 1587. When Mary first escaped to England, Jane convinced her husband to send the Scottish queen substantial money to help her. In the years after her husband's death, Jane did everything she could to convince Philip to aid the imprisoned Scottish queen.

Philip II and his third wife, Isabella, sister of Francis II, gave the count and countess an enthusiastic welcome when they arrived in Spain. The couple set up housekeeping, and everyone at Philip's court was impressed by their mutual love. Philip was so impressed by Feria he raised his status to that of a duke in 1567. In 1571 Philip planned to make Feria governor of the Low Countries, but Feria caught a violent fever and within three weeks he was dead. When Feria died, he left his only surviving son in the sole care of his wife, adding that he would give her no advice on how to raise their son and take care of his lands and house, as she would do it much better than he would know how to ask her to. The same year, Jane also lost her grandmother. Jane was thirty-four years old. The Duke of Feria had left enormous debts, and Jane worked hard in the next decade to free the estate from debts and raise her son well. Jane was also fighting her mother-in-law over the estate to protect the rights of her son. She also did all she could to help Catholic English exiles and supported the training of English Jesuits. She also worked with English exiles to aid Mary Stuart.

There was a lot of pressure for her to move to Flanders and assume the leadership of the English exiles attempting to restore Catholicism to England, which Jane seriously considered in the early 1590s. This greatly concerned her son, who saw that such a role for his mother would leave her open to abuse and danger. The splits and intrigues in the exile community put Jane at risk, not only for her reputation but also for her safety. At her son's insistence, Jane reluctantly gave up the plan and stayed in Spain. At the end of her life Jane spent most of her time in prayer. When she died in 1612, she was buried in a Franciscan habit. Jane Dormer had left her country as a young woman of twenty-one never to return. She was a devoted wife and mother. Her life touched many of the most politically powerful of her day, and her firm adherence to the Catholic faith shaped both her private and her public role.

BIBLIOGRAPHY

Clifford, Henry. *The Life of Jane Dormer, Duchess of Feria*. Ed. Rev. Joseph Stevenson. London: Burns and Oates, 1887.

Loomie, Albert J. *The Spanish Elizabethans: The English Exiles at the Court of Philip II*. Westport, CT: Greenwood Press, 1963.

Carole Levin

ELISABETH OF SCHONAU
(1129–1164)
Germany
Mystic, Writer

The medieval feminine ideal was simple: Women were to be "chaste, silent, and obedient." While many women were praised for upholding this ideal, many others chose to defy these expectations. Although the Church denied women the opportunity to publicly preach in the twelfth century, some found alternative ways to express their religious thoughts. One particularly dramatic medium of religious self-expression among some women was through visionary mysticism, revelations that were believed to be divinely inspired through supernatural means. Elisabeth of Schonau was one such woman whose visionary experience afforded her the opportunity to be heard.

Little is known about Elisabeth's family. During this time, unmarried women of wealthy and influential families typically entered nunneries, and it is probable that Elisabeth's own family was moderately affluent. She entered the Benedictine monastery at Schonau when she was twelve. The Benedictines, a monastic order that began during the high Middle Ages and often maintained separate communities for both men and women, emphasized the rule of St. Benedict and recognized the supremacy of the Pope and the Roman Church.

In 1152 at the age of twenty-three, Elisabeth, a devout and pious believer, experienced visions after suffering from a serious illness. Although she was able to eloquently tell her visionary experience in Latin, she was not literate enough to record her own visions and shared her revelations with the other sisters at the monastery. Her ability to speak such eloquent Latin despite her lack of an education offered proof to the people of her time that her visions were of a divine origin: Elisabeth dictated her religious, visionary experiences so that they could be preserved. The visions revealed her focus on the heavenly realm. Initially she was spiritually transported to heaven, where she witnessed the angels and other heavenly beings. In these early visions, which are recorded in her book *Liber Visionum Primus*

(*Visions, Book One*), Elisabeth was a more active participant in the visions. Elisabeth watched as scenes revealed heaven in all its splendor, and souls in purgatory earnestly begged prayers from her to end their torments.

Elisabeth's brother, Egbert, learned of his sister's visions on his visits to the monastery. She had for some time tried to convince him to be ordained, and she even had a vision where the Virgin Mary compelled him to do so. His devotion to his sister and his belief in her visions prompted him to leave Bonn in 1155 and enter the monastery at Schonau. Once there, he served as Elisabeth's secretary and strongly encouraged her to share all her visions, which he recorded.

The focus of Elisabeth's visions changed once Egbert joined her. While in the earlier ones she was a witness to the heavenly sights, the latter ones emphasized her theological beliefs. Although Elisabeth was sometimes referred to as a prophet, she for the most part refrained from prophetic insights. In 1154, shortly before her brother's arrival in Schonau, Elisabeth foresaw destruction of the world by Satan and shared her prophecy with Abbot Hildelin of Schonau. He in turn told other ecclesiastics, and word of Elisabeth's vision spread. The prophecy, however, was never realized, and the embarrassment this caused Elisabeth left her greatly concerned about her reputation. Not surprisingly, Egbert chose to omit this vision from his collection of Elisabeth's teachings.

Egbert compiled six books of Elisabeth's visions and teachings. In addition to these, Egbert also wrote *De Obitu Elisabeth* (*Concerning the Death of Elisabeth*), our only contemporary biography. The books containing her visions are *Libri Visionum Primus, Secundus, and Tertius* (*Visions, Books 1, 2, and 3*); *Liber Viarum Dei* (*On the Ways of God*), her account of the ten roles in which a person can live a Christian life; *Visio de Resurrectione Beate Virginis Marie* (*Revelations of the Holy Band of Virgins of Cologne*), revelations on the spiritual and bodily assumption of the Virgin Mary; and *Revelatio*, the revelations about Saint Ursula and the legend of her 11,000 virgins. The revelations contained in this book were written when Abbot Gerlach of Deutz asked Elisabeth to verify that the relics from a grave in Cologne belonged to Ursula and her women. Through her visions, Elisabeth was able to confirm Gerlach's hopes. The last collection that Egbert compiled contained her letters.

Perhaps through Egbert's involvement in her life and her own development as a mystic, Elisabeth's visions changed. In *Libri Visionum*

Secunda and Tertius, she focused on this world and the Church. Elisabeth readily challenged the Church, its leaders, and their failings, believing it in part her own responsibility to correct the corruption. She was deeply concerned about the spread of heretical movements; at the time of her visionary experience, the Cathars, a heretical Christian group, were considered to be a threat to the Church because they denounced the Mass, baptism, marriage, and to a large extent, the Church itself. Elisabeth, through her visions, spoke out against the Cathars and chastised Church leaders who chose to ignore them. Also, Elisabeth took issue with simony, the buying and selling of Church offices.

Although Elisabeth rarely left the monastery at Schonau, her message was widely circulated and well accepted. Even when her revelations differed from accepted Church traditions, Elisabeth encountered little opposition. In a vision, an angel told Elisabeth that the date for Mary's bodily Assumption was forty days after her recorded physical death on August 15. Although the Church recognized only August 15 as the Feast of the Assumption, the monastery at Schonau accepted Elisabeth's word and acknowledged September 23 as Mary's bodily Assumption and August 15 as the date of her death. Elisabeth's modern biographer Anne Clark has noted that monasteries at Mainz, Regensburg, and other cities followed Elisabeth's revelation.

In spite of her established reputation as a highly respected spiritual leader and mystic, Elisabeth sought the encouragement of another well-known visionary of her time, Hildegard of Bingen. Letters of their correspondence survive today, documenting Elisabeth's need for support and approval from this knowledgeable woman. In her letters, Hildegard readily offered advice and criticism to the young novice.

For a woman who rarely traveled beyond the walls of the Schonau monastery, Elisabeth's reputation was far-reaching. Surviving translations of her texts attest to her popularity and appeal to not only laypeople but ecclesiastical readers as well. Roger of Ford, a Cistercian monk, was credited with introducing some of Elisabeth's works into France and England. Translations also exist in Anglo-Saxon and even Icelandic versions.

Her brother Egbert's discussion of her death focused on her spiritual qualities and the nature of her visions. He wrote *De Obitu* as a tribute to her remarkable life and accomplishments. Elisabeth died at the age of thirty-five, but she managed, along with Hildegard, to establish a female voice within religious circles, giving credence to her ideas. Although she never officially preached a sermon, her words were widely circulated and better remembered than those of many of her male contemporaries.

BIBLIOGRAPHY

Brown, Raphael. *The Life of Mary as Seen by the Mystics.* Rockford, IL: Tan Books and Publishers, 1991.

Bynum, Caroline Walker. *Jesus as Mother: Studies in the Spirituality of the High Middle Ages.* Berkeley: University of California Press, 1982.

Clark, Anne. *Elisabeth of Schonau: A Twelfth-Century Visionary.* Philadelphia: University of Pennsylvania Press, 1992.

Petroff, Elisabeth Alvida, ed. *Medieval Women's Visionary Literature.* New York: Oxford University Press, 1986.

Stephanie Witham

ELIZABETH OF BRAUNSCHWEIG
(1510–1558)
Germany
Protestant Political Leader

Despite his insistence on the spiritual equality of all persons and his bold repudiation of papal sovereignty and the rule of celibacy that served as a distinguishing feature of the Roman Catholic ministry, Martin Luther maintained a very traditional view of women. Refusing to draw distinctions between noblewomen and commoners, he considered all women inferior to men in abilities and subject to their husbands in the marriage bond. Additionally, these chaste, silent, and obedient women were not to be permitted any political or teaching ministry in the Church. Even with these strictures, however, Luther's reform ideas continued to receive the warm support of a number of women ranked among the German aristocracy. Elizabeth of Braunschweig was one of these noblewomen, a devotee who knew Luther and who dedicated her adult life to the cause of promoting his reform program.

Born the third of five children into the leading family of Brandenburg, Elizabeth's Protestant credentials were anything but newly minted. Her mother, Elizabeth of Brandenburg, was sister to Christian II of Denmark, the prince who introduced Lutheranism into that state. Elizabeth's maternal grandmother Christine was the sister of Frederick of Saxony, the elector who protected Luther from Roman Catholic Emperor Charles V. On the opposite side of the religious divide was her father, the Elector of Brandenburg Joachim I. His strident opposition to Luther at two Church councils, one at the city of Worms (1521) and again at Augsburg (1520), marked him as one of the leading political figures in the early efforts to undermine the Protestant cause. Elizabeth's mother, unwilling to renounce her Lutheran beliefs, abandoned her husband for a seventeen-year exile in

Saxony. At one point she even took up residence in Luther's household in Wittenburg.

In 1525, at the age of fifteen, Elizabeth of Braunschweig was married to Duke Erich of Braunschweig-Calenberg. During the first decade of her marriage to a man forty years her senior, Elizabeth remained firmly within the Roman Catholic communion, this despite the fact that her mother had converted to Lutheranism. But in 1538, after visits from her mother, her brother John of Kustrin, and the Lutheran pastor Antonius Corvinus, Elizabeth announced her conversion to the Reformed faith. Identifying more specific theological reasons for her decision is problematic since women could neither attend universities nor receive any formal theological training. And as historian William Monter has pointed out, sixteenth-century women did not often convert to Protestantism on an individual basis. Instead they were more likely to join Reform communions in the company of male relatives. But women were encouraged to read the Bible and to share in the "priesthood of all believers," and Elizabeth seems to have regarded this principle as foundational. Surprisingly, her husband was more understanding than her father had been toward his wife; Duke Erich allowed Elizabeth the free practice of her beliefs so long as she did not attempt to disturb the established faith. This position was really quite exceptional in a strongly patriarchal age, for it was commonly thought that women who demurred from their husbands on religious matters were challenging age-old assumptions about proper gender roles.

When Erich died in 1540, Elizabeth became regent for her twelve-year-old son, a position enjoyed by a select few noblewomen of the period. She held this post for the next five years, supervising a household staff of officials and servants numbering upwards of 200 persons. Her power to initiate substantive change, therefore, was largely set by "personal" factors of marital status, inherited power, and social class. In her privileged capacity, she undertook a concerted effort to disseminate the Lutheran vision of Reformed religion throughout Braunschweig-Calenberg. Turning for assistance in this work to Philip of Hesse, the political leader of the Schmalkald League, a coalition of Protestant princes in the Empire, Antonius Corvinus was again dispatched to her household. Corvinus was both theologian and administrator, having already composed numerous expository *postillae* on the Gospels, Epistles, and Psalms. These sermon aids were printed in numerous Low German dialects and were instrumental in the spread of the Reform movement. As an administrator, he had served Philip of Hesse as a delegate to the Regensburg Colloquy in 1541. After his arrival, Corvinus composed a Church order that attacked concubinous priests and permitted those in cloisters to leave whenever they wished. He undertook a series of extensive visitations, often accompanied by the regent, to churches throughout the territory in an attempt to introduce Lutheran belief and practice.

Elizabeth had carefully schooled her son Erich II in the Lutheran faith and arranged his marriage to the Lutheran sister of the Duke of Saxony. But at age eighteen the young man allied himself with the Catholic Emperor Charles V and began the process of undoing his mother's Reform efforts. He imprisoned the pastor Corvinus in 1549, not least because the pastor advocated complete church autonomy from state control, and rebuffed his mother's entreaties to uphold the Lutheran cause. Although he later recanted his beliefs and rejoined his mother, Erich was defeated in battle in 1553 by his Catholic cousin Heinz, and Elizabeth was expelled from the Calenberg duchy of Braunschweig. Spending three years in exile and poverty before returning home to die at the age of forty-eight, her efforts while regent did not go unrewarded in this northwestern German territory. Eventually, all of Braunschweig accepted the Lutheran Communion. The political patronage and support of Elizabeth, although limited to a few brief years in the 1540s, provided the essential groundwork for subsequent Lutheran ministers.

BIBLIOGRAPHY

Bailey, Teresa. "From Piety to Politics: Elizabeth of Braunschweig and the Introduction of the Reformation." Ph.D. dissertation, Stanford University, 1987.

Bainton, Roland H. *Women of the Reformation in Germany and Italy.* Minneapolis: Augsburg Publishing House, 1971. 111–144.

Monter, William. "Women in the Age of Reformation." In Renate Bridenthal, Claudia Koonze, and Susan Stuard, eds., *Becoming Visible: Women in European History.* 2nd ed. Boston: Houghton Mifflin, 1987. 203–219.

Wiesner, Merry E. "Nuns, Wives, and Mothers: Women and the Reformation in Germany." In Sherrin Marshall, ed., *Women in Reformation and Counter-Reformation Europe: Public and Private Worlds.* Bloomington: Indiana University Press, 1989. 8–28.

W. M. Spellman

ISABELLA D'ESTE
(1474–1539)
Italy
Patron of Arts and Letters and Political Activist

Isabella d'Este distinguished herself during the Italian Renaissance as an avid patron of the arts and as a consummate politician. Variously referred to as the "First Lady of the Renaissance" and as a "Machiavelli in skirts," Isabella d'Este endeavored to live life on her own terms, cultivating the recognition and admiration of artists and writers, statesmen and Popes. While historians disagree as to which of Isabella's interests deserve the most recognition—her cultural patronage or her political intrigues—they agree that she pursued both activities with remarkable vigor.

Despite being the eldest child of Ercole d'Este, Duke of Ferrara (1431–1505), and his wife, Leonora of Aragon (1455–1493), Isabella d'Este's future did not include, as it would have if she had been a first-born son, ruling the independent Italian city–state of Ferrara. Instead, Duke Ercole arranged a politically advantageous marriage for his daughter with Francesco Gonzaga (1466–1519), the son of and heir to the ruling dynasty in Mantua. Because of its strategic location, an alliance between Ferrara and Mantua could help protect Ferrara against the Venetians' desire to expand their territory into the mainland. The marital alliance would also help Ferrara maintain its sovereign status, by strengthening its ties to the neighboring state of Mantua. Duke Ercole formally announced the engagement of Isabella and Francesco in May 1480. Ten years later, at the age of sixteen, Isabella d'Este became Marchesa of Gonzaga.

Upon arriving in Mantua, Isabella forged her most enduring friendship with Francesco's sister, Elisabetta Gonzaga Montefeltro, Duchess of Urbino (1471–1526). Elisabetta suggested by her own example how a lady at her social level should conduct herself. After visiting Elisabetta's court at Urbino, a renowned cultural center, Isabella strove to entice intellectuals and artists to participate in Mantua's courtly activities. Isabella then embarked upon a lifelong

Cartoon for the portrait of Isabella d'Este by Leonardo da Vinci. Credit: Alinari/Art Resource, NY. Reprinted with permission.

endeavor to design and decorate her own personal chambers—a private study, a museum, and a library—rooms in which her well-connected guests could be graciously entertained and, should the need arise, politically manipulated.

With the help of her numerous connections, Isabella amassed a private collection composed of antiquities as well as contemporary masterpieces. A lover and patron of the arts, Isabella relied on the advice and assistance of Christoforo Romano, the sculptor, who served as her artistic guide for many years. She frequently appealed to artists, like Leonardo da Vinci, musical instrument craftsmen, like Lorenzo da Pavia, and men of letters, like Baldassare Castiglione (the author of *The Book of the Courtier*) and Pietro Bembo (the classical and Italian scholar and poet), whenever she sought help to judge the worth of, or to expedite the acquisition of, any "excellent thing."

Isabella's artistic interests also extended to the new printing industry. Aldo Manuzio (ca. 1450–1515), the humanist-turned-printer, made available to an increasingly educated public printed works by classical authors, such as Ovid, and Italian authors, such as Petrarch and Dante. Isabella delighted in ordering and buying books from Manuzio's acclaimed Aldine press. Works by contemporary authors provided Isabella with special pleasure, and she supported the work of the poet Ludovico Ariosto (1474–1533). In recognition of her patronage, Ariosto personally paid Isabella a visit to present her with a copy of his famous poem *Orlando Furioso*.

Isabella's impressive collections ultimately helped to enhance the social status of the Gonzaga family; and when the need arose, Isabella fully understood the political advantages to be gained by bestowing a gift upon a potential ally. Such political alliances held great significance for families like the Gonzagas because of the unstable political climate that dominated Italy during Isabella's lifetime. As the French house of Valois competed with the Spanish house of Hapsburg for control of the Italian peninsula—in a conflict known as the Italian Wars (1494–1559)—both Francesco and Isabella found ample opportunities to play active political roles.

Francesco earned a living by hiring himself as a *condottierre*, a professional soldier. Although Francesco's duplicitous political intrigues often called his loyalty into question, his various employers nevertheless valued his skill as a soldier. Pope Julius II (ruled 1503–1513), however, must have felt the need to provide himself with some means of guaranteeing Francesco's loyalty, because he extended an "invitation" to Isabella's ten-year-old son Federico (1500–1540) to attend upon him in Rome. Unable to refuse the Pope's request, the tearful mother kissed her favorite son good-bye, while the shrewd politician frequently wrote to counsel him to make the most of his opportunity. The years Federico spent at the court of Pope Julius II (1510–1513) proved to be profitable ones, as he had the opportunity to make important social and political connections.

During Francesco's military absences, Isabella took advantage of her unique opportunity to reign in Mantua. Isabella demonstrated a gift for rule accompanied by genuine regard for her subjects. The skillful manner in which Isabella governed Mantua earned her the admiration of her contemporaries.

Always on the lookout for an alliance that might assure the Gonzagas' continued sovereignty, Isabella actively cultivated the goodwill of the most influential figures of her time. A significant opportunity arose for Isabella when Cardinal Giovanni de' Medici was elected Pope Leo X (ruled 1513–1521). Isabella lost no time in endorsing the new Pope. Before he became Pope, Leo had stood as godfather to Francesco and Isabella's youngest son, Ferrante (1507–1557). An art enthusiast like Isabella, Leo surrounded himself with cultivated men, many of whom Isabella counted among her close personal friends. Isabella knew she could rely on her friends to promote a Gonzaga alliance with the new Pope, and she undertook a journey to Rome, where her intimate friends—Giuliano de' Medici, the Pope's brother; Pietro Bembo; and Baldassare Castiglione—greeted her with pleasure. After successfully establishing an amicable, politically expedient relationship between the Gonzagas and Leo X, Isabella found herself compelled to return to Mantua from Rome to nurse her husband, whose health had deteriorated to the point that he was no longer physically able to serve as a soldier.

With the death of King Louis XII of France (ruled 1498–1515) and the ascension of Francis I (ruled 1515–1547), Isabella took advantage of another political opportunity by sending her fifteen-year-old son Federico to pay his respects to Francis I, the new ruler of Milan. Isabella responded with enthusiasm when Francis invited Federico to accompany him to France. Federico, who had already profited from the years he had spent at the court of Pope Julius II, now had a prime opportunity to continue developing his network of political connections. Upon Federico's return from France in 1517, Isabella arranged a financially advantageous marriage contract between Federico and Maria Paleologa, the eight-year-old daughter of the Marquis of Monferrato.

By 1519, Isabella's husband, Francesco, recognized that his health was rapidly failing. On his deathbed, Francesco acknowledged Isabella's political talents. After her husband's death, Isabella lent her capable assistance in administering the affairs of Mantua to her son Federico. When Pope Leo X appointed Federico as captain-general of his papal forces in 1521, Isabella personally oversaw the signing of the contract.

Isabella's insistence that Mantua maintain its neutrality during the conflicts that ravaged the Italian peninsula ultimately prolonged the survival of Mantua as an autonomous state; however, Isabella's plans to govern Mantua's affairs as regent with her son Federico came to an abrupt end when he rebelled against her authority. Federico assumed complete control over his inheritance upon turning twenty-two, and he began paying more attention to his mistress, Isabella Boschetti, than he did to his mother. As a result of this slight, Isabella transferred her attentions to her second son, Ercole (1505–1565), whom she sent to the University of Bologna. Isabella's youngest son, Ferrante, left Italy to follow a military career in the service of Charles V (Holy Roman Emperor, 1519–1556).

With the military conflicts between the French and Spanish steadily escalating, Pope Clement VII (ruled 1523–1534) found it politically expedient to ally himself with Italy's ruling families. Isabella, who was always sensitive to Italy's political situation, responded by arranging a trip to Rome. Upon her arrival in 1525, Isabella received Clement VII's cordial welcome. Soon after her arrival, Charles V's army, which included Spanish and German soldiers, began marching toward Rome as part of a military offensive. In spite of the accelerating danger, Isabella chose to ignore Federico's warning, deciding to remain in Rome until she had achieved her goal of obtaining a cardinalship for her son Ercole.

Isabella was unable to leave Rome when Pope Clement VII found himself forced to issue an order to close the city gates. In a desperate effort to raise the money needed to buy off the advancing soldiers, Pope Clement announced his decision to create five new cardinalships, which he offered for sale. Isabella saw her chance, raised the asking price of 40,000 ducats, and received a red cardinal's hat for her son Ercole.

Instead of yielding to panic, Isabella turned her attention to securing provisions and to fortifying the palace where she had been lodging. She also undertook the protection of hundreds of her friends, including many of the Italian ambassadors to Rome. Isabella's residence was one of the few buildings to escape the 1527 sack of Rome by Charles V's soldiers, due in large part to her sensible preparations and to her courage. Although she had not seen her son Ferrante (who was a soldier in Charles's army) for almost three years, she knew that he would find and protect her. Ferrante succeeded. He engineered a daring escape and rescued his mother and her companions. While still in Rome, Ferrante accepted a cavalry command, as a general, in the Emperor Charles V's imperial army.

An astute politician, Isabella foresaw the eventual triumph of Charles V's forces over the Italian peninsula, and she arranged to be present during the meeting between Charles V and Pope Clement VII. Charles personally honored Mantua with a visit, and Isabella had the satisfaction of seeing the Holy Roman Emperor bestow a dukedom upon her eldest son, Federico II.

The sudden and unexpected death of Maria Paleologa threatened

Federico's future marriage plans, but Isabella swiftly negotiated a new contract for Federico with Maria's younger sister, Margherita (1510–1566). Federico and Margherita wed in 1531, and Isabella graciously welcomed her new daughter-in-law to Mantua.

Isabella had also arranged what she hoped would be a politically advantageous marriage for her daughter Leonora (1493–1543), her eldest child, with Francesco Maria Della Rovere, the Duke of Urbino (1490–1538). Of Isabella's other daughters, two died while still children (Margherita and Livia), and two became nuns (Ippolita and Paolo).

Throughout her long life, Isabella distinguished herself as a consummate politician. She successfully steered the Gonzagas' fortunes through the many political upheavals that culminated in Charles V's domination of the Italian peninsula. In the end, Mantua retained at least the appearance of an autonomous state. Her supposed deathbed declaration to Federico sums up Isabella's estimation of her achievements: "I am a woman and I learned to live in a man's world" (Marek 234).

BIBLIOGRAPHY

Cartwright, Julia (Mrs. Ady). *Isabella d'Este: Marchioness of Mantua (1474–1539)*. 2 vols. New York: Dutton, 1923.

Kolsky, Stephen. "Images of Isabella d'Este." *Italian Studies* 39 (1984): 47–62.

Marek, George R. *The Bed and the Throne: The Life of Isabella d'Este*. New York: Harper & Row, 1976.

Martindale, Andrew. "The Patronage of Isabella d'Este at Mantua." *Apollo* 79 (1964): 183–191.

Meyer, Edith Patterson. *First Lady of the Renaissance: A Biography of Isabella d'Este*. Boston: Little, Brown, 1970.

Debra Barrett-Graves

JACQUELINE FÉLICIE
(Jacoba Felice)
(1290–d. after 1322)
France
Physician

Jacqueline Félicie de Almania was a woman of great skill and great courage who was successful at healing people, but that very success led her to be brought before the Inquisition in 1322 in Paris for practicing medicine without a license. Félicie's background is obscure; she was born around 1290 and may have been originally from Florence and emigrated to Paris. Some sources suggest that she was of Jewish descent and may have come to Paris from the Holy Roman Empire. A number of Jews, both men and women, are mentioned in a variety of European archives as practicing medicine in Europe in the fourteenth century, and Jewish women seem to be particularly adept as healers. Jews were known for their scholarship, which may have made some people more assured about their skills. There were several Jewish women who studied medicine at Salerno. Félicie managed to receive some training as a physician and practiced medicine in Paris in the early fourteenth century. But it was illegal for a woman to practice medicine—being successful made it all the more a crime—and at first she was admonished to stop and forced to pay a fine. When she continued her work in 1322, she was arrested and threatened with excommunication. She was tried before the bishops of Paris and the Dean of the Medical Faculty at the University of Paris.

Félicie had been visiting the ill in Paris and the surrounding suburbs. She had felt people's pulses and examined their urine. She had promised to cure them if they had faith in her and then had given them various syrups and potions and other concoctions and visited them regularly. She had received payment for her work, but only if she cured her patients. Enough of them survived to allow Félicie to earn a good living, and her refusal to accept payment unless her treatment was successful made her very popular.

At her trial, John of Padua, who had been a surgeon for King Philip IV of France, was one of the witnesses for the prosecution. He argued not only that what she was doing was illegal but that she could easily cause someone's death and that for this potentially appalling happening, she should be excommunicated.

But defending counsel showed that Félicie had treated and in fact cured many people who had been ill. She had brought comfort to her patients and had visited them regularly until they had regained their health. Many of Félicie's former patients came forward to testify on her behalf. They claimed that she had done more for them than any other physician and that since she had not taken payment until they were cured, they had not worried about inquiring into her credentials. One witness stated that many people had said that she was wiser in the art of medicine than the greatest master doctor in Paris. She was certainly willing to invest more time in each of her patients.

A number of patients explained they had tried other physicians first, but when none helped them, they turned instead to Félicie. Many of them had been referred to her by friends. Yvo Tueleu related how ill she had been, how no one else could help her until Félicie had given her a purge that had brought her fever down. Not only laypeople but churchmen had also sought Félicie's help. Dominus Odo de Cornessiaco, a friar, had failed to find a cure even after being visited by several notable physicians. Félicie had stayed by his side. She gave him massages with hot oil, steam baths, and poultices made from healing plants. She had worked tirelessly until he was cured.

Though Félicie worked with both men and women, Félicie claimed that it was especially important for her to be a physician for women. She argued that it was far better and more seemly for a wise woman who was learned in the art of medicine to be the one to visit a sick woman instead of a male physician. Many women would be horrified if a man were to touch their breasts, belly, feet, or other private parts. They would rather allow themselves to die than reveal their secret infirmities to a man. Women needed women practitioners; as Félicie perceived it, it was really a matter of life and death.

Yet Félicie's success and her arguments for women's health care were dismissed as unimportant, and she was found guilty of willful disobedience. She was told she could no longer practice medicine on pain of death and was excommunicated. Félicie's punishment came in large part not because she was incompetent but rather because she was so successful. Part of her sentence was to withdraw her statement that she cured many sick people whom the masters could not cure. Such a claim, they stated, was frivolous, since the court knew that any man trained in the art of medicine could cure the sick better than any woman. Unfortunately, Félicie disappears from the records after her trial. We don't know what became of her and if she continued her practice despite the harsh threats.

BIBLIOGRAPHY

Bourdillon, Hillary. *Women as Healers: A History of Women and Medicine.* Cambridge: Cambridge University Press, 1988.

Brooke, Elisabeth. *Women Healers: Portraits of Herbalists, Physicians, and Midwives.* Rochester, VT: Healing Arts Press, 1995.

Hurd-Mead, Kate Campbell. *A History of Women in Medicine: From the Earliest Times to the Beginning of the Nineteenth Century.* Haddam, CT: The Haddam Press, 1938.

Kibre, Pearl. "The Faculty of Medicine at Paris, Charlatanism, and Unlicensed Medical Practices in the Later Middle Ages." *Bulletin of the History of Medicine* 27, 1 (January–February 1953): 1–20.

Carole Levin

LAVINIA FONTANA
(1552–1614)
Italy
Portraitist and Altarpiece Painter

Lavinia Fontana has recently received recognition for being the first female painter in Italy to enjoy a successful career as an artist working in an urban setting. Throughout her career as an independent master, Lavinia accepted both private and public commissions, painting numerous portraits and public altarpieces.

Being born the daughter of the successful artist Prospero Fontana (1512–1597), a provincial painter with a solid reputation, had numerous advantages. During Lavinia's apprenticeship, Prospero shared with his daughter the artistic skills he had mastered during his early training in Genoa. The time Prospero had spent working in Florence and Rome, prior to returning to Bologna, undoubtedly contributed to the overall quality of Lavinia's early studies. Lavinia's apprenticeship in her father's studio provided her with ample opportunities to contribute to her father's commissioned works as well as to produce works of her own design. The first recorded works attributed to the hand of Lavinia date from 1575. Lavinia also profited from being born in the Italian city–state of Bologna, which was a prominent Italian artistic center during her lifetime. In Bologna, Lavinia could study distinguished works of art at her convenience.

Lavinia enjoyed a reputation as a successful portrait painter early in her career. Her attention to the details of the elaborate costumes worn by her aristocratic clients helped contribute to her unique status as an artist with uncommon promise and skill. Known to her contemporaries primarily as a portraitist, Lavinia's *oeuvre* also included a wide range of subject matter. Her works frequently drew on biblical and mythological settings, which incorporated numerous figures, including male and female nudes. Lavinia enjoyed a highly successful, professionally active career prior to the marriage her father arranged for her.

Lavinia's marital alliance in 1577 with Gian Paolo Zappi, a minor

Lavinia Fontana, self-portrait. Credit: Alinari/Art Resource, NY. Reprinted with permission.

painter who had trained in her father's workshop, raised her social status. Lavinia, who belonged to the artisan class, married into a family with noble origins. As a condition of the contract, Zappi remained in Bologna with Lavinia and her family, and he agreed to work in Prospero's studio. Lavinia, a more gifted artist than her husband, soon found herself in the position of supporting her family, whereas Zappi assumed the duties of running the house, a role reversal quite unusual for the period.

Prior to the 1570s, it was rare for a woman to earn a commission to work on a large-scale project, but Lavinia broke artistic ground by accepting and completing several large-scale public commissions. The Spanish court provided Lavinia with her first chance to execute such a work. In 1589, King Philip II of Spain (ruled 1556–1598) commissioned Lavinia to complete an altarpiece painting of the Holy Family for the El Escorial, the Spanish royal palace located near Madrid. Philip's previous association with **Sofonisba Anguissola** (ca. 1532/1535–1625), the Cremonese artist, may have played a role in his decision to entrust Lavinia with such an artistically prestigious and financially lucrative commission. Lavinia's own fame throughout Italy, at age thirty-seven, may have contributed to Philip's decision as well. The altarpiece painting that Lavinia completed for Philip—*Holy Family with Sleeping Christ Child*—is still considered a masterpiece today. After 1589, Lavinia accepted additional commissions for large-scale altarpiece works in Bologna and Rome. Around this time, Fontana gained the further distinction of becoming the first woman to maintain workshops in both of these cities.

In addition to securing the patronage of the Spanish king, Lavinia's fame as an artist earned her the patronage of a succession of Popes. Younger than Anguissola by approximately twenty years, Lavinia had established herself by the 1590s as a successful, independent artist, a rare accomplishment for a woman of her time. Pope Gregory XIII (ruled 1572–1585), himself originally from Bologna, ardently admired Lavinia's work. Another pope, Clement VIII (ruled 1592–1605), honored Lavinia by employing her for a time in the capacity of court painter.

The fortuitous circumstances surrounding her birth combined with her amazing artistic gifts explain Lavinia's ability to work as an independent artist. Contemporary records also document Lavinia's impressive academic achievements, indicating that she earned the degree of *dottoressa* (Doctor of the University) from the University of Bologna in 1580, another one of her many praiseworthy accomplishments.

Lavinia, along with her artist husband, Gian Paolo Zappi, may have moved her family to Rome around 1603, the period during which she executed her best-known public commission. Lavinia's large-scale painting *The Stoning of St. Stephen Martyr* (ca. 1603–1604) was created for the altarpiece in the church of San Paolo Fuori le Mura, an important pilgrimage church. Upon its completion, her work proved a disappointment for her contemporaries. Unfortunately, its destruction in a fire in 1823 makes evaluating the success of this significant, large-scale work (over twenty feet high) impossible today.

In 1611, a medal was struck in honor of Lavinia's artistic accomplishments. Her contemporaries and patrons held both her and her work in high regard, so much so that Lavinia received the honor of being elected to membership in Rome's celebrated Academy. The admirable quality of her work enabled Lavinia to ask and receive for her works a price equivalent to that commanded by male artists of significant stature.

In spite of what amounted to a lengthy career, during which time Lavinia produced over 100 works—including portraits, smaller religious and mythological commissions, and large-scale commissions of religious works—only about 30 or so signed and/or dated works can now be attributed to Lavinia Fontana with certainty.

A portraitist and an altarpiece painter, Lavinia Fontana enjoyed a prominent career as a respected artist. Lavinia Fontana's unusual achievements suggest that, with the appropriate circumstances, a talented woman could enjoy a career as a successful artist. What seems even more amazing is that Lavinia accomplished this feat while bearing eleven children. Sadly, only three of Lavinia's children outlived their illustrious mother. Lavinia Fontana's striking career, spanning approximately four decades, ultimately set a precedent for the later artistic achievements of **Artemisia Gentileschi** (ca. 1593–1652/1653).

BIBLIOGRAPHY

Greer, Germaine. *The Obstacle Race: The Fortunes of Women Painters and Their Work.* New York: Farrar, Straus and Giroux, 1979.

Harris, Ann Sutherland, and Linda Nochlin. *Women Artists: 1550–1950.* New York: Knopf, 1981.

Heller, Nancy G. *Women Artists: An Illustrated History.* New York: Abbeville, 1987.

Kortenhorst, Cynthia. "The First Truly Professional Female Artist?" In Els Kloek, Nicole Teeuwen, and Marijke Huisman, eds., *Women of the Golden Age: An International Debate on Women in Seventeenth-Century Holland, England and Italy.* Hilversum, Netherlands: Verloren, 1994. 183–185.

Murphy, Caroline. "Lavinia Fontana: The Making of a Woman Artist." In Els Kloek, Nicole Teeuwen, and Marijke Huisman, eds., *Women of the Golden Age: An International Debate on Women in Seventeenth-Century Holland, England and Italy.* Hilversum, Netherlands: Verloren, 1994. 171–181.

Debra Barrett-Graves

VERONICA FRANCO
(1546–1591)
Italy
Poet and Courtesan

Veronica Franco was a poet and citizen of Venice and one of that city's most famous *cortegiane oneste*, or honored courtesans, a distinction given to higher-class courtesans known for their intellectual gifts, wit, and fashionable appearances. The *cortegiane oneste* enjoyed a unique status apart both from the lower-class prostitutes and from the married women of Venice's upper class who were generally confined to private, domestic lives.

Although Franco and her three brothers were not born into the Venetian nobility, they did belong to a respectable class of merchants and professional men. When Veronica was young she was married to Paola Panizza, a physician; although the reasons are not known, they soon separated. Franco and Panizza did not have any children together, but Franco later had six children, three of whom died in infancy. The father of one of her children was Andrea Thon, a prominent Venetian nobleman.

Although marriage was considered the more socially and economically prudent choice for women, Franco remained single for the rest of her life, supporting herself and her children through her own career as a courtesan. Venice had a particularly high number of courtesans; this may have been due to the fact that the city was a crossroads for a variety of foreign travelers or because of the custom of relatively late marriages among Venetian upper-class men. Scholars have also suggested that the government may have condoned the *cortegiane oneste* because of the tax revenues they produced. The city's attitude toward this class of women, however, was generally ambiguous; Venice both boasted and lamented the *cortegiane oneste*, who were said to rival the upper-class matrons in their sumptuous wardrobes and surpass them in their conversational gifts. It was apparently Franco's mother who introduced her to the profession, for by the time Franco was twenty, she and her mother were both among the

215 women identified in a catalog published in 1565 listing the names, addresses, and prices of Venice's upper-class courtesans.

By the time Franco was in her late twenties, she was associated with the literary salon, or *ridotti*, of Domenico Venier, a poet who was even more noteworthy as a patron of various writers. Franco's poems and letters attest to the importance this connection to Venier and his circle had for her literary production and reputation. It was during the decade from 1570 that all of Franco's literary works were published. In 1575, she edited a collection of poems that she solicited from various authors, including nine of her own sonnets, in memory of Estor Martinengo, a Venetian nobleman who had fought valiantly against the Turks. This publication is an indication of Franco's association with the Venetian literati. Shortly after, she published her own book of poems, *Terze Rime*, dedicated to the Duke of Mantua, Guglielmo Gonzaga. This volume includes twenty-five *capitoli*, or poems of varying length; most of them are by Franco, but a few of them are by an unnamed author with whom she engages in a debate or dialogue on the subject of love. The *capitoli* are written in *terza rima*, three-line rhyming stanzas; in using the stylistically demanding *terza rima* form, Franco is departing from the more conventional form for lyric poetry, the Petrarchan sonnet.

Franco also published, in 1580, a collection of fifty of her personal letters that she had written over a period of several years, *Lettere familiari a diversi*. Several Italian authors had published collections of letters in the previous decades, though few of them were women. Franco's letters, conversational in tone, are filled with advice to various friends and discussion of various social issues. One of the most famous is a letter to a woman urging her not to allow her daughter to become a courtesan. While Franco does not appear to regret her position as a *cortegiana onesta*, she is also well aware that such a life can also involve oppression, inequality, and abuse, and she rails against a society that takes such advantage of impoverished young women who have no other means of support. In 1577 Franco had written a petition to government officials urging them to build a home for women who needed assistance in living chaste and honest lives. Whether through Franco's pleas or the influence of others, the Casa del Soccorso was soon established; it provided shelter for impoverished women who, because they were mothers or wives, were ineligible for similar charitable institutions for younger, unmarried women. Franco herself was familiar with the financial hardships women often endured. She was responsible for supporting not only her own children but the children of her deceased brother, and she also provided some assistance to her parents.

At the peak of her career, Franco associated with many of the leading political, intellectual, and artistic personages of her day. One of the crowning events of her life was in 1574 when Henri III de Valois, on his way from Poland to France to be crowned king, traveled through Venice and spent an evening with her. She gave him a miniature enameled portrait of herself and wrote two sonnets in his honor to mark the occasion. In 1580, when French essayist Montaigne visited Venice, Franco sent him a copy of her volume of letters, a gift he recorded in his journal. She was also the subject of a portrait by the Venetian painter Tintoretto.

While she circulated comfortably among many of the highly placed men of her time, she was also the subject of some slanderous attacks. Maffio Venier, a nephew of her literary patron, Domenico Venier, attacked Franco in three vicious poems that circulated in manuscript among the Venier salon; Franco used her poetic and rhetorical skills to defend herself and other courtesans through her own poetry. Another challenge to Franco's reputation came in 1580 when Redolfo Vannitelli, her children's tutor, brought charges against her for heresy. Property had been stolen from Franco's household, and when she suspected some of her servants, they sought to defend themselves by accusing her of heretical incantations and witchcraft. Although many such trials at the time often originated in domestic discord, penalties for those found guilty were severe and humiliating. Franco was brought to trial, but in two hearings she again used her rhetorical skills to defend herself, and the charges against her were eventually dropped. Support from her friend and patron Domenico Venier may also have helped to exonerate her, but her own eloquent self-defense was nonetheless critical in determining the outcome of the trial.

Veronica Franco died in Venice of an illness at the age of forty-five; although she bequeathed some gifts of jewelry and money to her sons, her financial and social standing were much less prosperous in the last decade of her life. Her more enduring legacy is a fascinating body of writing that reveals the complex status of women in sixteenth-century Venice.

BIBLIOGRAPHY

Jones, A., and M. Rosenthal. *Veronica Franco: Poems and Selected Letters.* Chicago: University of Chicago Press, 1998.

Rosenthal, M. *The Honest Courtesan: Veronica Franco, Citizen and Writer in Sixteenth-Century Venice.* Chicago: University of Chicago Press, 1992.

Jo Eldridge Carney

VERONICA GAMBARA
(1485–1550)
Italy
Patron of Artists and Poet

As the presiding figure over a lively court frequented by the leading artists, writers, and political figures of sixteenth-century Italy, Veronica Gambara represents the quintessential Renaissance woman. At her fashionable salon, she provided patronage for musicians, painters, poets, and intellectuals and also produced an impressive body of her own poetry in an era in which most of the literature was written by men.

Gambara was born into a noble family near Brescia in 1485; she was connected to numerous prominent aristocratic families. Her aunt, Emilia Pia, was praised as the paragon of feminine virtue in Castiglione's *The Book of the Courtier*, the famous Renaissance treatise on courtly life; her great-aunt was the humanist Isotta Nogarola. As a child, Veronica received a solid humanist education in Greek, Latin, philosophy, and theology. She also displayed an early interest in poetry, especially that of Petrarch and Virgil.

When she was twenty-four, Gambara was married to Count Giberto X, who was the ruler of the northern Italian Correggio region; although the marriage was arranged, it was a seemingly happy one. They had two sons, Ippolito and Girolamo, and Gambara's references to her marriage in her letters and her poetry are positive. Like her friend, the poet and patron **Vittoria Colonna**, Veronica Gambara married a man who had an impressive military career; however, unlike Colonna's husband, Count Giberto X gave up his military expeditions after his marriage and settled into a life of domesticity and administration of his estate.

Veronica seemed to be contented in her life as countessa of a beautiful estate and salon where poets and political figures alike gathered for social and intellectual interchange. The Casino, their castle of 360 rooms, included an impressive library and was lavishly decorated; guests were drawn there not only because of the comfort and opulence of the palace but also because of Gambara herself. It was said that she was not a great beauty, but she was quite vivacious and colorful, even flamboyant; she loved beautiful clothing, sumptuous decor, painting, and sculpture.

In 1518, Gambara's husband died; she was only thirty-two. Although her grief was genuine, her reaction was typically dramatic. She went into seclusion for several months; when she came out, not only was she dressed in mourning, but she had her rooms decorated in black cloth and refused to go anywhere unless the horses driving her were "as black as night." Like her countrywomen Vittoria Colonna and **Giulia Gonzaga**, Veronica Gambara decided never to remarry.

After her husband's death, Gambara was left to manage their state of Correggio, a task for which she proved quite able. She was concerned with literacy among her people, and she also aided widows and orphans who had lost husbands and fathers in the frequent wars Italy then experienced. She defended her city against invaders, figured out how to feed them in time of famine, and wrote to political leaders of the day, especially her friend Emperor Charles V, ruler of the vast Holy Roman Empire, advocating peace. She also promoted the careers of her sons: Ippolito followed a military career under Charles V, and Girolamo entered the Church and eventually became a cardinal.

Gambara also continued to welcome artists and intellectuals to her Correggio estate. She befriended the painter Antonio Allegri, whom we now refer to simply as Correggio. Gambara tirelessly promoted his work; his successful career was in part due to her procuring of commissions and patrons for him. Among other well-known figures who frequented her salon were the humanist and poet Pietro Bembo; the famous satirist Pietro Aretino; and the illustrious patron of the arts **Isabella d'Este**. Even the famous monarchs King Francis I of France and Emperor Charles V, both great patrons of the arts themselves, visited Gambara's estate. For the first visit of Charles V, Gambara ordered a two-mile roadway built leading to the estate to make the emperor's arrival more convenient and comfortable. Charles returned two years later for another stay at the Casino; for this visit, Veronica commissioned Correggio to decorate some of the walls of the castle with his paintings.

In addition to providing patronage for other artists, Gambara was herself a poet. When she was seventeen, she began writing to Pietro Bembo and eventually sent him her poems. He became a literary adviser and then a friend; they eventually met and corresponded for the rest of Gambara's life. Gambara's poetry comprises about eighty extant poems on a variety of subjects: Most of them are in sonnet form, though she did experiment with other forms as well, such as the madrigal and the ballad. Many of them are love poems to her husband; like most poetry of the day, these poems are influenced by the fourteenth-century Italian lyric poet Petrarch. Other poems deal with the effects of war on Italy; through her own experience as a ruler of Correggio and through her acquaintance with political leaders, Gambara had direct knowledge of military matters. In some of these poems she implores her friend, Charles V, to establish peace in his realm; in another sonnet, she urges the enemies Charles V and Francis I, "Conquer your wrath and ancient hatred." Other sonnets were written in praise of Vittoria Colonna, whose own poetry was widely admired. There are also poems on pastoral and spiritual themes.

Gambara's reputation as a poet was not as great as Vittoria Colonna's, but her work is certainly worthy of greater consideration than it has received. Gambara was also a lively correspondent; there are about 150 letters extant, written to family and friends, including Pietro Bembo, Vittoria Colonna, Isabella d'Este, and Pietro Aretino.

Veronica died in 1550 at the age of sixty-four and was buried next to her husband in the Church of San Domenico. In 1556, her tomb, the church, and her beloved Casino were all destroyed by an invasion of Spanish soldiers. In her lifetime Gambara had tirelessly appealed to her friend Charles V for peace, and he had assured her that he would always protect Correggio, but he had abdicated in 1556 in favor of his son, Philip II of Spain. While no memorial remains of Gambara's splendid court, her love of the arts lives on in the works of the artists she patronized and in the writings she has left behind.

BIBLIOGRAPHY

Allen, Beverly, Muriel Kittel, and Keala Jane Jewel, eds. *The Defiant Muse: Italian Feminist Poems from the Middle Ages to the Present.* New York: Feminist Press, 1989.

Jerrold, Maud F. "A Sister Poet: Veronica Gambara." In *Vittoria Colonna with Some Account of Her Friends and Her Times.* New York: E. P. Dutton, 1906.

Poss, Richard. "Veronica Gambara." In Katherina M. Wilson, ed., *Women Writers of the Renaissance and Reformation.* Athens: University of Georgia Press, 1987.

Jo Eldridge Carney

ARTEMISIA GENTILESCHI
(ca. 1593–1652/1653)
Italy
Artist

Among the leading contributions of Artemisia Gentileschi to the history of Western art is the influential role she played as a transmitter of Michelangelo Merisi da Caravaggio's (1573–1610) innovative artistic techniques. Along with her father, Orazio Gentileschi (1563–1639), Artemisia carried Caravaggio's use of simplified forms, his use of realistic portrayals, and his use of dramatic lighting throughout Italy, to Florence, Genoa, and Naples.

Born into the artisan class, the daughter of Prudentia Montone and the painter Orazio Gentileschi did not enjoy the humanistic training that **Sofonisba Anguissola** (ca. 1532/1535–1625), the Cremonese painter, had received from her father. Nor was Artemisia able to attend a prestigious university and earn her doctoral degree, as did **Lavinia Fontana** (1552–1614), the Bolognese painter. In spite of a limited formal education, Artemisia received superior artistic training, serving as an apprentice to her father. Artemisia enjoyed the benefit of having as her teacher an artist whose work was highly regarded. Orazio's eldest child and sole daughter, Artemisia alone of his four children demonstrated an amazing gift for painting. Fortunately for Artemisia, the circumstances of her birth enabled her pursuit of a serious artistic career. Artemisia also found herself living in an important Italian artistic center during a period of artistic prominence. The abundance of major historical artistic monuments located in Rome, which Artemisia could study at her leisure, proved to be especially beneficial for her early training.

From the start of her career, Artemisia worked on full-scale compositions, many of which featured dramatic subjects. Artemisia has been most widely recognized for her dramatic studies of Judith and Holofernes. Her engaging paintings of the Old Testament heroines Susanna, Esther, and Bathsheba have also received praise.

Artemisia's most successful paintings, completed before 1630, in-

Artemisia Gentileschi, *Self-Portrait as La Pittura*. Cat. no. ML 499 BP 2652. The Royal Collection © 1999, Her Majesty Queen Elizabeth II. Reprinted by permission of the Royal Collection Picture Library.

corporate Caravaggesque realism and *chiaroscuro*, a painting technique using varied tones of light and dark paint to suggest three-dimensional space. A hallmark technique of the *caravaggisti*, also known as the "night painters," was the use of *tenebrism*, light and dark contrasts used for dramatic intensity; Artemisia—the sole *caravaggista*—incorporated this technique into her own compositions with striking results.

In 1612, Artemisia had to endure what became a sensational trial, when her father formally accused Agostino Tassi (ca. 1580–1644), the artist he had hired to teach his daughter perspective, of repeatedly raping his daughter. At the time, Tassi had already been found guilty of arranging the murder of his wife. In spite of the questionable nature of Tassi's character, the examining judge chose to subject Artemisia to torture, ordering that metal rings (*sibille*) be tightened around her fingers to extract a confession of guilt. She also had to endure an internal physical examination to determine whether she was still a virgin. Even though Artemisia refused to recant her accusation of rape, the court still acquitted Tassi, who had spent less than a year in prison for the crime he committed against Artemisia.

To avoid further shame, Artemisia married a Florentine by the

name of Pietro Antonio di Vincenzo Stiattesi not long after the trial
had ended. The couple probably moved their household to Florence
shortly after being married. Artemisia had at least one daughter, variously referred to as Prudentia or Palmira, born in Florence around
1618. Artemisia's surviving correspondence suggests that she had a
second daughter, born sometime after 1624.

Throughout her career, Artemisia used her unique position as a
woman, which allowed her ready access to female models, including
herself, to full advantage. Artemisia's paintings often contain unusually striking depictions of female nudes. By 1615 Artemisia had established herself in Florence as a well-known artist. The lucrative
commission awarded to Artemisia by Michelangelo Buonarroti the
Younger to paint a nude figure, *The Allegory of Inclination* (ca.
1615), suggests his recognition of and admiration for Artemisia's talent in rendering the female nude with anatomical realism. Unfortunately, Leonardo, Michelangelo's heir, had another artist—Baldassare
Francheschini, Il Volterrano—cover the figure's nudity at a later date.

While in Florence, Artemisia also enjoyed the patronage of the
Medici family, the city's dynastic rulers. Artemisia's aristocratic patrons may have facilitated her ready acceptance, at the age of twenty-
three, into the prestigious Florentine Accademia del Disegno, which
had originally been founded by the artist Giorgio Vasari (1511–1574)
and others in 1563. Artemisia became an official member of the Florentine Accademia in 1616. Since the Accademia del Disegno had
received no women as members since opening, Artemisia's status as
a member constitutes an extraordinary achievement.

After Artemisia's marriage failed, she left Florence. She is believed
to have spent time in Genoa, when her father worked there between
1621 and 1624. She also produced some additional commissions in
Venice during the 1620s.

Artemisia's contemporaries recognized her skill as a portrait
painter; however, only one portrait painting (the so-called *Portrait of
a Condottieri*) remains today that can be attributed with confidence
to her. Artemisia's *Portrait of a Gonfaloniere* (1622) verifies her presence in Rome by 1622; its superb rendering further illustrates why
her contemporaries esteemed her work as that of a first-rate portraitist. Artemisia would remain in Rome until the end of the decade. A
drawing by Pierre Dumonstier le Neveu, dating from this period, of
Artemisia's hand holding a paintbrush is another testament to Artemisia's status as a prominent artist.

In her surviving letters, Artemisia mentions executing commissions for the kings of France, Spain, and England. Artemisia is believed to have taken up residence in England around 1638 in order to assist her father's work on an important commission for England's King Charles I (ruled 1625–1649) and Queen Henrietta Maria. Artemisia helped her ailing father complete work on Queen Henrietta Maria's palace, called the Queen's House, at Greenwich.

After 1630, Artemisia lived in Naples for a period of approximately twenty more years, except for the brief sojourn in London already mentioned. Artemisia's fame was such that when she arrived in Naples, according to legend, she was treated like a celebrity.

Artemisia's *Self-Portrait* (ca. 1630) represents one of her particularly unique and distinctive paintings. Her unusual choice to emphasize her role as a working artist contributes to the painting's singular appearance, as does Artemisia's inclusion of symbols typically associated with the subject of her allegory, the personification of painting. The symbols—a medallion on a chain, the artist's disordered hair, and her varicolored gown—imply imitation, the artistic frenzy of the creative act, and skill, respectively.

By the 1630s, Artemisia's Caravaggesque style had lost much of its fashionable appeal. Because Artemisia was both knowledgeable about and sensitive to contemporary trends, she successfully adapted her commissions to accommodate the preferences of her clients and patrons.

What little is known about the final decade of Artemisia's life comes from the correspondence she exchanged with Don Antonio Ruffo, a wealthy Sicilian patron, who employed her services as an artist. Thirteen letters, dating from around 1649–1651, have survived from their dealings. A singularly interesting detail included in Artemisia's correspondence with Don Ruffo is her stern insistence that he treat her fairly by paying her the price she quoted for her work.

The date of and the circumstances surrounding Artemisia's death are still unknown today. A possible date for her death is circa 1652–1653, around the time when some verses that refer to Artemisia in less than flattering terms appeared in print.

Artemisia Gentileschi is the first female Italian artist determined to compete with the male artists of her time. She claimed to have "the spirit of Caesar" in the soul of a woman, an unusual expression of personal self-worth by an exceptional woman. Refusing to accept a conventional role, she demonstrated through her many paintings her impressive status as an influential artistic genius.

BIBLIOGRAPHY

Garrard, Mary D. *Artemisia Gentileschi: The Image of the Female Hero in Italian Baroque Art.* Princeton: Princeton University Press, 1989.

Greer, Germaine. *The Obstacle Race: The Fortunes of Women Painters and Their Work.* New York: Farrar, Straus and Giroux, 1979.

Harris, Ann Sutherland, and Linda Nochlin. *Women Artists: 1550–1950.* New York: Knopf, 1981.

Heller, Nancy G. *Women Artists: An Illustrated History.* New York: Abbeville, 1987.

Debra Barrett-Graves

GIULIA GONZAGA
(1513–1566)
Italy
Patron of Artists and Religious Reformists

Giulia Gonzaga was a member of the illustrious Gonzaga family of
Mantua; her intellectual interests and beauty, as well as her affiliation
with the contemporary religious controversy and reform movement
in Italy, earned her a reputation in her day as one of the most fascinating women of the Italian Renaissance.

As a child, Giulia received a classical education along with her aristocratic brothers. When she was twelve, she was chosen to accompany her cousin **Isabella d'Este**, a famous patron of artists, to Rome
as one of her ladies-in-waiting; there Giulia met Vespasiano Colonna,
a widowed prince from southern Italy. A marriage was soon arranged;
at the time Giulia was fourteen and Colonna was forty-one. Just two
years after their marriage, Colonna died, leaving his vast property to
Giulia on the condition that she remain unmarried. Colonna's will
stipulated that if Giulia chose to remarry, she would have to forfeit
the property to her stepdaughter Isabella. Although Giulia had many
suitors, including Ippolito de' Medici, the nephew of Pope Clement
VII, she chose to remain single. Her stepdaughter, Isabella Colonna,
married Luigi Rodomante Gonzaga, Giulia's beloved brother.

Although Giulia seems to have preferred the quiet life, the early
years of her widowhood were not without incident. After her husband's death, Giulia's villa at Fondi became a salon for artists, writers,
and religious figures, and she herself inspired praise from such literary
giants as the novelist Bandello and the poets Ariosto and Tasso.

One of the most tragic events of Giulia's life took place when she
was just twenty years old. Giulia's reputation for talent and beauty
was known even outside of Italy. A notorious pirate, Kheyr-ed-din,
known in Europe as Barbarossa, was in the service of Sultan Süleyman
II, leader of the vast Ottoman Empire; he decided to kidnap Gonzaga
and take her back to Turkey as a present for Süleyman. During a raid
on the Italian coast, Barbarossa landed near Fondi, massacred many

of the inhabitants of the nearby village, and continued his march toward Giulia's castle. Fortunately, a vigilant servant alerted her of the impending danger, and Giulia managed to escape to a nearby fortress. Barbarossa's anger at Giulia's escape led him to further pillaging and killing until he was stopped by an army headed by Cardinal Ippolito de' Medici.

Giulia returned to her castle at Fondi to supervise repairs and restore order. Soon after this devastating episode, Giulia was troubled by litigious attacks from Isabella, her stepdaughter and sister-in-law. Luigi Gonzaga, Isabella's husband and Giulia's brother, had died in battle, leaving the young Isabella widowed and mother of a young son. Though well provided for, Isabella had long disputed her father's will that left everything to Giulia. Isabella continued her litigation for years, even after she was remarried to a wealthy general in the service of Charles V. Upon Isabella's remarriage, she lost custody of her son, Vespasiano Colonna, to Giulia and her father. For the rest of her life, Giulia looked after her beloved nephew, who grew up to become a famous and talented soldier–prince. Giulia also suffered another loss at this time when her longtime friend and defender Cardinal Ippolito de' Medici died.

In 1534, Giulia moved to Naples, where she met two men who would have a profound influence on her life: Juan de Valdes and Bernardino Ochino, members of the Italian reform movement. Juan de Valdes was a Spanish humanist who had fled to Italy to escape persecution for his reformist beliefs, even though he did not consider himself a Protestant. His teachings focused on the importance of inner spiritual values instead of external expressions of faith and extreme asceticism. Bernardino Ochino was the charismatic leader of the Capuchins, an austere order of the Franciscans; his sermons drew vast crowds, for his preaching, according to Emperor Charles V, "would make the stones weep."

When Gonzaga first heard Ochino preach, she was extremely moved, and she shared her responses with her friend, Valdes. In response, Valdes wrote for her the *Abecedario Christiano*, the "Christian Alphabet," a work that contributed significantly to the dissemination of reformist principles in Italy. Valdes dedicated a number of his other works to Gonzaga as well. From this point on, Gonzaga's principal interest was the Catholic reform movement. Although she could have lived in a more luxurious and fashionable manner, Gonzaga retired to the monastery of San Francesco delle Monache where she lived a simple, quiet life. She chose not to take formal vows, but she lived in the monastery for over thirty years, doing charitable works for local hospitals and the poor and serving as a resident patron for her religious home. She dedicated her life to carrying on the work of Juan de Valdes after his death in 1541. She maintained many of the friends she had made through her alliance with Valdes, including several women also interested in reformist ideas: **Vittoria Colonna**, Isabella Bresenga, Caterina Cibo, and **Veronica Gambara**. The poet Marcantonio Flaminio and courtier Pietro Carnesecchi were also close friends in the reformist circle.

Gonzaga accepted many of Valdes's reformist teachings, but she did not consider his works or her acceptance of them to be heretical. Many religious authorities disagreed, however, and in the 1540s, efforts were under way to eradicate the alleged heresy of Valdes's circle. Several reformists, including Bernardino Ochino, Peter Martyr, and Isabella Bresenga, fled to Geneva to escape persecution. Gonzaga offered emotional and financial support to her friends in exile, particularly to her close friend Isabella Bresenga, to whom she sent clandestine letters and money for years.

For a long time, Giulia herself had been strongly suspected by the Italian Inquisitors, but despite the urgings of many of her friends, especially Pietro Carnesecchi, she refused to flee. In January 1566, the Grand Inquistor Pius V was elected Pope; he quickly brought Carnesecchi to trial and condemned him to be beheaded and burned. After Carnesecchi's death in July, many letters from Giulia were found among his papers. Upon learning about this correspondence, the Pope declared, "Had I known this, she would have been burned alive." Pius V never had the opportunity to condemn Giulia Gonzaga to death, for she had already died in her monastery on 19 April 1566.

A famous beauty, painted by such famous artists as Sebastiano del Piambo and Titian, and praised by numerous poets, Gonzaga's true legacy was her remarkable generosity to her family and friends and her brave support of the religious ideals she believed in so strongly.

BIBLIOGRAPHY

Bainton, Roland. *Women of the Reformation in Germany and Italy.* Minneapolis: Augsburg Publishing House, 1971.
Hare, Christopher [Marian Andrews]. *A Princess of the Italian Reformation,*

Giulia Gonzaga, 1513–1566, Her family and Her Friends. New York: C. Scribner's Sons, 1912.

Nieto, J. C. *Juan de Valdes and the Origins of the Spanish and Italian Reformation.* Geneva: Librairie Droz, 1970.

Jo Eldridge Carney

ARGULA VON GRUMBACH
(1492–ca. 1563)
Germany
Protestant Activist

Noblewomen who sponsored and protected Protestant reformers were often successful and respected leaders, but women who took the next step and began speaking or writing publicly on issues of theology and church government were almost always thought to be operating beyond their legitimate sphere. During the first decade of the Reformation in Germany, Argula von Grumbach set aside the injunction of St. Paul that women should be silent in the presence of men and entered into the public controversies generated by the Reformed message. Her letters and appeals to a variety of public authorities won the tacit support of the Protestant leader Martin Luther and placed her at the center of discussion over the role of women in the spiritual life of the Christian community.

Born into the noble Bavarian family of Hohenstaufen and twenty-six years old when, in 1517, Luther began his criticisms of the Roman Catholic Church, Argula had learned to read and to write German as a young girl. Due to the impoverishment of the family, she had spent her teen years as a maid-in-waiting to the mother of the Duke of Bavaria. Upon the loss of her parents to the plague around 1505, she became a permanent member of the Duke Albrecht IV's household, and in 1516 she was married to Friedrich von Grumbach, a caretaker of ducal estates at Dietfurt and Lenting in Bavaria. She began to read Luther's works as they became available in German, and she corresponded with a number of early Protestant reformers: Andreas Osiander in Nuremberg, Paul Speratus in Würzburg, and Luther's friend George Spalatin in Wittenberg. Although technically of noble birth, Grumbach inherited nothing from her parents, and she considered herself to be common both in terms of education and with respect to her access to political power.

Grumbach's brief public career began in 1523 when an instructor at the University of Ingolstadt, Aracius Seehofer, was forced to renounce elements of his teaching that he had learned under one of Luther's disciples, Philip Melanchthon. Reports had surfaced that young students were being tainted by the *Colloquies* of Desiderius Erasmus. Erasmus remained within the Roman Catholic fold, but he was very critical of the many abuses in the Church, and his writings were considered dangerous by many leaders within the Roman Church. Ingolstadt was the home of Luther's adversary Johannes Eck, and the investigation into Seehofer's alleged heretical teaching could have resulted in serious punishment for him. Writing to the rector and faculty of the university, Grumbach challenged and criticized those who denied a hearing to Luther's theological principles. Refuting the authority of the Roman Church, she likened Seehofer's treatment to Rome's refusal to put the Bible into the hands of the people. According to Grumbach, Church authorities had given broad license to preachers pending the deliberations of a future Church Council. Inviting the faculty to discuss her position publicly, she cited examples of churchmen like St. Jerome who were not ashamed to write to women and pointed to Christ's instruction of Mary Magdalene as precedent for her own exceptional activities.

Rather than respond directly, the university sent a copy of her appeal to the two Dukes of Bavaria, Wilhelm and Ludwig. Grumbach also wrote to Duke Wilhelm, calling upon him to condemn the evil academics and to embrace the Gospel message alone. Following Luther's call for the reform of the Roman Church in his address *To the Christian Nobility*, she admonished the duke to reform the corruptions within the Church without recourse to Rome. Her disdain for the clergy, both secular and regular, was intense. She joined with other pamphleteers in calling for an end to celibacy, monasticism, and clerical absenteeism. Indeed, her letters can be grouped among other lay pamphleteers who in the four years between 1521 and 1525 published a wide range of reformed ideas with the support of clergy. At this early point in his career, Luther was eager to win the support of common laypeople, and he referred to Grumbach as "a special instrument of Christ." This tolerance of lay publishing in areas previously reserved for male clergy ended once Luther took a firm stand against those common people who abused their Christian freedom.

Neither university nor government saw fit to reply directly to Grumbach's criticisms in the Seehofer case. Unintimidated by official indifference to her letters, in October 1523 Grumbach wrote to the mayor and city council of Ingolstadt and to the leader of Saxony,

Frederick the Wise, requesting that she be given a hearing at a general meeting of the princes of the Holy Roman Empire scheduled for the fall of 1523 at Nuremberg. In her letter to the city council, Grumbach insisted that despite her lack of formal education, she belonged to the universal priesthood of all believers and would not be silenced in her testimony. Her letters were published without her knowledge and subsequently mocked in a satirical poem by an anonymous student at Ingolstadt who advised the noblewoman to stick to spinning.

Argula responded to the anonymous personal attack with her own satirical verse, calling her opponent a coward and citing biblical examples of women who were called on to give witness for Christ. More important, she was invited to attend the Imperial Diet. There is little extant evidence of her activities there beyond some deprecatory remarks about the debauchery of the assembled delegates. In 1524 she sent what became her final public letter to the Diet meeting at Regensburg, declaiming against the condemnation of Luther, and in 1530 she met the reformer for the first time. She had earlier encouraged Luther to marry, sent reports to him on the activity of fellow evangelicals in Bavaria, and later sent her own sons to study under Melanchthon at Wittenberg. Grumbach's theology mirrored Luther's very closely in its emphasis upon the need for all to read Scripture, and she skillfully used her attacks on the Roman clergy as a means of politicizing the literate commoner.

While she trusted that other women would follow her example into print, few were willing to break free of the age-old injunction that women restrict themselves to private, domestic, and familial reform. Pamphlet and pulpit decried against women's public involvement in matters involving theology or ecclesiology. After the death of her first husband in 1530, Grumbach remarried but ceased her public involvement in religious affairs. Only toward the end of her life, in 1563, did she reemerge on the public stage, this time briefly imprisoned by the Duke of Bavaria for circulating anti-Catholic books, officiating at funerals, and holding religious meetings in her home. While no longer involved in the print wars of the Reformation, Grumbach apparently continued to advance the Reform movement irrespective of "appropriate" female roles in the life of the Church.

BIBLIOGRAPHY

Bainton, Roland. *Women of the Reformation in Germany and Italy.* Minneapolis: Augsburg Publishing House, 1971. 97–110.

Russell, Paul. *Lay Theology in the Reformation*. Cambridge: Cambridge University Press, 1986. 191–201.

Wiesner, Merry. "Women's Response to the Reformation." In R. Po-Chia Hsia, ed., *The German People and the Reformation*. Ithaca: Cornell University Press, 1988. 148–171.

W. M. Spellman

ANNE HALKETT
(1623–1699)
Britain
Diarist and Political Activist

Intrigue, scandal, and romance fill the pages of Lady Anne Murray Halkett's memoirs, and through her personal accounts, the reader learns of a remarkable woman who enjoyed neither aristocratic status nor financial security but achieved an unusually independent and exciting lifestyle in the early modern period. Although her diaries were not published until 1701, Anne began writing them in 1677. By writing them later in her life, she was able not only to record the daily events of her life but also to reflect upon those moments that were more significant to her. It is only through her memoirs that the details of her life survive today.

Anne Murray admired her parents, Thomas Murray, provost of Eton College, and Jane Drummond Murray, governess to the Duke of Gloucester and the Princess Elizabeth. Even more remarkable, her mother was asked to serve as provost for one year following her husband's death. With her father's death in April 1623, three short months after her birth, the responsibility for her education fell to her mother who "spared no expense in educating all of her children in the most suitable way to improve them," as Anne said later. Anne, along with her sister, learned to write, speak French, play the lute, dance, sew needlework, and read, a task that she readily employed with the Bible and her devotions. As a remarkably learned woman, Anne acknowledged her debt of gratitude to her mother's commitment to her daughter's education.

It is clear from Murray's writings that aside from being highly educated she was extremely attractive, a fact attested to by the number of men who courted her. She first fell in love with Thomas Howard, the eldest son of Edward, Lord Howard of Escrick. His title and fortune were well above Anne's, and she did not have a sufficient dowry. However, her mother, upset that Anne would even consider such a match, ordered Howard to either marry another's daughter or leave England, threatening to throw Anne out of her house, should she ever see Howard again. Obedient to her mother but passionately in love with Howard, Anne agreed to her mother's terms but vowed never to marry anyone until he died. Only two years later, she learned that Howard had privately married Lady Elizabeth Mordaunt, a woman more equal to his station.

The mysterious beginnings surrounding her second relationship with Colonel Bampfield, a member of the king's service, merely intensified their involvement. Anne was devoutly loyal to Charles I and the Royalist Party. In the 1640s, England was engulfed in a civil war between the king and Parliament. In the midst of the struggle Parliament kept Charles's son James under house arrest. Anne was intrigued by and participated in Bampfield's work. In 1648, Bampfield received a letter informing him of the king's desire to see his second son, James, the Duke of York, freed from St. James' Palace where he was detained. Anne and Bampfield devised the escape plan that included sending Bampfield to visit York with a ribbon whereby he could obtain his measurements. Anne passed them along to her tailor with the instructions to make a petticoat and waistcoat for a young and rather "large" gentlewoman. Her tailor, though obedient to her command, exclaimed that while he had made many gowns, he had never seen a woman of this size.

With dress in hand, Anne and Bampfield proceeded with their plan. While the traditional after-dinner "hide and seek" games were being played, Bampfield escorted the fifteen-year-old James, a most skilled player who was not likely to be missed for some time, to Anne at the designated area. She dressed him in the tailored women's apparel, and then Bampfield escorted the "maid" by boat to freedom in Holland, where he remained for the rest of the war. Anne took a coach to her brother's house to hide temporarily to avoid any connection with the plot.

Bampfield told Anne that his wife, an heiress, had just died, but he had to keep it a secret or Parliament might seize her wealth. He asked Anne to marry him, as he, he claimed, loved her very much. Anne returned his feelings and accepted his proposal but agreed to keep the engagement a secret. Although Anne believed him, his wife, in fact, was still living. Rumors spread about Anne's relationship with Bampfield, who kept assuring Anne that his wife had died. Anne felt humiliated and did not know what to believe but for a number of years stayed loyal to Bampfield and her commitment to marry him. She could not believe the man she loved was lying to her.

In 1649, following the death of her brother Will, Anne, still believing herself engaged to Bampfield, accepted an offer from a friend, Sir Charles Howard and his wife. Anne was destitute, so Howard's generous invitation to stay at Naworth castle proved very helpful. While there, she learned that Bampfield had been arrested as a Royalist but had managed to escape. Anne was also humiliated by the rumors about her relationship with Bampfield. At this time a woman's honor rested on her reputation, and Anne feared that she had lost hers.

The year 1649 was devastating for those who supported the monarchy. Oliver Cromwell and Parliament put Charles I on trial. He was executed for treason, and Cromwell assumed rule over the Commonwealth. Royalists now gave their support to Charles I's oldest son, the young Charles II. In 1650, because of her support of the Royalist cause, sympathizers in Scotland invited Anne to join them. Sir Charles provided Anne with the funds to allow her to go.

Her arrival in Scotland is almost legendary. Sir James Douglas invited her to Aberdeenshire, and upon her arrival, she was greeted by Douglas and Laird of Maines, who offered her help walking over the rocky ground. But Anne took a misstep and fell flat on her face. Each man blamed himself, but Anne remarked, "I think I am going to take possession of it," suggesting the land would now become her home. This comment is especially appropriate considering the life she established in Scotland.

Word reached the Dunfermeline estate where Anne was staying that King Charles II would soon arrive there. Fearful that the king had heard the rumors about her relationship with Bampfield, Anne drafted a letter to her only contact, Mr. Seamor, one of the King's Groomsmen of the Bed Chamber and a former servant to her family, asking him to inquire of the king if she might kiss his hand. Seamor promptly replied that the king would willingly receive her; however, Charles took little notice of Anne during his stay at Dunfermeline. Undaunted, she again inquired of a servant as to why the king did not take notice of her. She explained her service in helping his younger brother, the Duke of York, escape. On the morning of his departure, Charles obligingly told Anne, "I am ashamed I have been so long a'speaking to you, but it was because I could not say enough to you for the service you did my brother." His graciousness satisfied Anne, and soon she would do him further service.

Shortly after the king's departure, Anne accompanied Lady Dunfermeline to Kinrose where the Royalists and the Commonwealth forces were fighting. They encountered wounded soldiers who, after being injured in battle, were left unattended. Anne could not tolerate such obvious neglect and invited the soldiers to Kinrose to be treated. In all, Anne, along with two other women, dressed and cared for thirty soldiers that day. Anne had invited only a few, but word had spread among the men, and Anne would not turn anyone away untreated. At a council meeting, Charles heard of this act of bravery and compassion and realized that measures were needed to care for those wounded in his cause. As a direct result of Anne's actions, the king ordered that surgeons be placed in several small towns to care for the wounded, and he awarded her with fifty pieces of gold, in recognition of her service. A grateful Anne was able to pay some of her debts.

For the next two years, Anne continued to care for the wounded. In 1652 her mother died, and she went to Edinburgh to collect her inheritance, but the money was tied up in a litigation. While staying with another Royalist in Edinburgh, Anne was introduced to Sir James Halkett, a friend of her host. His visits became more frequent, and he quickly proposed. Anne, despite the reports that Bampfield's wife was still living, chose to believe Bampfield that his wife was dead and still considered herself engaged to him. Halkett himself investigated, and Anne was forced to recognize the truth. Now nothing would stand in the way of Halkett's proposal. He, a widower with two sons and two daughters, had already given care of his daughters to Anne. It was a responsibility she willingly undertook because although she had refused his offers of marriage, she did care for him. In 1653, she agreed to marry Halkett on the condition that she first settle her debts in London. Because of her Royalist connections, she was never able to gain all of her inheritance, but on 2 March 1656 she married Halkett. She bore him four children and recorded her life with him as a happy one until his death in 1670.

This extraordinary life is contained in the pages of her memoirs. Little is known about Anne Halkett's last years, but it is clear that she was not forgotten by the people who knew her. In 1685, James II awarded her a pension of £100 yearly in recognition of the service she had done for him when he was the Duke of York. Anne died on

22 April 1699. Her memoirs, published in 1701 and again in 1778, give us the life of a courageous and loyal woman who lived on her own terms.

BIBLIOGRAPHY

Fraser, Antonia. *The Weaker Vessel.* New York: Alfred A. Knopf, 1984.

Loftis, John, ed. *The Memoirs of Anne, Lady Halkett and Ann, Lady Fanshawe.* Oxford: Clarendon, 1979.

Nichols, John Gough, ed. *The Autobiography of Anne Lady Halkett.* Westminster: Camden Society, 1875.

Stephanie Witham

ELIZABETH HARDWICK
(Bess of Hardwick)
(ca. 1527–1608)
Britain
Builder and Matriarch

Elizabeth Hardwick, better known as Bess of Hardwick, grew up in a family with grave financial difficulties, but through her single-minded dedication, Bess became one of the wealthiest women of her age and was known for her building: both of a family dynasty and some of the finest manor houses of Elizabethan England. Hardwick Hall is still standing today. She survived four husbands and saw her children married to people of high rank and influence. Although she failed at her goal to have a grandchild become monarch of England, by taking risks and making choices, she was able to attain her major aim of securing wealth and status for herself and her children. From humble beginnings, she rose to become Countess of Shrewsbury.

Bess grew up in a small country home, Hardwick Hall, in Derbyshire. She had three sisters and a brother. Her father died in 1528, and the family lost much of their land. Although Bess learned to read and write, she had a fairly limited education: no foreign languages or musical training. Bess was not an intellectual, nor was she more than conventionally religious. Literature and theology meant little to her; wealth and power a great deal.

When she was in her early teens, Bess went to live with a distant relative, Lady Zouche, to act as companion to the children. While in this household she became further acquainted with Robert Barley, who was a year or two younger than she. The two young people married early in 1543. Robert died, however, in 1544, leaving Bess a widow at sixteen.

It seems that at this time she was able to secure a place as a lady-in-waiting to Frances Grey, the niece of Henry VIII. There Bess met Sir William Cavendish, a man more than twice her age and already twice widowed who had had a long career in service to the Crown.

Elizabeth Hardwick, Countess of Shrewsbury. Hope Collection, HP 2737. Copyright Ashmolean Museum, Oxford. Reproduced by permission of the Ashmolean.

Bess had little to offer materially, but Cavendish recognized her ambition and resolve, and the two were married in 1547. They had three daughters and three sons who survived infancy. This was the only marriage for Bess that produced children, and from that time forward, her first loyalty was to provide well for them. Sir William bought the estate of Chatsworth in 1549, and Bess spent many years rebuilding the manor house. From her husband, Bess learned accounting and estate management, lessons she would never forget.

Cavendish and his family managed to weather the political crisis of 1553, when on the death of King Edward VI the Duke of Northumberland attempted to place Protestant Lady Jane Grey on the throne in place of Edward's older sister, the Catholic Mary I. Despite the close connections with the Greys, Cavendish converted to Catholicism and kept his position as Treasurer of the Royal Chamber. For the next few years, Bess and her husband divided their time between London and Chatsworth, rebuilding and furnishing the manor house as lavishly as they could, a project that was not completed when Sir William suddenly found himself under attack.

In 1557 Sir William was called before the Lord Treasurer to explain the huge discrepancies in his accounts. While Cavendish probably had used his position to enrich himself, it seems that Mary's government was politically motivated in its move against Cavendish. Mary wanted anyone whose loyalty she doubted out of office. In the midst of the investigations, Cavendish died. Bess was left a widow again. She had six children and two stepdaughters and now owed the government £5,000, a sum she did not possess. Bess gave up the London house and kept her family together in the country. Seeing Mary was in ill health, Bess kept up relations with the Princess Elizabeth, which was to prove helpful.

When Elizabeth I became queen in 1558, she appointed Bess to be one of her ladies-in-waiting. Bess was delighted by the opportunity. She was hoping that Elizabeth would forgive the debt to the Crown. Bess also wanted a new husband—one who was well connected and would be helpful to her and her children. She found him in Sir William St. Loe, the queen's Captain of the Guard and Chief Butler of England. St. Loe, immensely loyal to the queen and a man of wealth, fell deeply in love with Bess. They were married in the fall of 1559, a fortunate turn of events for Bess, given her financial problems and the number of daughters who would require dowries.

Once she had remarried, Bess and her children spent much of their time at Chatsworth and St. Loe would visit her there when he could be relieved of his duties at court. Despite St. Loe's deep affection for his wife, there were problems. William's younger brother Edward, who had been his heir, was furious about the marriage and determined to do something about it. Edward had already been suspected of poisoning an old man so that he could marry his widow and then poisoning her two months later when the possibility of a more advantageous marriage occurred. When Edward visited William and Bess in early 1561, he attempted to poison them. They survived, but William then decided to draw up a legal document so that he and Bess held all their lands jointly, and she inherited them all upon his death. St. Loe and Bess also continued to beg Elizabeth to abate or cancel the Cavendish debt to the Crown. Elizabeth finally did so in the summer of 1563; St. Loe paid £1,000, and the rest was forgiven. St. Loe seems to have been happy with his marriage and not begrudged his wife the funds she required for dowries for her daughters or her building plans for Chatsworth. He died in early 1565. In his will he left his soul to God and his body to the earth: everything else to Bess.

After being widowed three times and now left comfortably off, Bess might have retired to the country with her children. But this was not her plan. As a widow in her late thirties she returned to court to find another husband. The wife of George Talbot, Earl of Shrewsbury, had died in late 1566, leaving him with seven surviving children. In 1567 Bess married him. Shrewsbury was one of the wealthiest men in England. As part of the marriage agreement, her oldest son Henry married his daughter Grace, and his son Gilbert married her youngest daughter Mary. Thus the advantage to Bess and the Cavendish children of the Shrewsbury wealth and estates would not end with the death of Talbot. In the early years the relations between Bess and her fourth husband were cordial and affectionate, and the earl, as did her third husband, signed a document that left a great deal of wealth and land in Bess's hands. Later, he was to deeply regret this move.

Shrewsbury was a deeply loyal man, and in January 1569 when Elizabeth needed someone she could trust, she turned to him. Mary Stuart had been forced to abdicate the crown of Scotland and had been imprisoned after the scandal of the murder of her second husband and her marriage to his probable murderer. In 1568 Mary had managed to escape to England. Elizabeth kept Mary in England as an unwilling guest and needed a loyal subject who would guard her. The guardianship of Mary was to have painful consequences. It was one factor in the destruction of the good relations between Bess and her last husband.

Being Mary Stuart's custodians caused Bess and the earl deep distress. This burden was to last for fifteen years. Mary had a huge household that had to be accommodated, which caused financial problems since Elizabeth never paid enough to cover all the expenses. It was also a terrible psychological strain since the earl and Bess had to worry about all the plots to assassinate Elizabeth, free Mary, and place her on the throne.

In 1574 the marriage Bess arranged for her daughter Elizabeth upset Shrewsbury. Elizabeth secretly married Charles Stuart, the only surviving son of Margaret, Countess of Lennox, the daughter of Henry VIII's older sister. Bess saw the marriage as a triumph—her grandchild could potentially be the next monarch of England. And for Margaret the Shrewsbury wealth was very appealing. Bess hoped that her husband's services to the Crown would cause the queen to forgive her presumption. The earl wrote to Queen Elizabeth about the marriage, explaining he had not been consulted either. The Countess of Lennox was sent to the Tower for a few months. Although Bess may well have gained the queen's displeasure, we have no evidence that she was also punished, but the earl was angry that Bess had been involved in such a plot. Charles and Elizabeth had one daughter, **Arbella** (Stuart), born in 1575. Charles died the next year and Elizabeth in 1582. Bess raised Arbella, hoping she would be the next queen of England. Bess's plans for Arbella enraged their "guest" Mary Stuart and led to further ill feelings. While Bess called Arbella her "jewel" during her childhood, the two fought bitterly as Arbella grew up. Mary Stuart's son James succeeded Elizabeth, not Arbella, and Bess failed in her effort to have her granddaughter become queen.

In 1583 Bess bought Hardwick Hall, her father's old estate. Shrewsbury was upset about the time and money Bess was spending on Chatsworth and now Hardwick. At the same time, rumors began to circulate that the earl and Mary had had an affair. The earl was convinced that the rumors had been started by Bess and her sons, and he was furious. Some historians argue that Bess may well have begun the rumors as a desperate means to have Mary Stuart removed from the earl's care. Queen Elizabeth sent for the earl and believed his protestations of innocence, but Shrewsbury insisted on a formal separation from Bess. In 1584 Elizabeth finally released him from his guardianship of Mary Stuart. The queen also attempted to force Bess and the earl to reconcile, but she met with only limited success.

In 1590, the year of the earl's death, Bess decided to pull down the old Hardwick Hall and began to build a magnificent new structure in its place. Because of arrangements they had made soon after the marriage, Bess as widow controlled a great deal of wealth. The new Hardwick Hall was imposing, with an innovative long gallery and many windows. Each of the towers was topped with an elaborate monogram of *ES* for Elizabeth of Shrewsbury. Bess was claiming Hardwick Hall as her creation and signing it for all the world to see. Legend has it that she was told in her youth that she would live as long as she kept building. In the winter of 1608 the weather stopped the construction on Hardwick Hall, and Bess, a woman who constructed elaborate houses and dynasties, died. She was at least eighty. The inscription at her tomb, probably composed by her son William, listed her husband and children and described her as a magnificent builder.

BIBLIOGRAPHY

Durant, David. *Bess of Hardwick: Portrait of an Elizabethan Dynast.* London: Weidenfeld and Nicolson, 1977.

Hogrefe, Pearl. *Women of Action in Tudor England.* Ames: Iowa State University Press, 1977.

Williams, E. Carleton. *Bess of Hardwick.* London: Longmans, 1959.

Carole Levin

HÉLISENNE DE CRENNE
(Marguerite Briet)
(ca. 1510/1520–ca. 1552)
France
Author and Defender of Women

Hélisenne de Crenne is the pseudonym of one of the most important female authors of the French Renaissance. She is the author of what has been called the first sentimental novel in French; she also wrote a dream allegory, a collection of letters, and a translation of Virgil's *Aeneid*.

We have very few biographical facts about Hélisenne de Crenne; even the dates of her birth and death are uncertain. Her real name was Marguerite Briet, and she was born in Abbeville, a small village in Picardy. At a young age she married Philippe Fournel, who was a country squire of the area of Crasnes or Crenne, thus the last part of her pen name. It appears that Hélisenne, who was from a wealthy family, brought a considerable dowry to the marriage. They had a son, but we do not know any other information about their marriage other than the fact that it appeared to be very unhappy. A document from 1552 indicates that sometime before that year Hélisenne and her husband had legally separated and that she still maintained her property. For some time she resided in Paris, where her works were published. Much of the biographical information about Hélisenne is surmised from her writings, although scholars still debate how much of her writing is autobiographical and how much of it is fictional.

Hélisenne's first major work, *Les Angoysses douloureuses qui procedent d'amours* (*The Torments of Love*), is a long novel about a young girl named Hélisenne who is married to a husband for whom she initially felt some affection. The first part of the novel describes how she falls in love with another young man named Guenelic; out of despair and jealousy, her husband, whom she refers to as Argus after the mythological giant of a hundred eyes, imprisons her in one of his castles. The first part of the novel focuses on the nature and consequences of obsessive love, but it is nonetheless written in a realistic mode; the second and third sections follow the pattern of the chivalric romance. The second part, narrated by Guenelic, recounts the series of adventures he undergoes as he and his loyal friend Quezinstra travel throughout Europe looking for Hélisenne. In the third section, the character Hélisenne dies of a fatal illness. In the tradition of tragic love tales, this work seems particularly indebted to Boccacio's *Fiametta*, a fourteenth-century tale of obsessive love.

Les Angoysses was published in 1538 by Denys Janot, a Parisian printer; the work was a popular success and went through several reprintings. Hélisenne dedicated her novel specifically to female readers, although historical evidence indicates that the book was widely read by both men and women. In addition to debate over the extent to which the novel is autobiographical, contemporary critics have also addressed the ambiguous tone of *Les Angoysses*. At times the author sounds a cautionary note as she warns her female readers to "avoid the dangerous snares of love," whereas at other times, she seems to celebrate the experience of mad, passionate love. Current scholarship on *Les Angoysses* has also focused on matters of style: Many readers have found Hélisenne's writing pretentious and verbose, but others have argued that her prose is colorful, exuberant, and impressively learned.

Even though the character Hélisenne had died at the end of *Les Angoysses*, Hélisenne de Crenne continued to write under that pen name, publishing three more works in three consecutive years. Her second work appeared in 1539, *Les Epistres familieres et invectives* (*Personal and Invective Letters*). This collection of letters comprises thirteen personal letters written to relatives and friends and five invective letters; some scholars argue that collectively the letters form an epistolary novel that recounts the story surrounding her previous novel. The personal letters include letters of consolation, gratitude, and congratulations; these missives offer an interesting glimpse into sixteenth-century everyday life. The invective letters include an exchange between Hélisenne and her husband in which she defends herself and women in general against his slanderous, misogynistic attacks and letters in which she defends the right of women to pursue their literary interests. Of particular interest to literary history is the fourth invective letter in which Hélisenne describes many learned women of antiquity and then praises Marguerite de Navarre as a contemporary exemplar of the praiseworthy learned woman. Her tone in these invective letters is unequivocally defensive, spirited, and determined as she vows to speak out for women whose detractors say "their only pastime should be to spin."

In 1540 her third work appeared, *Le Songe de Madame Hélisenne* (*The Dream of Madame Hélisenne*). The work is an allegorical dream vision, a genre previously used by fourteenth-century author Christine de Pizan in *Le Livre de la Cite des Dames* (*The Book of the City of Ladies*) and by other medieval writers. In this dream vision, figures representing Reason, Chastity, Shame, and Sensuality have a debate over questions of virtue and dignity in men and women. Hélisenne's last work was *Les quatres premiers livres des Eneydes* (*The First Four Books of the Aeneid*); this was the first complete translation of these books into French. Hélisenne dedicated the work to the king of France, François I.

In spite of the popularity and frequent reprintings of her works during her lifetime, Hélisenne's literary reputation was forgotten after her death. The nineteenth century brought some renewed interest in her writings; this interest has increased among scholars of literature and history in the twentieth century. Once again, Hélisenne de Crenne is being recognized as one of the most powerful and unique voices of early modern women.

BIBLIOGRAPHY

H. de Crenne. *The Torments of Love*. Ed. and with an introduction by Lisa Neal; trans. Lisa Neal and Steven Rendall. Minneapolis: University of Minnesota Press, 1996.

A Renaissance Woman: Hélisenne's Personal and Invective Letters. Trans. and ed. Marianna M. Mustacchi and Paul J. Archambault. Syracuse: Syracuse University Press, 1986.

Jo Eldridge Carney

HROTSVIT OF GANDERSHEIM
(Roswitha, Hrosvitha)
(ca. 932/935–1001/1002)
Germany
Poet, Dramatist, and Historian

Hrotsvit, the Canoness of Gandersheim, lays claim to a host of extraordinary achievements. In the introduction to her dramas, Hrotsvit calls herself the strong voice of Gandersheim (*Clamor Validus Gandeshemensis*). Hrotsvit is the first known nonliturgical dramatist of Christianity. Based on hagiography (the writing of saints' lives), her innovative dramas anticipate the revival of theater in the Middle Ages by approximately one and a half centuries. In addition to her original contributions to drama, Hrotsvit has earned a place in the history of women as the first female German poet and historian.

The benefactors of the religious foundation of Gandersheim (ca. 852)—Duke Liudolf and his wife Oda—also have the distinction of being the ancestors of the illustrious Ottonian Dynasty, whose monarchs first consolidated their rule in Saxon Germany. During the reign of the Ottos, Germany became one of the strongest and most enlightened European states. Otto I, known as Otto the Great (912–973), received a succession of imperial crowns and titles: King of the Germans (936), King of the Lombards (951), and the title of Holy Roman Emperor (962). Not only was Otto I an exceptionally gifted statesman; he was also an avid patron of learning and of the Church.

Imperialism, learning, and faith thrived under the Ottos in a cultural renaissance regarded as a continuation of the ninth-century revival of learning known as the Carolingian Renaissance. Otto's brother, Bruno, the Archbishop of Cologne, brought artists and scholars from Constantinople to the German court. When the emperor's son, Otto II, took Theophano, a Greek princess, as his wife, Greek culture and philosophy continued to influence the German court.

In 947 Otto I decreed the foundation of Gandersheim free from imperial control. Gandersheim's abbesses maintained an army and a court of law, they coined money, and they enjoyed the privilege of having representation in the Imperial Diet. Hrotsvit is reputed to have entered Gandersheim under Gerberga II's rule (ruled ca. 965–1001). The daughter of Henry of Bavaria and the niece of Otto I, Gerberga II reigned during a time when devotion to learning and service flourished. As a thriving center of spiritual and intellectual activities, Gandersheim was an ideal setting for its members, who were free to cultivate their unique gifts.

The canonesses of Gandersheim generally lived a communal life, and regulations obliged them to observe the canonical hours; however, canonesses did not take vows of poverty, only vows of chastity and obedience. As a canoness, Hrotsvit could actively participate in Gandersheim's stimulating intellectual climate. Hrotsvit would have been allowed to own books and property, and with permission she could even travel.

The details of Hrotsvit's life and career derive for the most part from statements she provides in her dedicatory epistles and from her literary canon itself. Hrotsvit must have been descended from noble Saxon parentage, since Gandersheim admitted only daughters of the aristocracy.

We know that Hrotsvit received an exemplary education. She identifies Rikkardis as one of her teachers. Rikkardis is believed to have provided Hrotsvit with instruction in the liberal arts, which in the Middle Ages included seven branches of learning: grammar, logic, rhetoric, arithmetic, geometry, music, and astronomy. Gerberga II, Hrotsvit's abbess and other teacher, introduced Hrotsvit to Roman authors and patristic writers.

Hrotsvit's writings indicate familiarity with both ancient and medieval literature. She knew the works of the Roman authors Virgil, Horace, Ovid, and Terence, among others. Boethius, the sixth-century Roman philosopher and statesman, seems particularly to have captured Hrotsvit's imagination with his works. Her readings included works from Christian writers and legends of the saints and martyrs. Hrotsvit also knew and used the Vulgate Bible, liturgical texts, and various apocryphal acts and gospels.

The cultural advances that occurred as a result of the Carolingian and Ottonian Renaissances provided Hrotsvit with a solid foundation for her work. She wrote in Latin, the language used by tenth-century European churchmen, statesmen, and teachers. Gerberga II's family ties to the imperial court guaranteed the reception of Hrotsvit's writings by an appreciative audience of leading intellectuals, such as Gerberga's friend, Otto II. Hrotsvit's contemporaries highly regarded and praised her many intellectual accomplishments. Hrotsvit's legends and historical epics are written in verse, and her plays, written in imitation of Terence, are composed in rhymed prose. Hrotsvit's ability to use sophisticated Latin meters demonstrates her familiarity with grammatical and metrical textbooks.

Until the beginning of the twentieth century, an incomplete manuscript constituted the only surviving copy of Hrotsvit's work. Conrad Celtes, the German poet laureate and humanist, is credited with discovering in 1493 the incomplete text of Hrotsvit's work: a manuscript known as the *Emmeram-Munich Codex* that dates from the eleventh century. Today, with the fortunate recovery of additional fragments and manuscripts, Hrotsvit's literary canon includes eight legends, six plays, and two historical epics. Several prefaces and dedications, along with a thirty-five-line poem, complete the rest of her canon.

Hrotsvit's works have been grouped into three books, which include her sacred legends ("Maria," "Ascensio," "Gongolf," "Pelagius," "Basilius," "Theophilus," "Dionysius," and "Saint Agnes"), her dramas (*Gallicanus, Dulcitius, Calimachus, Paphnutius, Abraham*, and *Sapientia*), and her epic poems (*Carmen de Gestis Oddonis Imperatoris* and *Primordia Coenobii Gandeshemensis*).

In her writings, Hrotsvit seeks to glorify the ways of God, while offering literary models of Christian virtue for emulation by the faithful. Because of their originality, many consider Hrotsvit's six dramas as her most important literary contributions. Another singular accomplishment that deserves recognition is Hrotsvit's conscious effort to create positive literary portraits of women, especially in her plays, in response to the antifeminist tradition prevalent in the tenth century. A remarkable poetess, dramatist, and historian, Hrotsvit of Gandersheim deserves her prominent place in the history of women.

BIBLIOGRAPHY

Haight, Anne Lyon, ed. *Hroswitha of Gandersheim: Her Life, Times, and Works, and a Comprehensive Bibliography.* New York: Hroswitha Club, 1965.

Sperberg-McQueen, M. R. "Whose Body Is It? Chaste Strategies and the Reinforcement of Patriarchy in Three Plays by Hrotswitha von Gandersheim." *Women in German Yearbook* 8 (1992): 47–71.

Sticca, Sandro. "Sin and Salvation: The Dramatic Context of Hroswitha's Women." In Douglas Radcliff-Umstead, ed., *The Roles and Images of Women in the Middle Ages and Renaissance*. University of Pittsburgh Publications on the Middle Ages and Renaissance. Pittsburgh: Center for Medieval and Renaissance Studies, 1975. 3: 3–22.

Wilson, Katharina M. *Hrotsvit of Gandersheim: A Florilegium of Her Works*. Ed. Jane Chance. Cambridge: Brewer, 1998.

Wilson, Katharina M. "The Saxon Canoness: Hrotsvit of Gandersheim." In Katharina M. Wilson, ed., *Medieval Women Writers*. Athens: University of Georgia Press, 1984. 30–63.

Debra Barrett-Graves

HÜRREM SULTAN
(Roxelana)
(fl. 1520s–1558)
Turkey
Political Adviser, Diplomat, and Imperial
Benefactress

In 1453, the Conqueror Mehmed II (ruled 1444–1446, 1451–1481) achieved a great triumph for the Turkish House of Osman when he captured Constantinople, the capital city of the decaying Byzantine Empire. Renaming the city Istanbul, the Ottoman Sultans, over the years, constructed a number of impressive architectural buildings, adding to the city's unparalleled collection of monuments. Famous for capturing numerous territories, the Sunni Islamic Ottoman Turks soon ruled over an enormous empire.

The reign of the Sultan Süleyman the Magnificent (ruled 1520–1566) represents a high point in Ottoman fortunes, with Süleyman being viewed as having played an instrumental role in elevating the Ottoman Empire to its status as one of the sixteenth century's greatest powers.

Süleyman similarly elevated a favorite slave girl to a position of unprecedented influence and power. Her remarkable career would last for the majority of Süleyman's reign, from the birth of her first child (1521) to the time of her death (1558).

While her origins remain obscure, a Polish tale reports that she was born in a village located on the Dniester River, an unstable region located on the borders of Poland, Hungary, and Moldavia. Traditional accounts relate how "Aleksandra Lisowska," the daughter of a poor Ruthenian priest, was carried off during one of the region's frequent raids and then sold into slavery.

"Aleksandra Lisowska" would eventually become known to Western Europeans as "Roxelana," a term loosely translated as the "Russian-born woman" and more specifically translated as the "Ruthenian

Portrait of Roxelana (Hürrem Sultan). Courtesy of the Topkapi Palace Museum, Istanbul. Reprinted with permission.

maiden." The Turks, however, called her Hürrem ("Laughing One") in recognition of her pleasant disposition.

The institution in which Hürrem served, Süleyman's *harēm*, had a definite, intricately developed female hierarchy. Each member of the *harēm* held a distinct position within this hierarchy, dependent primarily upon status and age. By virtue of its rigid structure, the *harēm* was similar to a sanctuary that enforced the chastity of most of its members. Within the *harēm*, the Sultan's mother, the Sultan Validé ("royal mother"), possessed the greatest amount of power.

Hürrem's prestige in the *harēm* increased when she became Süleyman's *kadin* ("recognized concubine"). Precisely when Hürrem became a member of Süleyman's *harēm* is unknown; however, she is believed to have become Süleyman's concubine around 1520. Her status increased even more dramatically the following year when Hürrem gave birth to Süleyman's son. Dates for the births of Hürrem and Süleyman's children remain conjectural; however, the consensus is that the births of Mehmed, Mihrimah, Abdullah, Selim, and Bayezid occurred rapidly over the next four to five years. Although their last child,

Jihangir, was born a hunchback, Hürrem had presented Süleyman with enough healthy sons to assure the dynasty's continuation.

After securing a primary place in the Sultan's affections, Hürrem's intimate relationship with Süleyman allowed her to serve as his confidante. This position had been formerly enjoyed by Süleyman's previous favorites, especially by his chief counselor the Grand Vizier İbrahim (Grand Vizier, 1523–1536), a Greek slave, and possibly by the mother (another *kadin*) of his first son, Mustafa. Süleyman seems to have regarded Hürrem as a companion with whom he could discuss his interest in the lands in the north, an area about which Hürrem had personal knowledge.

Süleyman's familiar relationship with Hürrem would eventually lead to an unimaginable breach of tradition. By Süleyman's reign, the Ottoman dynasty's practice of perpetuating its line through slave concubinage was regarded as binding tradition. Further, Ottoman Sultans practiced serial concubinage, limiting male offspring to one per mother to give each prince an equal chance when the time came to vie for the throne. Tradition, then, weighed heavily against a Sultan who wished to contract a legal marriage, especially since no Sultan had done so since the reign of Bayezid I (1389–1402). Süleyman's decision to marry Hürrem further enhanced her unique status when she became the Sultan's acknowledged legal wife. When this marriage occurred is not certain, although speculation has placed it around 1534. In choosing to make Hürrem his legal wife, Süleyman abandoned the practice of serial concubinage. An unenthusiastic public regarded Süleyman's private attachment and public commitment to Hürrem with concern, and Süleyman's servants whispered their fears that Hürrem had somehow managed to bewitch their Sultan.

Various accounts relate that around 1541 Hürrem Sultan moved her train of slave girls and eunuchs into the Grand Seraglio, where the Sultan himself resided, when a fire broke out and gutted the residence that had housed the *harēm*. Once installed in the Grand Seraglio, also the seat of administration, the acknowledged wife of the Sultan succeeded in securing permanent lodgings there. Since the Conqueror Mehmed II had specifically decreed that no women should be allowed to sleep in the same building where government business was conducted, Hürrem Sultan is regarded as having accomplished a remarkable triumph. Other accounts associate the move with Hürrem Sultan's marriage to Süleyman. Whichever version one accepts, Hürrem Sultan's reception chambers soon became so well established that the palace slaves began referring to them as the "Throne Room Within."

Hürrem Sultan continued to strengthen her unique position by securing the appointment of Rüstem Pasha, who had married her daughter Mihrimah, as Süleyman's Grand Vizier (ca. 1544). Hürrem's alliance with her daughter and son-in-law contributed even further to her considerable power and influence, an alliance scholars believe may have helped Hürrem Sultan to secure the succession to the throne for one of her own sons. Scholars believe that the intrigues of Hürrem Sultan and Rüstem Pasha at least partially contributed to Süleyman's decision to have his eldest son, Mustafa, strangled. Popular with the soldiers, and generally acknowledged to be a vigorous and capable young leader, Mustafa represented a clear danger to Hürrem Sultan and to her children. With the execution of Mustafa, and his son, Hürrem Sultan's position, along with her sons' position, would be virtually unassailable. Playing upon Süleyman's insecurities, Hürrem Sultan and Rüstem Pasha seem to have succeeded in convincing the Sultan that Mustafa could conceivably seize power for himself, prematurely wresting control from his father. While the Sultan may have succumbed to the considerable influence of others, Süleyman alone gave the command and watched as his henchmen strangled Mustafa to death. In the end, the order to murder his eldest son was his decision alone.

Hürrem Sultan's unusual position provided her with many opportunities to participate in Ottoman politics. Functioning as Süleyman's confidante and as his trusted political adviser, Hürrem Sultan provided Süleyman with reliable, valuable news from the capital during his absences. Süleyman seems to have initiated political contacts through Hürrem Sultan whenever he preferred a peaceful solution instead of an inopportune military conflict. Hürrem Sultan never traveled anywhere as Süleyman's agent, but she is believed to have spoken on his behalf as a foreign diplomat through various spoken and written exchanges.

Hürrem Sultan's steady ascent at the Ottoman court (*harēm* slave, *kadin*, trusted confidante, and the Sultan's acknowledged wife) verifies her unique position. Another of Hürrem Sultan's familiar titles—*haseki* ("the Sultan's favorite")—further indicates her privileged status.

By providing services for the poor, Hürrem Sultan earned additional recognition as an imperial benefactress. The monuments and charities associated with Hürrem Sultan, such as the Haseki complex located in Istanbul, which Süleyman built in her honor, constitute public displays of imperial benevolence, whereas the charitable foundation Hürrem

Sultan personally sponsored in Jerusalem indicates another public expression of benevolent imperial support.

When Hürrem Sultan died, Süleyman lost both a personal companion and a confidante. The Sultan privately mourned the loss of his wife; as a final public statement of his respect and devotion, Süleyman had Hürrem Sultan interred in a separate tomb situated near his own burial monument.

The prestige she earned and the power expressed for and by Hürrem Sultan clearly set a precedent. The dynastic women of succeeding generations would become increasingly involved in the government of the Ottoman Empire, exercising more political leverage than ever before, during what is referred to as the reign of women (*Kadinlar Sultanati*).

BIBLIOGRAPHY

Clot, André. *Suleiman the Magnificent.* Trans. Matthew J. Reisz. New York: New Amsterdam, 1992.

Peirce, Leslie P. "Behind Harem Walls: Ottoman Royal Women and the Exercise of Power." In Dorothy O. Helly and Susan M. Reverby, eds., *Gendered Domains: Rethinking Public and Private in Women's History.* Ithaca, NY: Cornell University Press, 1992. 40–55.

Peirce, Leslie P. *The Imperial Harem: Women and Sovereignty in the Ottoman Empire.* Studies in Middle Eastern History. New York: Oxford University Press, 1993.

Penzer, N. M. *The Harēm.* London: Spring, 1965.

Zilfi, Madeline, ed. *Women in the Ottoman Empire: Middle Eastern Women in the Early Modern Era.* Leiden: Brill, 1997.

Debra Barrett-Graves

ESTHER INGLIS
(Esther Kello)
(1571–1624)
Britain
Professional Calligrapher and Miniaturist

Esther Inglis was a talented calligrapher and miniaturist at a time when both art forms were highly prized in England. She is one of the few women of sixteenth-century Europe who can be considered a professional writer and artist; in order to support herself and her family, she presented her illuminated manuscripts to various patrons in hopes of receiving some financial reward or further employment.

Inglis was born of French parents who had moved to Scotland in 1569; they were Huguenots, or Protestants of the Calvinist persuasion, who left their homeland in the atmosphere of religious persecution that would lead to the St. Bartholomew's Day Massacre in 1572, the killing of thousands of Protestants in Paris. Esther's father, Nicholas Langlois, and her mother, Marie Presot, established a French school in Edinburgh, for which they received a small yearly pension from King James VI of Scotland. Though we have little information about Esther's childhood, we do know that she received an education from her parents; she also learned calligraphy, most likely from her mother, whose accomplished hand is evident in a surviving manuscript.

When she was in her twenties, Esther married a minister, Bartholomew Kello. Kello's father was also a Presbyterian minister who had killed his wife in 1570 and was then executed. With no financial support from their families, Esther and Bartholomew always suffered financial problems even though they both worked very hard. They left Scotland in 1604 and moved to London; in 1607 Bartholomew was appointed rector at a parish in Essex. In addition to his ministerial duties in England, Kello supervised the copying of government documents; Esther often worked as his scribe. There is some evidence that prior to the death of Queen Elizabeth of England in March

Esther Inglis Kello by unknown artist. In the collection of the National Museums of Scotland, Cat. no. Ph L18, Scottish National Portrait Gallery. Reprinted with permission.

1603, Bartholomew Kello served as a go-between for Elizabeth's eventual successor, King James of Scotland, and her secretary, Robert Cecil; such activity would explain Kello's access to the many aristocrats to whom his wife dedicated her works. Esther and her husband had six children, four of whom survived: a son, Samuel, and three daughters, Mary, Esther, and Elizabeth. Although they were constantly plagued by poverty, their marriage seems to have been a happy one, and we have some verses that Bartholomew Kello wrote in praise of his wife.

Esther did not assume her husband's last name for the purpose of her work; rather, she anglicized *Langlois* to *Inglish*, or *Inglis*. Her talents as both a calligrapher and a miniaturist were put to use in her various manuscripts, which she presented to various dedicatees in hopes of patronage. Queen Elizabeth, King James, and his sons, Prince Henry and Prince Charles, were all recipients of her manuscripts, as were several other courtiers and aristocrats, including Queen Elizabeth's favorite, the Earl of Essex, and members of the famous aristocratic families, the Sidneys and the Herberts.

Over fifty of Inglis's manuscripts have been traced, though there are references to several more. Inglis wrote or transcribed verses and then illuminated them; the texts are usually religious or devotional in content and include psalms, proverbs, and a discourse on the Reformation. Of even greater interest than the content of her verses is their artistic rendering. Most of the books themselves are miniature, only a few inches wide with microscopic lettering and intricate decorative borders of flowers, fruits, insects, and animals. They were usually bound in leather, velvet, or silk; many of the extant manuscripts retain their original bindings. Some of the covers are embroidered; Inglis was praised by her contemporaries for her skill with the needle as well as the pen.

It is for her remarkable talent as a calligrapher that Inglis is most known. She was capable of producing several different hands, or styles. Besides the popular Roman and italic scripts, Esther could also write in the more difficult, intricate hands described in sixteenth-century handwriting treatises. The detailed nature of her work is most evident in the smaller manuscripts: In one four-inch line, she could write up to twenty-three words.

Inglis's presentation of her work embodied some of the contradictions present in the works of other early modern women who published their own writings or translations. At the same time they assert their own status as writers in a largely male literary world, they also apologize for assuming to present their work to the public, since they are only women. Many of Inglis's manuscripts include such self-deprecating statements, and yet she concludes many of her works with a vigorous emblem: two golden pens forming a cross with the words "Vive la plume!" Furthermore, in twenty-four of her manuscripts, she includes a miniature self-portrait in pen or water color, surely a sign of pride in her own artistry and an assertion of self-identity.

In spite of all the patronage Esther Inglis sought and received for her manuscripts, she was in debt when she died in 1624 at the age of fifty-three. Her portrait was painted in 1595 and is now displayed in the Scottish National Portrait Gallery.

BIBLIOGRAPHY

Goldberg, Jonathan. *Writing Matter: From the Hands of the English Renaissance.* Stanford, CA: Stanford University Press, 1990.
Scott-Elliott, A. H., and Elspeth Yeo. "Calligraphic Manuscripts of Esther

Inglis (1571–1624): A Catalogue." *The Papers of the Biographical Society of America* 84 (March 1990): 11–86.

Williams, Robert. "A Moon to Their Sun: Writing Mistresses of the Sixteenth and Seventeenth Centuries." *Fine Print* 11, 2 (1985): 88–98.

Jo Eldridge Carney

IZUMI SHIKIBU
(ca. 966/979–1030?)
Japan
Waka Poet and Heian Diarist

Izumi Shikibu, along with **Ono no Komachi**, has received praise for being one of Japan's two most gifted female poets. When Ono no Komachi (ca. 830/835–899) began writing her poems, the unique cultural advances associated with the court at Heiankyō, during what is known as the Heian period (794–1192), had started to flourish, having been initially stimulated by two continental cultures: China and Korea.

Heian literature reached an unusually high level of achievement during the late tenth and early eleventh centuries. Izumi Shikibu, along with **Sei Shōnagon** (fl. late tenth century) and **Murasaki Shikibu** (fl. early eleventh century), produced works of exceptional quality, in poetry and in prose. The literary output of this extraordinary trio of women constitutes an almost unparalleled contribution to the history of Japanese literature.

The proliferation of literary masterpieces created at the turn of the century (ca. 1000) can partially be attributed to the existence of the phonetic writing system known as *kana*, which provided women with a means of composing poems (*waka*) and diaries (*nikki*).

The dominant poetic form in the Japanese language from approximately the ninth century on was the *waka*, or "Japanese poem." *Waka* contained thirty-one syllables, presented in five lines, which consisted of five, seven, five, seven, and seven syllables, respectively. *Waka* collections, or *shū*, begin with the *Kokin[waka]shū* (*Collection of Old and New Japanese Poetry*, ca. 905–920), a royally commissioned imperial anthology that brought together the best works of Japanese poets.

Izumi Shikibu's poems represent some of the best *waka* poetry to have been written in the years following the *Kokinshū*'s publication. Throughout the Heian period, men created the majority of works with significant literary status. The work of Izumi Shikibu, the extraordinary female *waka* poet, should therefore command great respect. Izumi Shikibu's extensive collection of *waka* constitutes a singular achievement, both for its descriptions of erotic love and for its expressions of a devout religious consciousness.

Izumi Shikibu's parents probably met while serving the Lady Shōshi (950–1000), the eldest daughter of Emperor Suzaku (923–952; ruled 930–946), and, later, the imperial empress to the Emperor Reizei (950–1011; ruled 967–969). Izumi's father, Ōe no Masamune, and her mother, Suke no Naishi, belonged to the ranks of the middle bureaucracy. Izumi's date of birth occurred sometime in the last half of the tenth century, with suggested birthdates ranging from around 966 to 979. Izumi spent her early years at court, during which time her recorded name is Omotomaro.

Izumi Shikibu derives part of her adult name—"Izumi"—from Tachibana no Michisada (d. 1016), her first husband, who served as governor of Izumi province. "Shikibu" is a title that perhaps designated her father's rank or position, but its real meaning still eludes scholars. Izumi's daughter, Koshikibu no Naishi ("Little [Handmaid] Ceremonial"), like her mother, also earned acclaim as a poet.

Sei Shōnagon, Murasaki Shikibu, and Izumi Shikibu all held positions at the imperial court. Sei Shōnagon served at the imperial court of the Empress Fujiwara no Teishi (Sadako) (ca. 976–1000) in the capacity of lady-in-waiting for a period of seven to ten years (ca. 990/993–1000). Sadako was the royal consort of the sixty-sixth emperor, Ichijō Tennō (980–1011; ruled 986–1011), as well as the daughter of Fujiwara no Michitaka (d. 993). When Sadako's father died, his successor, Fujiwara no Michinaga (966–1027), the new leader of the powerful Fujiwara clan, married the Emperor Ichijō Tennō to his own daughter, Fujiwara no Shōshi. This marriage of political convenience resulted in the establishment of a rival court that soon eclipsed the glory formerly associated with the Empress Sadako's court. Izumi Shikibu and her contemporary Murasaki Shikibu served as their mistress this rival empress, Fujiwara no Shōshi (Akiko/Jōtōmon'In) (988–1074). Izumi is believed to have joined Empress Akiko's court around 1009.

High-ranking ladies-in-waiting enjoyed ideal conditions in which to write. Life at court allowed them to participate in and benefit from a stimulating social environment conducive to the production of their literary works. They had adequate leisure time in which to write, along with access to paper, which was a relatively scarce commodity.

The emergence of such authors as Izumi Shikibu, Murasaki Shikibu, and Sei Shōnagon has also been attributed to their marginal status at court. Their male contemporaries could use their considerable writing talents to advance their careers at court. Women, for whom such career advancement was not an option, nevertheless valued the enjoyment they derived from writing poems and diaries, technically superior works of unusual beauty in which the author's passionate sentiments found unique expression. Impressive writings certainly flowed from the pens of Sei Shōnagon, Murasaki Shikibu, and Izumi Shikibu.

Scholars have used inferences drawn from Izumi Shikibu's poetic canon in concert with the circumstances known to have surrounded her literary output to reconstruct what can only be regarded as an exceptional life. Izumi Shikibu's reputation as a woman of intense passion definitely contributed to her reputation as a poet of immense skill. Izumi Shikibu had love affairs with two princes of the imperial blood: Prince Tametaka (977–1002) and Prince Atsumichi (981–1007). As a result of the scandal associated with her first affair (with Prince Tametaka), her husband, Tachibana no Michisada, divorced her, and her family disowned her. Less than a year after the sudden death of Prince Tametaka, Izumi Shikibu began a romantic liaison with Prince Atsumichi, who turned out to be the great love of her life.

Izumi Shikibu's most outstanding *waka* are those in which she explores her amorous experiences. When Prince Atsumichi died suddenly, Izumi Shikibu mourned him in over 100 poems. Izumi Shikibu's poems have also been warmly embraced for their skillful adaptation of Buddhist themes.

After leaving court service, Izumi Shikibu is believed to have married Fujiwara no Yasumasa (958–1036), a man presumed to be one of Fujiwara no Michinaga's retainers.

In recognition of Izumi Shikibu's considerable poetic skills, the compilers of the fourth imperial anthology, *Goshūi [waka]shū* (*Later Gleanings*, ca. 1086), chose sixty-seven of her poems for inclusion, the largest number by any single poet. Izumi's personal collection of poems, the *Izumi Shikibu Shū*, exists in five versions and contains from over 500 to less than 1,000 poems, depending on the text consulted.

The romantic adventures of Izumi Shikibu additionally inspired another significant work, a Heian romance known as *Izumi Shikibu nikki* (ca. 1004–1008, *The Poetic Memoirs of Izumi Shikibu*). Authorship of the *Izumi Shikibu nikki* has been attributed to Izumi Shikibu, but the attribution remains controversial. Some prefer to view the work as a fictionalized romance based on the life of the poetess Izumi Shikibu and her notorious love affair with Prince Atsumichi.

Like Ono no Komachi, Izumi Shikibu has become a figure of Japanese legend. Both her amorous nature and her religious longings have provided subject matter for a variety of tales, plays, and histories. An unforgettable personality, Izumi Shikibu is one of Japan's most gifted *waka* poets.

BIBLIOGRAPHY

Cranston, Edwin A., trans. *The Izumi Shikibu Diary: A Romance of the Heian Court*. Cambridge: Harvard University Press, 1969.

Hirshfield, Jane, and Mariko Aratani, trans. *The Ink Dark Moon: Love Poems by Ono no Komachi and Izumi Shikibu*. New York: Vintage, 1990.

Hulvey, S. Yumiko. "Izumi Shikibu." In Chieko I. Mulhern, ed., *Japanese Women Writers: A Bio-Critical Sourcebook*. Westport, CT: Greenwood, 1994. 153–160.

McCullough, Helen Craig, ed. *Classical Japanese Prose: An Anthology*. Stanford: Stanford University Press, 1990.

Morris, Ivan. *The World of the Shining Prince: Court Life in Ancient Japan*. New York: Kodansha, 1994.

Shuichi Kato. *A History of Japanese Literature: The First Thousand Years*. Trans. David Chibett. Tokyo: Kodansha, 1979.

Debra Barrett-Graves

JADWIGA OF POLAND

(1373–1399)
Hungary
Queen and Political Leader

One of the most popular monarchs in Polish history, Jadwiga sacrificed her personal happiness in order to convert one country to Catholicism and to provide political stability for another. She was Hungarian by birth, but once she ascended to the throne of Poland, she became completely devoted to the concerns and interests of the Polish people.

Jadwiga was the youngest daughter of King Louis the Great of Hungary, who ruled that country for forty years; but while he was a beloved and effective king of Hungary, he was also the ineffective absentee king of Poland for twelve years. In his absence, Louis's mother ruled Poland. Louis had no sons, but he made a pact with the Polish nobles that one of his three daughters would inherit the throne; the other two daughters would become the rulers of Hungary and of his territory in Naples. Given their illustrious destinies, the future husbands of these young princesses were carefully chosen: When Jadwiga was only five, she was betrothed to William, one of the Hapsburg princes of Austria, and her sister Maria was contracted to marry Sigismund of Luxembourg. The eldest sister, Catherine, died in childhood.

When Jadwiga was only nine, her father Louis died, leaving Hungary in a state of grief and chaos. Louis's mother Elizabeth, who had been ruling in Poland in his place, had died the previous year, so Poland was in even greater turmoil. Jadwiga's sister Maria was supposed to become the next ruler of Poland along with her betrothed, Sigismund of Luxembourg, but Poland did not relish the possibility of another absentee monarch. The Polish nobles were also opposed to the Germanic power represented by Maria's husband Sigismund, so they determined that instead of Maria, Louis's second daughter, Jadwiga, should reign in Poland, but only on the condition that she live there permanently. Jadwiga's mother, Elizabeth, hesitated to accept their proposal: She did not want to abandon the Polish crown for Jadwiga, but she was not yet ready to part with her young daughter. The Poles, dissatisfied that Jadwiga did not come to Poland immediately, threatened to replace her. After a series of angry meetings and anxious communications with Hungary, the Polish nobles remained committed to Jadwiga as their queen, but they insisted that she come to Poland without further delay for her coronation. Negotiations had been taking place for two years, and Poland would not wait any longer for its queen.

Thus, Jadwiga and her elaborate cortege set out for Cracow in the fall of 1384; she was not quite eleven years old. On October 15 she was crowned amidst much pomp and festivity in the cathedral next to the royal palace on Vavel Hill. The ornate crown of Poland was so heavy that two servants remained at her side throughout the coronation ceremonies, holding the crown above her head. The next day she went down into the city to be crowned again and celebrated by the local officials and merchants.

Jadwiga adopted her new country and its attendant responsibilities with enthusiasm and dedication. Many of the nobles at her father's court and many of her relatives were of Polish ancestry, so Jadwiga spoke Polish with ease; the excellent education her father had provided her also served her well in her new role. Within a few days of her coronation, Jadwiga was signing documents, listening to petitions, and attending to the internal problems of her new kingdom.

External affairs, however, were troubling Poland. The neighboring pagan state of Lithuania was a constant threat, so the Polish lords attempted peaceful negotiations with the Lithuanian leader, the Grand Duke Jagiello. They urged Jagiello to join his kingdom to Poland and to persuade Jadwiga to accept him as her husband and joint ruler. Not only would this solve the tension between Lithuania and Poland, but together they would form a united block against their enemies. Jagiello agreed, promising that he and his entire country would convert to Catholicism; he also promised financial security to Poland.

This proposal had much to offer both countries, but Jadwiga was not eager to accept it. As a child, she had been betrothed to William of Hapsburg, an arrangement that they had both taken seriously. They had spent much time together as children, and Jadwiga fully intended to marry him. William, hearing that the Polish nobles were arranging a marriage between Jadwiga and the Lithuanian ruler Jagiello, rushed from Vienna to Cracow. The Austrian prince was not allowed access to Jadwiga's castle, so Jadwiga came down to the city to meet him.

In the next month, Jadwiga and William met several times, using a Franciscan convent for their rendezvous and waiting anxiously to receive word from Hungary that Jadwiga's mother, Elizabeth, supported their marriage. But Elizabeth refused to help her daughter, and the Poles insisted that Jadwiga accept Jagiello instead as her husband. William and Jadwiga were adamantly opposed to breaking their engagement; eventually William gained access to the castle by disguising himself, but he was soon discovered and an alarm was sounded. In the ensuing melee, he managed to escape because Jadwiga lowered him down from the castle by a rope.

William hid in the city of Cracow for several months; with the help of secret messengers, he and Jadwiga contrived a plan of elopement. Late one night Jadwiga and a few of her ladies-in-waiting tried to escape from the castle but were stopped by a guard. Jadwiga took the ax from the guard and tried to break down the door, but the noise alerted one of her oldest and most faithful servants. He implored the young queen to abandon her foolish plan, to think of her responsibilities to her people, and to accept Jagiello as her king for the security of Poland and for the conversion of Lithuania to Catholicism.

Thus, the young queen gave up her beloved William and married Jagiello, who then became King of Poland. Jagiello remained true to his promise to convert pagan Lithuania, which was an enormous comfort to his devout queen. With his help, Jadwiga was also able to recover some Polish property from its southeast border that Jadwiga's father Louis had appropriated for Hungary. Although this involved a conflict with her sister Maria, Queen of Hungary, Jadwiga again put her personal concerns aside for the good of her country; she led an army to the province of Galicia and won the land back through peaceful means. The young queen of Poland thus accomplished two great goals through her marriage: the conversion of Lithuania and the restoration of lands to Poland that provided her country with a gateway to the Orient and fertile lands for farming.

Jadwiga was also instrumental in warding off the threat of the Teutonic Knights; she went directly to meet with their Grand Master to request the restoration of Polish lands. Adept at peaceful negotiations, she also served as an arbiter in the conflicts between her husband and his politically ambitious brothers. Although the marriage between Jadwiga and Jagiello was not one of love, it was eventually one of harmony and mutual concern for their people.

Jadwiga's commitment to her public duties as queen never flagged, even in the midst of great personal anguish. In Hungary, Jadwiga's mother Elizabeth had been conspiring against her daughter Maria's husband, Sigismund, but her plot failed, and she herself was brutally murdered. Jadwiga was also the target of some vicious slander, much of which originated with her former and embittered betrothed, William of Austria. Then in 1395, her sister Maria died; even though the sisters were sometimes political rivals, they were still very close. After Maria's death, Jadwiga became extremely ascetic, adopting plain garments, a hairshirt of rough animal skin, and a veil. In spite of her generous giving of gifts and her splendid, glamorous court, she herself withdrew from festive activities, fasted more frequently, spent more time in prayer, and reproached herself for not having a child, since the inability to conceive was considered a punishment for one's sins.

Jadwiga also became increasingly devoted to charitable activities for the sick and the poor; her admirers claimed that her kindness to the downtrodden was unsurpassed, and there are a number of legends surrounding her generosity. She and Jagiello founded several churches, and she supported the performance of more church music. She wanted religion to be more accessible to the people, so she encouraged the translation of religious services and devotional works into Polish instead of Latin. There are also records of the exquisite church vestments Jadwiga donated, many of which she had embroidered herself.

Her generosity extended beyond her religious contributions: Jadwiga continued the work begun by her great-uncle Casimir of founding a university at Cracow, the oldest university of central Europe, which would later produce such great scholars as the astronomer Copernicus.

In 1399 it seemed that her prayers for a child had been answered, but on June 22 of that year, she gave birth prematurely to a baby girl who died three weeks later. On July 17 Jadwiga herself died at the age of twenty-six from complications of childbirth. Even on her deathbed, she was concerned about her country, as she begged her husband to marry a cousin whose ancestry included both Lithuania and Poland. Jagiello later fulfilled her request, but he was devastated at the death of his queen. He removed the wedding ring from her finger and wore it for the rest of his life, claiming that it was his most treasured possession. In her will, Jadwiga requested that her sumptuous wardrobe and jewels be sold: Half of the wealth was to be distributed to the poor, and the other half was to be given to the university. She was buried in the Vavel Cathedral, and pilgrimages to her grave became very popular. Although canonization proceedings were never completed, the cult of Queen Jadwiga began immediately after her death and continued in subsequent centuries. To this day, she enjoys legendary status in Poland as the queen who sacrificed her personal happiness to ensure the stability of her beloved people.

BIBLIOGRAPHY

Gardner, Monica M. *Queen Jadwiga of Poland*. Dublin: Browne & Nolan, 1944.

Opfell, Olga S. *Queens, Empresses, Grand Duchesses and Regents: Women Rulers of Europe, A.D. 1328–1989*. Jefferson, NC: McFarland and Co., 1989.

Jo Eldridge Carney

JUANA OF CASTILE
(1479–1555)
Spain
Queen

"Juana la Loca" was queen of Castile from 1504 and of Aragon from 1516 to her death in 1555. Although technically queen, she spent most of her long reign imprisoned and declared mad by first her husband, then her father, and finally her son. Juana was the third child of Ferdinand of Aragon and Isabella of Castile, but the deaths of her older sister and brother meant that by 1500 she had become the heir to the combined thrones of Aragon and Castile. Juana always greatly preferred her father to her mother, and her loyalty to her father led to difficulties with her husband, whom she also passionately loved. Despite her deep feelings of affection, she was to be betrayed by all the men in her family. Although Juana did clearly have mental problems, many of the stories about her are myths developed by her enemies. Scholars debate just how "mad" Juana actually was and at what point in her life she really became irrational.

Isabella had insisted that all her children—daughters as well as son—be well educated, and Juana spoke French and Latin as well as Spanish. Juana may well have been the most brilliant of the five children. She also danced well and played a number of instruments. At sixteen Juana was betrothed to Philip the Handsome of Burgundy, the only son of the Holy Roman Emperor Maximillian; her brother Juan was at the same time betrothed to Philip's sister, Margaret. This alliance was part of Ferdinand's plan to secure allies against France. Philip and Juana married in October 1496 in Flanders; five months later the other wedding was celebrated in Spain. The marriage of Juan and Margaret was short-lived. Juan died in October 1497, six months after the wedding, leaving a pregnant wife. Three months later that child was stillborn. The Cortes of Castile (the equivalent of Parliament) recognized Juana's older sister Isabel, Queen of Portugal, as heiress to the throne, but the same year she died giving birth to a son Miguel. At first Juana and Philip's marriage looked to be much

Juana of Castile. From Special Collections, The Newark Public Library, New Jersey. Reprinted with permission.

more successful. Though this was an arranged marriage, Juana immediately fell deeply in love with her husband with an all-consuming passion that never left her.

Life in the Netherlands had some difficulties for Juana. She was furious about Philip's frequent affairs and did nothing to hide her rage. In 1498 she had her first child, a daughter Elinor. In February 1500 Juana gave birth to a son, Charles. Only a few months later, the two-year-old Miguel died, and Juana, again pregnant, was the heiress to the crowns of Castile and Aragon. Her second daughter Isabel was born in 1501.

With Juana now the heir to the combined thrones of Castile and Aragon, Isabella wanted to see her daughter and son-in-law and summoned them to Spain. They finally arrived in May 1502. Philip, bored and disliking the hot Spanish summer, stated he must return to Flanders. Juana was again pregnant, and Isabella insisted she stay until the baby was born. After her husband's departure, Juana sank into melancholy. In the spring of 1503 she had her second son, Fernando (or Ferdinand). Philip wanted her home. Juana, fearful of what he might have been doing in her absence, agreed. But Isabella wanted Juana to stay for an extended period in Spain and prepare for queenship. Isabella worried deeply that Philip would rule Spain as an appendage to the Holy Roman Empire and wanted Juana, not Philip, in control. Juana had no intention of staying. Juana and her mother quarreled dreadfully before Isabella at last consented to Juana's departure. Isabella was more and more concerned about Juana's instability and questioned if she would be competent to rule.

When Juana returned to Philip she was furious to find he had a mistress and attacked her, cutting off her long blond hair. Juana then requested magical help from the Moorish serving maids who had accompanied her and used their love potions on Philip. When Philip learned of his wife's machinations, he dismissed the serving girls, and Juana, confined to her chambers, went on a hunger strike. Although they soon reconciled, the pattern of behavior was set: Philip had affairs, and Juana, intensely jealous, quarreled violently with him.

In November 1504, Isabella died. She had left a codicil to her will that if Juana did not wish to rule Castile, or was incompetent to do so, her father Ferdinand was to rule for her. Isabella had been Queen of Castile in her own right and Ferdinand her consort. Ferdinand was eager to not simply be King of Aragon and father to the Queen of Castile. He had his officials graphically describe Juana's instability, and the Cortes, worried about how she would rule, named Ferdinand curator. Ferdinand also wrote to Juana asking for full authority to govern while she was out of the country. But Philip also wanted to control Spain and suppressed her father's letter, instead pressuring Juana to write that he as her husband should rule for her. Philip did all he could to isolate Juana so that Ferdinand's agents could not influence her. After the birth of yet another child, Juana and Philip set off to Castile, with a brief, unplanned stop in England due to stormy weather.

In Castile Juana insisted she had not come to take over from her father but only to consult with him. Philip was outraged and continued to isolate Juana. Philip managed to get Ferdinand to sign a treaty giving Philip control of Castile, although Ferdinand protested the treaty soon after he signed it. Ferdinand, however, soon left for Naples. Juana was upset by the treaty, but Philip managed to calm her, and the two made a state entry into Valladolid with Juana yet again pregnant. But once the members of the Cortes gave the couple their oath of fealty, Philip asked them to declare her incompetent and put the entire rule into his hands. Juana's supporters were outraged, and some scholars do argue that Juana at this time in her life was still clearly lucid, though unstable, and that Philip called her mad for the worst of political motivations. The Cortes denied Philip's request but allowed him to remain king consort. He used whatever power he had to replace Spanish officials with his own favorites.

Philip and Juana then traveled to Burgos, where Philip was determined to have Juana placed under constraint. But before he could carry out his plan, he became ill. Juana, still deeply in love with him despite all that had happened, stayed constantly at his bedside. Six days later in September 1506, he was dead at the age of twenty-eight. Juana was overwhelmed by grief.

Juana's enemies spread stories that she viewed his corpse daily, but in fact she did not have his coffin opened until five weeks after his death—and then because she had heard that Philip's courtiers had managed to smuggle away his body. But his body was there, cut apart and treated with lime, and must have been a horrible sight. Juana decided to honor Philip's request to be buried in Granada. Amid new reports that his corpse had been stolen, Juana had his coffin opened a second time. Juana and her entourage left Burgos in December, but dense fog prevented them from getting very far. They eventually reached Torquemada, about thirty-five miles from Burgos, but Juana, exhausted and ill, realized she could go no further until after her child was born and she recovered her strength. Although Catalina was born in January, Juana was not ready to continue her journey until April. While in Torquemada Juana had Philip's gorgeously draped coffin in front of the altar at the local church and frequently held midnight vigils there but forbade any other women to go near the coffin. Finally Juana had Philip all to herself. Although Juana and her entourage left Torquemada in April, they still did not get far. Out in a field in a storm, Juana, without giving a reason, again had the coffin opened.

Ferdinand and Juana met in Tortoles shortly thereafter, Philip's coffin still unburied, and Juana turned the government over to Ferdinand so that he could rule as regent. Ferdinand tried to convince Juana to marry the widowed Henry VII of England; Juana, however, had no interest in another marriage. But Ferdinand was concerned. What if she wanted to resume power? Ferdinand planned an expedition and was afraid some of the nobility would rally around Juana during his absence. To protect his position, he turned on his daughter. He had armed troops take her to a remote castle of Tordesillas in February 1509, where she was under the brutal control of Luis

Ferrer, one of Ferdinand's favorites, who may have had her beaten. Philip's coffin was placed in a nearby nunnery. When Ferdinand visited, instead of improving her situation, he ordered her moved to an inner room where she could no longer look out on the river. Juana was certainly unstable before, but certainly Ferdinand's calculating mistreatment was designed to worsen her mental condition. Later Ferdinand brought with him a group of prominent nobles who surprised a distraught Juana. Juana realized Ferdinand was attempting to make her look completely incompetent and went to dress appropriately, but the damage had already been done. Juana's one comfort was the company of her youngest daughter Catalina.

Ferdinand died in January 1516, although Juana was never informed and people consistently lied to her about it. Two years later, Juana's son Charles visited his mother. He had not seen Juana in twelve years and had little sympathy for her. The purpose of Charles's visit was to compel his mother to delegate to him the authority to rule. She did so, and the Castillian Cortes agreed but added as a stipulation that if Juana was restored to reason, she could then rule. Charles knew that he must keep his mother imprisoned and declared mad forever despite her desperate pleas that she be set free if he was to continue to rule Spain. Some scholars suggest he ordered her guardian, the Marquis of Denia, to do all he could to drive her completely insane.

Charles's grandfather Maximillian died in 1519, and Charles was crowned Holy Roman Emperor even though he was still determined to rule Spain from afar. Juana's incarceration made her a symbol of Spanish nationalism. When Castile was in revolt against Charles as an absentee ruler in 1520, the rebels vowed to set Juana free and restore her sovereignty. Although Charles had declared her insane and thus incompetent, his men asked Juana to issue an edict against the rebels. She refused. Juana, at last freed, presided over the Cortes for the first time in her life; she also finally learned of her father's death. But Juana, free after years of captivity, caught between loyalty to the rebels and to her son, felt paralyzed.

By the end of the year, Charles's forces had retaken Spain and Juana was again a prisoner. Denia kept Juana locked in a dimly lit room. No visitors were allowed, and Catalina was finally taken away from her. Philip's coffin, of such bizarre psychological importance to her, was taken from the nunnery near her and finally moved to its resting place in the royal chapel at Granada. Each year she deteriorated further, as she crouched on the floor and flung her dishes of food against the wall. She lived in this horrific way for many years, finally dying at the age of seventy-five in 1555. Although Charles had ignored and ill-used Juana during her lifetime, he had her body splendidly entombed next to Philip's. She and her husband were finally together.

BIBLIOGRAPHY

Miller, Townsend. *The Castles and the Crown.* London: Victor Gollancz, 1963.

Opfell, Olga S. *Queens, Empresses, Grand Duchesses and Regents: Women Rulers of Europe,* A.D. *1328–1989.* Jefferson, NC: McFarland and Co., 1989.

Prawdin, Michael. *The Mad Queen of Spain.* Trans. Eden Paul and Cedar Paul. Boston: Houghton Mifflin, 1939.

Carole Levin

ANNA KOMNENA
(1083–1153/1155)
Western Asia Minor (modern-day Turkey)
Scholar and Historian

The Byzantine princess Anna Komnena has been acclaimed as the medieval Greek world's most educated woman. Anna also deserves recognition for her encouragement of a group of scholars dedicated to the study of Aristotle's works. The greatest achievement of this brilliant daughter of Alexius I Komnenus (ruled 1081–1118) and Irene Ducas (d. 1133) is the history that she wrote about her father and his reign known as *The Alexiad*.

Toward the middle of the eleventh century, the Komneni, a military family of great power and wealth, assumed a leading role in the Byzantine world. Ruling as its emperor until his abdication, Isaac Komnenus (ruled 1057–1059) increased the Komneni's influential status. When Isaac's brother John refused the throne after Isaac's abdication, the Ducas family succeeded to power; however, the Komneni would soon regain control over the Byzantine Empire. With the persistent urging of his mother, Anna Dalassene (the wife of Isaac's brother John), Alexius seized the throne for the Komneni in a coup d'état (1081), approximately two years before Anna was born. Under the competent rule of Alexius I, the Komneni dynasty held its borders against a series of invaders, including the Normans and the Turks.

Anna's personal and family pride is legendary. Her birth in the purple chamber of Constantinople's imperial palace on 1 December 1083 earned for her the title *Porphyrogenete*, which means to have been "born in the purple." The eldest of seven children—Maria, John II Porphyrogenitous, Andronicus, Isaac, Eudocia, and Theodora—Anna had been led to believe that one day she, too, would reign over the magnificent Byzantine Empire. Alexius had even placed a crown upon Anna's head while she was still an infant. He had also betrothed her to the Empress Maria of Alania's son, Constantine Ducas, the rightful heir to the throne. Upon the birth of her brother John (ca. 1087), Anna's hopes of ruling an empire came to an abrupt end. Her father broke off her engagement to Constantine Ducas, and he designated Anna's brother John as the empire's acknowledged heir. Anna held her brother personally responsible for her plight, and he was destined to be the recipient of Anna's enmity for the rest of his life.

Anna's attempted revolt against her brother John II Porphyrogenitous shortly after her father's death in 1118 ultimately failed, even though Anna's mother had supported her eldest daughter's plan to seize the throne. In lieu of what could have been a more severe punishment, John II chose to exile Anna from the palace she had lived in since the time of her birth. John's punishment had the subsequent effect of severely limiting Anna's involvement in the political events of the empire. In 1097, Anna had been married to Nicephoros Bryennios, a distinguished historian and general, and it was presumably on her husband's behalf, to secure the throne for the two of them, that Anna had instigated her unsuccessful rebellion against her brother's rule. Anna and Bryennios had four children: Alexius Komnenus, John Ducas, Irene Ducas, and a daughter whose name is unknown.

When her husband died in 1137, Anna took up permanent residence in the religious retreat her mother had founded, the convent Kecharitomene, which means "all gracious." Prior to his death, Bryennios had begun writing a history to commemorate the Komneni's reign. Anna took up her husband's work after his death.

A highly educated woman, Anna devoted herself to her writing. While in her retirement, Anna held literary gatherings, and she supported the efforts of a group of scholars dedicated to Aristotelian studies, but her primary scholarly endeavor was focused on writing her history, *The Alexiad*. Anna's death has been dated around 1153–1155, when Georgios Tornikes, the metropolitan Bishop of Ephesus, may have delivered her funeral oration.

Three contemporary writers have left written testaments to commemorate Anna's astonishing intellectual accomplishments. Theodore Prodromos refers to Anna as the "Tenth Muse," Nicetas Chionates praises Anna's knowledge of "the sciences" and "philosophy," and Tornikes credits Anna with having reached "the highest summit of wisdom, both secular and divine." The numerous biblical and classical allusions that dominate Anna's history also support Anna's remarkable educational attainments.

When Anna first began her educational training, Byzantine scholars had dedicated themselves to the preservation of classical texts from antiquity. Anna, therefore, had a rare opportunity to study an unusual range of classical authors, along with a wide variety of disciplines. She received instruction in classical literature (especially Homer), in Scripture, in philosophy and rhetoric, and in the sciences, including the study of medical science, for which Anna demonstrated an unusual aptitude.

Anna's greatest contribution, however, is as a historian. Her prose epic composed in fifteen books—*The Alexiad* (ca. 1148)—represents a singular addition to the history of women. *The Alexiad*, an original work of Byzantine historiography, remains the most important book to have been written by a Byzantine woman, despite her somewhat confused chronology and her obvious partiality.

In some instances, *The Alexiad* is the only source for many of the events that occurred in Asia Minor. Anna's detailed accounts of Turkish incursions hold special value. In *The Alexiad*, Anna presents information about the Komneni, including details about their influential women, who lived at the center of power.

The Alexiad is primarily Anna's account of her father and the history of his reign. Among Anna's significant contributions is the three-dimensional portrait she presents of her father, as a monarch and as a military strategist. In this respect, *The Alexiad* constitutes a psychological study of particular importance. Anna also provides readers today with a Byzantine woman's views about herself and her world. Her admiring character sketches of a group of imperial women who influenced her father, Alexius—his mother, Anna Dalassena; the former empress, Maria of Alania; and his wife, Irene Ducas—indicate a personal conviction on Anna's part that women at the center of power did have significant contributions of their own to offer.

The Alexiad, as the only Hellenic eyewitness account of the First Crusades, is a work of indisputable historical importance. Anna's version of events surrounding the First Crusade is unique for several reasons. Her eyewitness account of the crusaders' arrival on Byzantine soil in 1096 eventually served to explode the previously accepted myth that religious reasons had chiefly motivated the Frankish counts. Her descriptions of liquid fire and the crossbow remain unique. Anna also includes important verbatim accounts of authentic documents not to be found in any other sources.

A remarkable scholar and Byzantine historian, Anna Komnena deserves the prominent place she holds in the history of women.

BIBLIOGRAPHY

Cavallo, Guglielmo, ed. *The Byzantines.* Trans. Thomas Dunlap, Teresa Lavender Fagan, and Charles Lambert. Chicago: University of Chicago Press, 1997.

Dalven, Rae. *Anna Comnena.* Twayne's World Authors Ser. 213. New York: Twayne, 1972.

Diehl, Charles. "Anna Comnena." In Harold Bell and Theresa de Kerpely, trans., *Byzantine Empresses.* New York: Knopf, 1963. 174–197.

Hanawalt, Emily Albu. "VITA: Anna Comnena." *Harvard Magazine* (March–April 1982): 38–39.

Kaegi, Walter E., ed. *Byzantinische Forschungen: Internationale Zeitschrift für Byzantinistik.* Proc. of 20th Annual Byzantine Studies Conf., Sept. 1994, Ann Arbor, MI. Amsterdam, Netherlands: Hakkert, 1996.

Sewter, E.R.A. *The Alexiad of Anna Comnena.* New York: Penguin, 1969.

Debra Barrett-Graves

HELENE KOTTANER
(1400–after 1457)
Austria
Writer of Memoirs and Royal Servant

Helene Kottaner was a dedicated servant and chambermaid to the fifteenth-century Queen Elizabeth of Hungary; at a time of factional politics and dynastic confusion, Kottaner's act of courage and loyalty to Elizabeth helped secure the succession for the queen's son. Kottaner's tale of her brave act is recorded in her own words in a remarkable account, the first memoir written by a woman in German.

Helene Kottaner's story is interwoven with that of her queen. In 1432 Elizabeth, the only child of Sigismund, the King of Hungary and the Holy Roman Emperor, was married to the Duke of Austria, Albrecht V. When King Sigismund died in 1438, his son-in-law Albrecht was elected to replace him as the King of Hungary and the Holy Roman Emperor. Elizabeth became the queen; their first child was a daughter also named Elizabeth.

We know very little about Helene Kottaner; born in Austria in 1400, she married, had several children, and served at Albrecht's court while he was still in Vienna. When he moved to Hungary to marry Elizabeth, Helene and her family remained in his service. She soon became Elizabeth's chambermaid, an important post that would have involved supervision of the ladies-in-waiting, care of the royal wardrobe, and advice and counsel to the queen.

Albrecht II's reign was successful but short-lived; in October of 1439 he died of dysentery; Elizabeth was thirty-one years old at the time and pregnant with their second child. Elizabeth claimed the regency, but Albrecht's advisers did not support the rule of a woman; they urged Elizabeth to remarry quickly so as to preserve their kingdom from invasion by the Turks. Wladislaus III, the sixteen-year-old King of Poland, was proposed to Elizabeth as a suitable marriage partner. Elizabeth, however, did not want to share her powers or to remarry; furthermore, she had faith that her unborn child was a male who could inherit the throne. Her hopes were fulfilled, for on 21

February 1440, her son was born. He was named Ladislaus Posthumous, and when he was twelve weeks old, Elizabeth had him crowned as the country's next king in spite of great political opposition.

This coronation would not have happened without the help of Queen Elizabeth's close confidante and chambermaid Helene Kottaner. Despite the pressure on Elizabeth to marry the King of Poland, she was intent upon securing the kingship instead for her son. During her pregnancy, Elizabeth contrived a secret plan to secure the precious Holy Crown of St. Stephen, the crown that was believed to confer the powers of kingship on the possessor, which had been locked and sealed in a vault for safekeeping at the stronghold at Plintenburg. Elizabeth and her court had moved twelve miles away from Plintenburg to Komorn, but she decided to send Kottaner back to Plintenburg to smuggle out the Holy Crown.

When Elizabeth first asked Kottaner to undertake the theft of the crown, the chambermaid realized that the plan was extremely dangerous; she was worried not only about herself but about the fate of her own young children if her mission was unsuccessful. She finally agreed to Elizabeth's request, because she was aware of its grave importance to her queen and to the security of the country. Kottaner requested the assistance of another loyal servant, but afraid of the potential danger, he refused. Another suitable servant agreed to help, and the two of them set off to Plintenburg with the necessary tools hidden in their clothing: keys for the doors leading to the vault, files to break into the vault itself, and the queen's insignia necessary to reapply the seals.

Kottaner's memoir recounts in fascinating detail their ordeal as she and her assistant arrived at the castle, ostensibly to accompany some of the ladies-in-waiting back to Komorn the next day. Kottaner asked to sleep that night in the room next to the treasure vault, and she managed to obtain candles on the pretext that she intended to stay awake for awhile and pray. While she kept an anxious watch, the other servant filed and burned through the several locks to get the crown; once the crown was secured, they threw the files in the ladies' privy and sewed the crown inside a feather pillow. In spite of some suspicious servants and various mishaps, they were able to smuggle the crown out of the castle successfully. Kottaner kept the pillow safe on their return trip, even when their sled overturned in the middle of the partially frozen Danube and many of their possessions were lost in the icy waters.

The very day Kottaner returned with the Holy Crown, the young king was born, and three months later, he was crowned. The coronation of the infant king was not enough, however, to ensure a smooth transition for his succession. Tension and disagreement among various factions continued, and the opposing parties still elected Wladislaus of Poland as the next king. This double coronation resulted in civil war. Fearing for her son's life, Elizabeth and her followers had to flee to Austria; during the perilous journey, Kottaner was in charge of the infant king and the crown. After all of the trouble that was taken to secure the crown, Elizabeth, destitute, was forced to pawn it to Frederick III, the Holy Roman Emperor, in exchange for a loan of 2,500 florins. The receipt for this transaction describes the ornate crown in great detail and is a valuable piece of evidence for historians. Elizabeth was never able to return to Hungary; she died in Austria in 1442. It was not until 1452, when Ladislaus was twelve years old, that he was reconfirmed as king. During his reign, rival factions continued their struggle for power. In 1457, King Ladislaus died; there were rumors that he had been poisoned. We do not know what happened to Helene Kottaner after Ladislaus's death.

Helene Kottaner's memoir also describes the events leading up to Ladislaus's coronation and their flight from Hungary. Some scholars believe that her motivation for writing the memoir was to remind Ladislaus of the services she had performed for him and his mother; she received a reward from the young king in 1452. The manuscript is now housed in the National Library of Vienna; while it has begun to receive attention from scholars, the work in its entirety has not yet been translated into English or even into modern German. An excellent English translation of excerpts from the manuscript by Professor Maya C. Bijvoet is available.

BIBLIOGRAPHY

Bijvoet, Maya C. "The Austrian Chambermaid." In Katherina M. Wilson, ed., *Women Writers of the Renaissance and Reformation*. Athens: University of Georgia Press, 1987.

Sugar, Peter F., ed. *A History of Hungary*. Bloomington: Indiana University Press, 1990.

Jo Eldridge Carney

LOUISE LABÉ
(ca. 1520–1566)
France
Poet

One of the finest lyric poets of the French Renaissance, Louise Labé was famous for her passionate love sonnets, her involvement in the cultural life of sixteenth-century Lyons, and her defense of these activities. She was both praised and attacked for writing love sonnets at a time when virtuous women did not declare their desire publicly in print.

Unfortunately, little is known about Labé's life. Scholars generally agree that she was born near Lyons, France, sometime around 1520 (between her parents' marriage in 1516 and her mother's death in 1523). Her father, Pierre Charly (also known as Labé), was a prosperous rope-maker; her mother, Etiennette, was his second wife. Labé had three brothers and a sister, as well as a half brother and a half sister from her father's third marriage. Labé's father provided her with an excellent education. She knew Latin, Italian, and probably Spanish and Greek, as well as conventionally feminine skills, such as needlework, spinning, weaving, and lute playing. Only a very small percentage of women were taught classical languages in this era, and most of them were from aristocratic families. Thus Labé's knowledge of Latin and Greek was not typical. One way that prominent nonnoble citizens like Labé's father could display their wealth and position was by training their children in aristocratic accomplishments and learning. Labé may have received her education from nuns at a nearby convent school (La Déserte), to which her mother's family had contributed money. In one poem, Labé refers proudly to her considerable skill at horsemanship and arms, as well as needlework. Some scholars suggest that Labé may actually have taken part in a tournament in Lyons held for the future King Henry II in 1542. If true, Labé's actions were certainly extraordinary, for the women's role at such events was to watch the men perform and *not* to participate themselves.

Around 1543, Labé was married to Ennemond Perrin, a wealthy rope-maker at least twenty years her senior. Little is known about their marriage, but Perrin apparently allowed his wife to run a sort of literary salon in their home, where nobles, merchants, and writers (mostly men) met for intellectual conversation. Rumors of Labé's marital infidelity circulated in her own time, although these allegations originated mainly with men who were opposed to her highly visible, public participation in Lyon's cultural life and who were especially antagonistic to her writing. At a time when male-authored conduct books and sermons encouraged bourgeois women like Labé to remain "chaste, silent, and obedient" at home, she was understandably a controversial figure, both admired and attacked for her poetry, display of learning, and public persona.

A single volume of her works was printed in Lyons in 1555 (*Euvres de Louise Labé Lionnoize*). It contained twenty-four sonnets (one in Italian), three elegies, and a prose dialogue (*Le débat de Folie et d'Amour*, or The Debate between Folly and Love). As was customary, a number of poems (two dozen) by admirers praising Labé's poetic talent and verse also appear in the volume. The book is dedicated to Clémence de Bourges, the daughter of a Lyonnese nobleman. In her dedicatory letter to de Bourges, Labé defends women's right to education and rejects their alleged inferiority to men. She urges women to put aside their expected duties, such as spinning, to become men's partners in both domestic and public affairs. In Labé's view, women should adorn themselves with intellectual accomplishments and the fame these bring, rather than with luxurious clothing and jewelry. Four editions of Labé's works appeared between 1555 and 1556, an indication of their considerable popularity. Labé died several years after her husband in 1566. It is likely that she had no surviving children, because her will mentions none, and it leaves a large sum to the children of her brother François.

In the early sixteenth century, the French city of Lyons was a vibrant hub of artistic and commercial activity. After Paris, it was the most important printing center in France. Proximity to Germany and Italy as well as the city's traditional trade fairs, which attracted buyers and sellers across Europe, combined to make Lyons an international trading and banking venue; a large silk industry also developed there. As a result, Lyons was a cosmopolitan city, both commercially and culturally. It felt the influence of Italian Renaissance thought, particularly the revival of classical learning known as humanism, much earlier than other French cities, including Paris. Lyons was the home of several well-regarded poets: Maurice Scève, Olivier de Magny, and Pernette du Guillet, the last like Labé a female poet. Labé knew these and other celebrated poets of her day, including Pierre Ronsard and Joachim Du Bellay of the influential Plèiade school of French poetry. The intellectual and artistic milieu available to Labé in Lyons was thus an especially rich and stimulating one.

Like many of the poets named above, Labé was influenced by the love poetry of Petrarch, a fourteenth-century Italian humanist, translator, and poet whose sonnets had an enormous impact on poets across Europe. For several centuries, Petrarch's sonnets were widely admired and imitated, particularly for their mixture of sensual and spiritual desire. Conventionally, the Petrarchan lover-poet is male and expresses passion for an unattainable, idealized mistress. The unrequited lover often celebrates his mistress's beauty in a blazon, a list that compares various parts of the woman's body to jewels, precious metals, flowers, or other rare objects. Labé's sonnets, however, rework Petrarchan poetic conventions in ways that some of her male readers found scandalously provocative. Her poems are spoken by an openly passionate female lover who seeks a more mutual, reciprocal love than tradition usually provided. Labé's descriptions of her male lover's body are quite sensual and thus shocking in a time when virtuous women did not admit to having strong physical desires. Although modern readers and scholars still speculate, the identity of the beloved addressed in Labé's sonnets remains unknown. Some critics suggest that Olivier de Magny is Labé's beloved, because he wrote several poems praising her, used lines from her second sonnet in one of his, and wrote an ode satirizing her husband.

Romances and love poetry were literary genres deemed unsuitable for chaste women to read, let alone to write and publish. Some of Labé's critics viewed her amorous poems as evidence of her immoral character, particularly given her unusually prominent position in Lyon's intellectual and artistic life. In a letter from Geneva, Protestant theologian John Calvin called Labé (who was a Catholic) a common whore and accused her of leading a noted surgeon's wife into debauchery and sin. A scurrilous poem circulated in 1557 that called Labé "la belle cordiere" ("the beautiful rope-maker") and accused her of sleeping with numerous men. Modern scholars, however, discount these charges and view them as hostile reactions to a highly talented, unconventional woman.

BIBLIOGRAPHY

Jones, Ann Rosalind. *The Currency of Eros: Women's Love Lyric in Europe, 1540–1620.* Bloomington: Indiana University Press, 1990.

Rigolot, François. "Louise Labé." In Eva Sartori and Dorothy Zimmerman, eds., *French Woman Writers.* Westport, CT: Greenwood Press, 1991.

Sharratt, Peter, intro., and Graham Martin, trans. *Louise Labé, Sonnets.* Edinburgh Bilingual Library. Austin: University of Texas Press, 1972.

Warnke, Frank J., ed. *Three Women Poets: Renaissance and Baroque.* Lewisburg: Bucknell University Press, 1987.

Gwynne Kennedy

AEMILIA LANYER
(1569–1645)
Britain
Poet

Aemilia Lanyer was one of the first English women to argue in print and in her own name against the long-standing, widely held belief in women's inherent moral, physical, and intellectual inferiority to men. Her remarkable verse collection *Salve Deus Rex Judaeorum* (*Hail Lord, King of the Jews*) makes a case for women's central role in Christian history and even for women's spiritual superiority to men.

Lanyer's social class position differed significantly from that of other notable women writers in early modern England, such as **Mary Wroth, Elizabeth Cary**, and Mary Sidney Herbert. They were members of the upper classes (the gentry or peerage), whereas Lanyer's family were middle-class professionals who made their living as artists or providers of entertainment. Lanyer's father was Baptist Bassano, a Jewish lute player from Venice; he was one of Queen Elizabeth's court musicians. Her mother, Margaret Johnson, was English. Her father died in 1576, when Lanyer was seven, and her mother died in 1587. Lanyer's older sister, Angela, was already married to Joseph Holland by the time of their father's death; nothing else is known about her. Lanyer inherited some goods from her mother and (at age twenty-one) £100 from her father, presumably for her marriage. Sometime before 1592, Lanyer became the mistress of Henry Carey, Lord Hunsdon, the Queen's Lord Chamberlain and a prominent figure at Elizabeth's court. Because Hunsdon was a patron of Shakespeare's acting company, one critic has argued that Lanyer is the "dark lady" of Shakespeare's sonnets, but there is little evidence to support this speculation. Lanyer may have met the queen during her time with Hunsdon, for she refers in one poem to having been "blessed" with the late queen's "favor" during her "youth." The popular astrologer Simon Foreman, whom many Londoners including Lanyer consulted for advice, mentions in his diaries that Lanyer was known at court and received favors from Elizabeth as well as money, jewels, and gifts from Hunsdon and other noblemen. When she became pregnant, Lanyer was married for appearance's sake to Alphonso Lanyer, another of Elizabeth's court musicians. Their son, Henry, was born in 1593; he followed Lanyer family tradition and became a court flautist. A daughter, Odillya, died at nine months old in 1599.

Both Lanyer and her husband were ambitious for social advancement. In addition to his court employment, Alphonso embarked on several enterprises, including the Earl of Essex's expedition to the Azores in 1597 and campaign in Ireland in 1599, in hopes of financial and social rewards. He eventually received some income from a patent granted to him by Elizabeth's successor, James I. Aemilia, on the other hand, took to writing. Her *Salve Deus Rex Judaeorum*, printed in 1611, contains dedications to nine prominent noble and royal women, including Queen Anne, as well as two others to "virtuous" readers and "virtuous women in general." Some surviving copies of *Salve Deus* have the dedications in different orders or with omissions, suggesting that certain volumes were tailored for particular recipients. Alphonso apparently gave one as a gift to the Lord Chancellor of Ireland, whom he may have met while in Essex's service. There is no evidence that the couple's appeals for patronage succeeded, however, and after Alphonso's death in 1613, Aemilia's financial position became precarious. She fought her husband's family in the courts over the income from the patent for more than twenty years. Her efforts to support herself in 1617 by running a school ended in legal disputes after a few years. Lanyer died in 1645 at the age of sixty-seven.

Salve Deus is a remarkable work in a number of ways. Lanyer's multiple dedications to potential female patrons are highly unusual in women's writings at this time; such appeals to patrons of either sex occurred principally in male-authored works. Lanyer may have known personally some of the women she asks to "grace" or favor her work (and herself), as several poems suggest. Her claims to have been with the Countess of Cumberland at an estate called Cookham or to have known the Countess of Kent from her youth should probably be viewed with some caution, as they have not yet been corroborated by evidence outside of the poem. Lanyer's dedications are fascinating for the skill with which she alternately praises the virtues of her social superiors, asks them for some material reward, asserts her worthiness to receive it, and insists that moral or spiritual wealth is superior to the material wealth they possess. These are tricky arguments, particularly given Lanyer's former status as the Lord Chamberlain's mistress and her desire for financial compensation. The poems display at various points both Lanyer's desire to be included among the elite and her anger at her exclusion from their society. Her dedicatory letter to the "virtuous reader," on the other hand, vigorously defends women against their detractors, both male and female. Boldly equating men who forget that they were born from and nourished by women with enemies of Christ and his apostles, Lanyer counters with a list of women important in both Old Testament and New Testament history. Misogyny, she implies, is akin to blasphemy—a radical claim for a woman to make in print.

The final poem in *Salve Deus*, "To Cook-ham," is the first English country-house poem, predating Ben Jonson's "To Penshurst," which was previously thought to be the earliest of its type. Whereas country-house poems generally praise the manor (and its male lord) as representing harmony with the natural world, "the good life," benign social class relations, permanence, stability, and magnanimity, Lanyer's "To Cook-ham" celebrates and bids farewell to an estate headed by a mistress (the Countess of Cumberland) who must leave a place where women, including Lanyer, shared each other's company for a short time. Cumberland and her daughter, **Lady Anne Clifford**, were at the time engaged in legal disputes over land that was rightfully the inheritance of the daughter but that her father bequeathed to his brother instead. Lanyer was well aware of the circumstances, and her poem thus offers an ironic commentary on later celebrations of patriarchal benevolence.

The longest section of *Salve Deus* narrates the Passion of Christ and praises the spiritual virtues of Margaret, the Countess of Cumberland. It argues not only for women's central role in Christian biblical history but also for their spiritual superiority to men. Lanyer's account of the Passion stresses women's understanding of and empathy with Jesus. Female characters, such as Pilate's wife, Mary, and the daughters of Jerusalem, understand the significance of the events and either try to stop or mourn the Crucifixion, whereas male characters like Peter the apostle or the guards by the cross do neither. In her poem, Lanyer lodges responsibility for Christ's death squarely with men. Like many early modern writers, Lanyer offers her own interpretation of the Fall of Adam and Eve. Lanyer's, however, is more radical than most. Through the character of Pilate's wife, she argues that Pilate's knowing participation in Christ's death more than cancels out Eve's unwitting temptation by the serpent, and thus, women's submission to men (one consequence of the Fall) should cease! At several places in the poem, Lanyer claims divine authorization for her account, as will John Milton in his own poetic rewriting of the Fall (*Paradise Lost*) later in the century.

BIBLIOGRAPHY

Grossman, Marshall, ed. *Aemilia Lanyer*. Lexington: University of Kentucky Press, 1998.

Woods, Susanne, ed. *The Poems of Aemilia Lanyer*. New York: Oxford University Press, 1993.

Gwynne Kennedy

LUCRETIA DE LEÓN
(1569–ca. 1596)
Spain
Prophet

Born the daughter of Alonso Franco de León and Ana Ordonez, Lucretia de León was raised in the city of Madrid, royal capital of the Spanish Empire. During her brief life, she became well known in Madrid as a prophet whose dreams forecast a number of difficulties for Spain in general and for the king, Philip II, in particular. Lucretia's father was a legal agent or solicitor who represented the Italian Genoese banking community in Madrid. There were a total of five children in the middle-class urban household, and while her stern father disparaged Lucretia's early dreams on political subjects, fearing that any public recounting of these might place his family under suspicion of disloyalty to the Crown, her mother encouraged her in hopes that her daughter's notoriety might improve the family fortunes. Lucretia most likely could read Spanish, although she would later represent herself during her trial as a "simple woman" and "without letters." Her rather extensive knowledge of contemporary and historical events was assisted by members of the clergy.

In 1587 two prominent Catholic churchmen sought Lucretia's permission to transcribe her dreams. Alonso de Mendoza, a theologian from an aristocratic family who was attached to the cathedral of Toledo, and Fray Lucas de Allende, head of Madrid's Franciscan convent, sought to coach the young woman in the art of dream interpretation, divination, apocalyptic thought, and other aspects of the occult. While initially reluctant to have her dreams transcribed, the young girl's mother encouraged this undertaking. Mendoza assisted the family with financial support and schooled Lucretia in the politics of the day until her arrest in 1590. Today virtually everything we know about Lucretia de León comes to us from trial records produced by the Spanish Inquisition over a five-year period beginning in 1590. Included in this source material are the transcriptions of over

400 dreams that the young defendant recalled in the three years prior to her arrest on the charges of heresy and sedition.

Three factors were at work undermining Lucretia's credibility at the time of her arrest. The first involved the fact that she had no religious vocation. Most female seers were nuns who benefitted from the support of a recognized religious order. Oftentimes the asceticism, chastity, and rigor of monastic life helped to dispel whatever suspicion might have been attached to would-be prophets and mystics. Lucretia's incapacity to claim any spiritual credentials undermined her efforts to be taken as a legitimate prophet. Indeed several months after her initial detention, she gave birth to a child out of wedlock. Early in 1590, at the age of twenty-one, she had become involved with Diego de Vitores Texeda, a Latin secretary to Lucretia's priest confessor. Their clandestine marriage, when made public after Lucretia's arrest, outraged religious opinion.

The second disadvantage concerned the fact that Lucretia's pictures of a kingdom on the brink of disaster under Philip II came to her as dreams and not as visions. Catholic theologians since the time of St. Augustine in the early fifth century argued that God most often worked through visions or the divine enlightenment of a human intellect—not through dreams. Augustine believed that it was difficult to differentiate divine dreams and those that had natural, bodily origins. In general, the early Church fathers had recognized that dreams could sometimes serve as instruments of divine communication, but only rarely. The thirteenth-century theologian St. Thomas Aquinas criticized those who used natural dreams for purposes of divination, and he attributed the desire to know the future to an express contract with Satan. Distinguishing between the true prophet and the false one was a very difficult enterprise.

Finally, the greatest problem facing Lucretia as she faced the Inquisition had to do with the overtly political messages contained in her dreams. Most earlier holy prophets had focused their attentions on reform in the Church or even spiritual renewal in the community at large. Indeed, prior to the Protestant Reformation, religious eccentrics who claimed a special relationship with God were often tolerated or merely dismissed without much notice. But by the middle of the sixteenth century, and particularly in strictly Catholic countries like Spain, the Roman Church, fearful of the spread of heresy, attempted to suppress most forms of alternate religious expression. The

Inquisition worked diligently to police the religious opinions of the entire populace, focusing attention especially in the urban centers. Female visionaries were thought to be the most dangerous due to the widespread belief that women, being of a weaker nature, could not successfully rebuff the delusions of Satan. And a woman whose visions became public knowledge was truly dangerous since only the devil could compel one to make public what was intended to be a private communication.

Lucretia lived during the later reign of the powerful Spanish monarch Philip II. Many of her recorded dreams contain strong social and political commentary, mostly hostile, of Philip's rule. The king is often shown as weak, aging, and irresolute. Corruption in the Church, high taxes, and widespread injustice with respect to the lives of the poor are all included. She predicted Spain's decline as a great power at the hands of its Protestant and Muslim rivals, and this, too, she attributed to the king's personal failings as a ruler. Lucretia was clearly operating within a centuries-old prophetic tradition, but the novelty involved her shift away from strictly spiritual and moral matters and into the much more dangerous arena of political commentary. And in her case, prophesying was clearly viewed as a threat to the political stability and integrity of Philip II's regime.

Lucretia's arrest had been ordered by the king himself, mainly because her dreams were thought to pose a direct challenge to the monarchy at a moment in Philip II's reign when the king had suffered a number of military and diplomatic setbacks. In 1588 the mighty Spanish Armada had failed in its goal of invading Elizabeth I's English kingdom. Despite the wealth of the Spanish colonial holdings in the New World, prosperity had given way to economic stagnation in Castile. During the 1580s thousands of impoverished peasants flocked to the major cities looking for work. When some of the king's advisers began to support her claims to extraordinary and prophetic dreams that warned of Spain's imminent collapse as a great power, Philip saw nothing but conspiracy against the monarchy.

Like Joan of Arc in fifteenth-century France or the Englishwoman **Elizabeth Barton**, who had visions warning King Henry VIII against his plan to end his marriage to Catherine of Aragon, political visionaries often found themselves facing charges of treason. Disgruntled churchmen like Mendoza and political opponents of the king used Lucretia's prophetic statements in order to move the king toward greater efforts at reform. By drawing upon unique spiritual gifts, Lucretia was able to enter into the realm of male-dominated politics, perhaps in the only manner available to women of the age.

During her trial, Lucretia sought to blame her misfortune squarely on the shoulders of the two priests who had transcribed her dreams. The trial of Lucretia and her alleged co-conspirators dragged on for almost five years, and on two occasions, the young woman was apparently subject to torture by her inquisitors. In the end she was charged with having made a pact with the devil, blasphemy, falsehood, sacrilege, and sedition. She was sentenced to receive 100 lashes, banishment from Madrid, and two years' seclusion in a religious house. We have no information on what became of Lucretia or her daughter after the completion of her sentence. Her brief attempt to influence the world of politics as a divinely inspired seer having been rejected by both Church and state, Lucretia de León returned to the obscurity that surrounds the lives of so many women of the sixteenth century.

BIBLIOGRAPHY

Kagan, Richard L. *Lucretia's Dreams: Politics and Prophecy in Sixteenth-Century Spain*. Berkeley: University of California Press, 1990.

W. M. Spellman

ANNE LOCKE
(1530–1590)
Britain
Puritan Writer and Scholar

Anne Locke was the daughter of a merchant and government agent who worked in the service of King Henry VIII. After the death of Anne's mother in 1545, her father, Stephen Vaughan, married the widow of a London mercer named Margery Brinklow. Anne's mother, stepmother, and father had decidedly Protestant leanings, and Protestant religious views were inculcated at home throughout Anne's earliest years. During the brief reign of Henry VIII's son, Edward VI (1547–1553), England was exposed to a wide range of Protestant influences. An English-language prayer book was introduced, and the sacraments were reduced to two, baptism and the Lord's Supper. In theory, the priesthood was no longer set apart from the laity; the Lutheran-inspired "priesthood of all believers" was advanced as clergy were now permitted to marry.

By the time of the young king's death in 1553, Protestantism had gained a large following, especially in London and the southeast more generally. Anne was taught to read and write, and although she received no formal education, she was familiar with Scripture and followed developments in reform theology quite closely. Sometime after her twentieth birthday, Anne married a neighbor and mercer by the name of Henry Locke. Her husband was also from a respected London family with a reputation for Protestantism. In 1553 the Scottish Protestant reformer John Knox (1513–1572) lived briefly in the Lockes' London home before the start of his exile on the Continent in the wake of the Catholic Queen Mary's accession after Edward VI's death.

Knox was clearly impressed by Anne's commitment to Protestant principles. From 1556 until 1562, he wrote thirteen letters to the pious Mrs. Locke. The earliest letters were sent from Geneva, and in them, Knox invites Anne to join his little band of Protestant saints in exile. England was now under a Roman Catholic monarch, and there seemed little hope that Protestantism would triumph so long as Mary remained queen. In fact, while Queen Mary has been treated unfairly by most historians, it is true that more than 300 Protestants were martyred for their beliefs during her reign, 55 of whom were women. Knox's frustration with the rule of Catholic leaders, both in England under Queen Mary and in his homeland of Scotland under the regent Mary of Guise, broke forth in his hostile *First Blast of the Trumpet against the Monstrous Regiment of Women* (1558). It was an unfortunate production, not least due to the fact that it earned for Knox the lasting enmity of the future Protestant Queen Elizabeth I.

In May 1557 Anne made the decision to leave her home, traveling with her two small children to Geneva and what Knox had described to her in a letter as "the perfect school of Christ." Her husband subsequently joined his family, a decision probably motivated in part by the fact that he had to complete some business transactions on the Continent. Anne quickly joined a small community of English Protestant exiles living in the city and busied herself translating some of John Calvin's sermons into English. Locke dedicated her work to Catherine, Dowager Duchess of Suffolk, who had converted to Protestantism in the 1540s, provided financial support for Protestant publications, and like so many others, went into exile at the accession of the Catholic Queen Mary. Knox continued his work as well, now writing diatribes calling for the right to resist unpopular and heretical monarchs. Anne stayed on in Geneva for a few months after Knox returned to Scotland early in 1559. Elizabeth I had acceded to the English throne the previous year, but the English Protestant exile community on the Continent was uncertain of the new queen's commitment to the reformed faith. Finally, Anne returned to her husband's house in London in midsummer 1559, and Knox's letters to her continued for another three years.

We know little of Anne's life during the 1560s. By the Act of Supremacy, Queen Elizabeth reclaimed leadership over the Church of England as established by her father Henry VIII, and an Act of Uniformity imposed a Book of Common Prayer on all of the queen's English subjects. Those who avoided church on Sunday were to pay a one shilling fine. With her *via media*, or middle way, in Church government and doctrine, Elizabeth hoped to temporize between the extremes of Roman Catholicism and the brand of reform or Puritan Protestantism endorsed by Calvinists like Anne Locke. Her husband Henry was by this time a well-to-do London businessman, and quiet conformity to the outward forms of Anglicanism was the path of many who hoped for further reform in the future.

After her first husband died in 1571, Anne married a young Cambridge graduate and preacher named Edward Dering. Dering had been a fellow of Christ's College, Cambridge, from 1560 to 1570, at a time when heated theological debate at the university was the norm. He was about ten years younger than his wife, but he had established himself as one of the most powerful young preachers in the country. However, just before marrying Anne, Dering became a forceful critic of the Established Church of England, even going so far as to criticize the queen's handling of religious affairs in a sermon preached in Elizabeth's presence in 1570. Despite this initial affront, he was appointed to a position as reader at St. Paul's Cathedral in London, where his reputation as a learned and engaging preacher spread rapidly. Dering's attacks on the clergy of the Church of England did not abate, however, and after repeated efforts to curb his harsh sermons in the pulpit, the queen had him silenced in 1573.

A number of Puritan preachers, laymen, and women were imprisoned during that year for their refusal to accept the doctrines and hierarchy of the Church as established by Elizabeth. Although Anne supported her husband's harsh Puritan critiques, she was not among those arrested. Dering wrote to his brother at the end of that year: "My wife hath been I thank God in no trouble, neither was any toward her that I know of; if any fall, God hath made her rich in grace and knowledge to give account of her doing" (Collinson, 285). Dering's anxiousness for his wife was not misplaced. Recent historians have shown that in defying ecclesiastical authorities, females put into jeopardy their reputations and were thought to be "masterless women" and therefore no better than whores. In 1576, at the age of thirty-six, Anne's second husband died after a brief illness but not before having led—with strong support from his wife—some of the strongest Puritan criticisms against the Anglican Church during the entire reign of Elizabeth I.

Anne Locke married for the third and last time around 1583. Her last husband, Richard Prowse, was a draper (cloth merchant) and former mayor of the city of Exeter in the southwest of the country. In 1584 Prowse was elected to Parliament and sided with the Puritan party in the House of Commons. During the final year of her life, Anne published a work of translation, Jean Taffin's *Of the markes of the children of God, and of their comfort in afflictions.* Its appearance in print at the very time when English Puritans were being hard-pressed by the Archbishop of Canterbury, John Whitgift, to conform to the Church of England indicates that Anne Locke was well aware of the precarious nature of the Reform movement in England. And like so many Protestant women who exercised considerable spiritual authority within the domestic setting, Anne's impact on the public debate was muted by social and cultural attitudes that continued to favor patriarchal control of religion in the public square. Protestant men continued to maintain that males alone were designed for sacred functions, whereas women were to remain within the domestic sphere.

BIBLIOGRAPHY

Collinson, Patrick. *Godly People: Essays on English Protestantism and Puritanism.* London: Hambledon Press, 1983. 273–289.

Crawford, Patricia. *Women and Religion in England, 1500–1720.* New York: Routledge, 1993.

W. M. Spellman

KATHERINE LUTHER
(1499–1550)
Germany
Protestant Reformer

Katherine von Bora Luther stands in the background behind her husband, the great reformer Martin Luther. Her strength and courage were for the most part in the private realm, but this should not detract from her worth. Katherine's father was a nobleman, Hans von Bora. Her mother died soon after Katherine was born; at the age of five when her father remarried, Katherine was placed in a nunnery, where her aunt was abbess, so that she could gain an education. At the age of ten she was moved to another nunnery, Nimschen, where another aunt was also a nun; and in about 1515, at the age of sixteen, Katherine took her vows as a nun. For centuries this was how many women became nuns. It was frequently not a deliberate choice out of religious devotion; rather, the nunneries were too often places for superfluous females who were no longer wanted or needed at home and this was the case for Katherine. Katherine von Bora was a young nun during the time when Germany was rocked by the monk Martin Luther's attack on the Catholic Church.

Luther's father had intended him to be a lawyer, but a crisis of faith had propelled Martin instead to take his vows. He entered a monastery in 1505 and was ordained a priest two years later. Luther was deeply concerned about the ways one comes to salvation, and he was upset by any practices that he felt stood in the way. In October 1517, in Wittenberg where he was professor of theology, he nailed to the church door ninety-five theses attacking the Church's stand on indulgences, prayers churchmen were paid to recite so that the souls of individuals' loved ones would spend less time in purgatory. Two years later, when Luther had refused to recant his beliefs, the Catholic Church excommunicated him and declared him to be an outlaw. But fortunately Prince Frederick of Saxony, where Wittenberg was located, protected Luther and for a year kept him safe at his castle at Wartburg. A number of the German principalities wished to assert

Marriage of Katherine von Bora and Martin Luther. From Gustav Just, *Lutherbuch* (St. Louis: Concordia, 1902). Reprinted by permission of the University Libraries of the University of Nebraska-Lincoln.

their independence of the Pope and the Holy Roman Emperor Charles V, and supporting Luther was one way to do this. With the aid of Frederick, Luther began his translation of the Bible into German and to further refine his ideas of what being a true Christian meant. One of his statements was that monastic vows ought to be abolished, which of course would then allow for clerical marriage.

By the early 1520s, Martin Luther's writings, with his appeal to the Scripture as the sole authority and his belief in Salvation by faith alone, were infiltrating even the nunneries of Saxony. Luther argued that there was no special grace to be found in leaving the world to be a monk or a nun and that there was a priesthood of all believers. Nine of the sisters at Nimschen, including Katherine, wrote to Luther, asking his advice and sharing their concerns about how to live in a way that could be justified by their consciences. Luther sent back word that if they wanted to escape the nunnery, he would make the arrangements. This was a difficult promise for him to make since Nimschen was in the section of Saxony ruled not by Prince Frederick but by Duke George, who hated Luther and his ideas. In fact, the duke had recently had a man executed for attempting to help some nuns escape their convent.

Luther found a man he trusted, Leonard Kopp, who on some occasions had delivered smoked herring to the nunnery and would then return to Wittenberg with the empty barrels. By some accounts, the nuns were smuggled out of the nunnery in empty herring barrels, which would have been an extremely uncomfortable as well as frightening experience. Other accounts suggest they were covered up in the wagons with the barrels. The Tuesday after Easter in 1523 they arrived in Wittenberg, where Luther felt responsible for them. The relatives of most of the women refused to accept them back into their families. Luther was able to arrange marriages or find positions for most of the women. For two years Katherine was a companion in the home of the artist Lucas Cranach in Wittenberg. She then met a young man of some wealth who fell in love with her and proposed marriage. But the young man backed out of the arrangement when his parents objected. Luther suggested an older man, Dr. Kasper Glatz, the former rector of the University at Wittenberg, as a replacement, but Katherine was adamant that she did not wish to marry him.

Luther, frustrated by what to do, asked Katherine whom she did want to marry. Katherine sent word to Luther through Dr. von Amsdorf that she did not want to be unreasonable, and if he wanted to know who she would accept as a husband, she would be willing to marry him, Martin Luther. Possibly she wished to marry Luther, or possibly Katherine did not really wish to marry at all at this point and thought that Luther, already over forty and unmarried, had no interest in marriage, so he would be a safe suggestion.

But when Luther thought it over, he decided it would be a good idea. It would please his father who had never been totally reconciled to his son's choice of a profession and wanted grandchildren. It would annoy the Pope, something Luther always enjoyed. Since he said that monks and nuns were not a special category and that they should live as everyone else did including marrying if they wished, it would seal his testimony, show that he practiced what he preached. And, he was convinced, his marriage would make the devils weep in rage and the angels laugh for joy.

The 1525 marriage of Martin Luther and Katherine von Bora was not, then, a romantic match, but they did come to deeply love one another. Luther ruefully admitted that in everyday affairs he relied more on Katie, as he called her, than on Christ. Over the years Luther's references to his feelings about his wife became more and more intense.

Katherine took care of Luther so well his health improved dramatically once he married. She worked to overcome his depressions, and she accepted his eccentricities. She was greatly skilled in the use of herbs, in what constituted a healthy diet, and in massage. Many years later their son, himself a physician, praised his mother for her care of his father and stated that Katie Luther was almost a doctor.

By marrying Luther, Katherine also took on the responsibility for an enormous household. The Black Cloister where Luther had once lived as a monk was given to Luther by Frederick the Wise. It had forty bedrooms, and pretty soon they were all filled. The Luthers had six children of their own and also raised a number of nieces and nephews as well as four orphans they adopted. Students came from all over Europe to study with Luther, and refugees turned up unexpectedly and needed a place to stay. While the students were supposed to pay for their keep, too often they did not. Katherine insisted that their household become self-sustaining. She ran a farm with livestock, herded, and milked the cattle. She had a garden and an orchard. She made butter and cheese and also ran a brewery attached to the farm. Martin was generous to a fault, but Katherine managed to keep the establishment going. For weddings and celebrations she sometimes had over a hundred people to feed at her table.

Luther's love for his wife grew stronger and stronger. He once wrote he would not exchange Katie for both Venice and France. He felt blessed that he had a wife who was true to him and a good and loving mother to his children. Both Katherine and Martin adored their children. Their second child, a daughter Elizabeth, died at the age of a year. Martin was devastated and wrote to a friend that he had never expected that parents could care so deeply for their children. His letters are filled with how much he and Katie loved their children. To their great grief, another daughter, Magdalene, nicknamed Lenchen, died at the age of thirteen.

Katherine, as a former nun, was well educated. She knew Latin and could follow the talk about theology that swirled around Luther. She talked through issues and encouraged his writing. When other theologians attacked Luther, she was furious and encouraged him to respond. They often talked about theology, and Luther acknowledged that Katie knew the Psalms better than any papist. She would often ask for instruction and discussed theological issues with him. In one instance, Katherine was in total disagreement with her husband. Martin was speaking about the agony Abraham felt when God commanded him to kill his son Isaac. Katherine responded that she did not believe that God would make such a horrible demand. But, Luther replied to her: Katie, he did. Martin's recognition of Abraham's anguish and Katherine's refusal to believe in such a God are telling insights into their own love of their children.

Katherine was aware that she was considerably younger than Martin and was deeply worried over how she would support herself and the children, should anything happen to him. After his death in 1546, Katherine insisted on keeping the Black Cloister, rented rooms to students, and did the planting and harvesting herself. But the world she was in was in crisis. The Catholic Holy Roman Emperor Charles V finally unleashed his army against Protestant Wittenberg. Katherine gathered up her children and fled. When she returned, her lands had been burned, her livestock devoured, and her gardens destroyed. With great determination, she set herself to rebuild, but in 1550 she died after an illness that came from being thrown from her wagon. Luther had never thought of marriage until Katherine suggested it, but in his letters and writings after his marriage, he is a powerful advocate for the meaning that it brings to one's life. Katherine von Bora Luther's care and support of her husband did much to humanize the reformer Martin Luther. As a wife and mother, she was also a woman of courage and compassion.

BIBLIOGRAPHY

Bainton, Roland. *Women of the Reformation in Germany and Italy.* Boston: Beacon Press, 1971.
Holland, Linda. *Alabaster Doves.* Chicago: Moody Press, 1995.
Smith, Jeanette C. "Katherine von Bora through Five Centuries: A Historiography." *Sixteenth Century Journal* 30, 3 (1999): 745–74.

Carole Levin

MALINCHE
(Doña Marina)
(ca. 1504–ca. 1528)
Mexico
Interpreter for Cortés

An Indian woman who became an interpreter and indispensable guide for the Spanish explorer Hernando Cortés during his conquest of Mexico, Malinche—also known as La Malinche—is one of the most controversial figures of early modern history. She is revered by some as a woman of remarkable courage and leadership and criticized by others as a traitor to the native people, but it is generally accepted that Cortés would not have been successful in defeating the Aztec Empire without her help.

We know little about her early life—not even her given name is certain—but she was born in the region of Coatzacoalcos in central Mexico in the early 1500s. Her father was a powerful lord, or cacique, but he died when Malinche was young; her mother remarried and gave birth to a son. According to one historical account, Malinche's mother wanted to ensure her son's inheritance, so she secretly sold Malinche to slave merchants and pretended that her daughter had died, although another account claims that Marina was kidnapped by the slave merchants. She was resold several times to chiefs of various tribes, which is most likely how she acquired her linguistic skill.

In 1519, Malinche was owned by a group of tribal lords on the Tabascan coast who decided to give some young slave women to the invading Spaniards; the gift was most likely intended to pacify the leader, Hernando Cortés, and encourage him to continue his march against Moctezuma, the feared leader of the Aztecs. Malinche was one of a group of twenty young Indian women who were presented to Cortés and his followers to provide domestic and sexual services. Cortés distributed the women among his officers; he first gave Malinche to one of his lieutenants, Alonso Puertocarrero, but soon after Cortés decided to take her for himself when her facility with languages became apparent. The women were soon baptized, and Malinche was given the Christian name Doña Marina; since the local dialect did not include the letter "r," the Indians called her Malin, or Malin-tzin ("tzin" being a title of honor equivalent to Doña), which sounded like Malinche to the Spaniards.

Doña Marina was fluent in Nahuatl, the language of the northern Aztecs, but she also knew the Mayan dialect of the non-Aztec communities, which made her a very useful interpreter. Cortés had already been using Jerónimo de Aguilar as a translator; Aguilar was a Spanish priest who had been captured and enslaved by Indians. During his eight years of captivity he had become fluent in Mayan, but he eventually escaped and found his way into Cortés's service, where he provided crucial assistance to his master. Doña Marina was even more valuable to Cortés since she knew Nahuatl as well as Mayan. Thus, a curious but effective chain of communication was established: Cortés spoke in Spanish to Aguilar, who then spoke in Mayan to Marina, and she in turn spoke in Nahuatl to the Aztec tribes. Doña Marina and Aguilar were constant and loyal servants to Cortés; when Aguilar died a few years later, fortunately by then Doña Marina had learned Spanish.

Doña Marina's value as an interpreter went beyond her knowledge of various languages. Within a given dialect there were variations in speech patterns and gestures according to status, and she was adept at recognizing these subtleties of communication and at negotiating in the "lordly speech" of the tribal leaders. She was also recognized as a persuasive and charismatic speaker in her own right; she did not merely repeat Cortés's words to the local people, but she delivered them in a powerful and effective manner. Many of the Indian tribes were trying to decide at the time whether they should fight Cortés or join him in league against the Aztecs; persuasive tactics were critical and could include intimidation, flattery, encouragement, and bribery. Doña Marina's rhetorical powers and her understanding of the cultural differences between the Europeans and the Indians were valuable tools in advancing Cortés's cause; without his Indian allies, Cortés would not have succeeded.

In September 1519, Cortés and his entourage arrived at the city of Tenochtitlán, the beautiful center of the Aztec Empire, ostensibly as Moctezuma's guests. Their situation was dangerous—they were outnumbered by the Aztecs and isolated in the city. Over the next several months, Doña Marina was instrumental in the continuous negotiations between Cortés and Moctezuma; some historians argue that it was due to her persuasive powers that Cortés managed to lure Moctezuma into captivity. After months of standoff, violence finally erupted; Moctezuma was killed, and the Aztecs forced Cortés and his men out of the city on 30 June 1520, a date that came to be known as *La Noche Triste* (The Night of Sadness) because of the many soldiers whose lives were lost. Cortés narrowly escaped capture, and in spite of his diminished troops and supplies, he began another assault on the city in December, and in the summer of the following year, the Aztec capital fell. Throughout the siege, Doña Marina was Cortés's constant companion and confidante, so much so that the natives used her name to refer to Cortés, calling him "Il Malinche." Soldiers commented on her bravery and equanimity in the midst of perilous conditions.

She was also Cortés's mistress. They had a son, Martin, though by his wife Cortés also had a son by the same name as well as children by other women. Cortés did assume responsibility for all of his children, both illegitimate and legitimate. Doña Marina accompanied him on another trip to Honduras where, according to one historical account, she visited her mother and her brother and forgave them for their betrayal. It was during this expedition that Cortés decided that Doña Marina should marry one of his men, Juan Jaramillo. At the time of her marriage, Cortés gave her an estate and several other properties. We do not know exactly why Cortés arranged the marriage, nor do we know how Doña Marina felt about being transferred from Cortés to another man, but we do know that she and Jaramillo had a daughter and that she died shortly after giving birth.

Malinche, or Doña Marina, is one of the most prominent female figures of Mexican history and legend. She has been depicted as a character in popular drama, poetry, fiction, and art, but the accumulation of cultural and artistic representations of Doña Marina often obscures the real woman. Nonetheless, while she has been vilified by some for her complicity with the conquistadors and for her willingness to exchange her beliefs for those of Christianity, she has also been praised throughout the centuries for her gifts as a communicator and a leader and for her extraordinary bravery.

BIBLIOGRAPHY

Cypress, Sandra Messinger. *La Malinche in Mexican Literature: From History to Myth.* Austin: University of Texas Press, 1991.

Karttunen, Frances. "Rethinking Malinche." In Susan Schroeder, Stephanie Wood, and Robert Haskett, eds., *Indian Women of Early Mexico.* Norman: University of Oklahoma Press, 1997.

Jo Eldridge Carney

MARGARET OF ANJOU
(ca. 1430–1482)
France
Queen Consort

Margaret of Anjou was a powerful queen who, in fighting to protect the interests of her husband and son of the house of Lancaster, lost them both but gained a reputation for both bravery and ruthlessness. Margaret was born about 1430 during the Hundred Years War between England and France. Earlier in the century English war efforts had been highly successful. The king of France, Charles VI, had periodic bouts of insanity, and the government was chaotic. Henry V of England, of the royal house of Lancaster, was a strong military leader who resumed the war. His triumph at Agincourt in 1415 had led eventually to the French signing the Treaty of Troyes in 1420. By the treaty, Henry married Charles VI's daughter Katherine, ruled as regent, and would be king after Charles's death. Charles's son, Charles the Dauphin, was disinherited. But Henry, strong and vigorous as he seemed, died only two years later, a few months before Charles VI. Henry and Katherine's son, Henry VI, at nine months, became King of France and England. Henry V's brothers fought among themselves as they tried to rule England and France for the infant king, while the Dauphin held court in exile at Bourges. During the 1430s the English allied themselves with the Burgundians, rivals of the Dauphin Charles's party. Around the time of Margaret's birth, the young peasant girl Joan of Arc, hearing the voices of the saints, persuaded the Dauphin to give her an army that relieved the siege at Orleans and then led Charles to Rheims to be crowned Charles VII, thus turning the tide of the war.

Margaret was the fourth surviving child of René of Anjou and Isabelle of Lorraine. René was the great-grandson of the French king John the Good, and his sister Mary was the wife of Charles VII, so Margaret was both cousin to the king and his niece by marriage. When Margaret was five she was sent to live with her paternal grand-

Margaret of Anjou. From Agnes Strickland, *Lives of the Queens of England* (London: H. Colburn, 1840–1848). Reprinted by permission of the University Libraries of the University of Nebraska-Lincoln.

mother, Yolande, and stayed with her until she was thirteen, when her grandmother died. While with her grandmother, she was educated and provided with the example of a strong and powerful woman. Contemporaries describe Margaret as a beautiful young woman. There was talk of marrying her to the Count of Nevers, but Charles VII had a better idea.

Cardinal Beaufort, Bishop of Winchester and Henry VI's great-uncle, came to France to try to arrange a lasting peace. He met Margaret at Chinon in 1442, and she impressed him deeply with her beauty and strong character. When he returned to England he was full of praises about her to the young king. The young Henry VI was a decent and pious man but also weak-willed and easily dominated. He became enamored with the idea of marrying the beautiful Margaret. There was one problem: Her father had impoverished himself with fighting profitless wars and could not provide a dowry. Nor was Charles VII willing to do so.

Henry VI's uncle Humphrey, Duke of Gloucester, led the opposition to the marriage. He was not in favor of negotiating a peace with France. The King's Council told William de la Pole, Earl of Suffolk, to lead an embassy to France and negotiate the marriage.

Suffolk was not pleased. He did not think that Charles VII would concede enough in the negotiations to make the marriage worthwhile. But he reluctantly agreed to go. The English and French signed a truce, and Margaret's marriage to Henry was part of it. The problem of Margaret not having a dowry was solved: René promised the islands of Minorca and Majorca, which he claimed to have inherited but in fact had no control over them. While this mythical dowry was of no value to the English, the signing of a truce that could lead to lasting peace was. Suffolk, perhaps thinking to have the loyalty of the future Queen of England, agreed to the terms.

On 24 May 1444 the solemn betrothal of Margaret and Henry was celebrated. Four days later the truce of Tours was signed between England and France and their allies. It lasted for nearly two years. Margaret thus brought no dowry but was the living symbol of the hope of future peace. The following year, Margaret came to England; Henry VI was twenty-three and his new queen was sixteen.

Margaret worked hard to further peace between England and France, though fighting again broke out between the countries as France attempted to expel England from the areas they still held, finally ending the Hundred Years War in 1453 with England's holdings in France reduced to the port city of Calais. Margaret soon exerted great influence on her husband. Her one great disappointment was that for a number of years she failed to conceive a child. The presumptive heir, Henry's cousin, Richard, Duke of York, had an alternate claim to the throne traced back to Edward III in the previous century. When Margaret was finally pregnant in 1453, Henry suffered from the first of several periodic bouts of insanity. York ruled for the incapacitated king and was more and more eager to gain power. While Henry was still incapacitated, Margaret gave birth to their only child, her son Edward, in October 1453.

Margaret was ambitious and, after the birth of her son, all the more eager to protect her family interests. She had great political power but was generally unpopular, particularly because she was so closely allied with the faction at court that wanted peace and strongly supported the Earl of Suffolk, the man who had helped negotiate her marriage. Although rumors of their love affair are probably false, they reflect the attitudes of the English people toward her, as did the reports, also highly unlikely, that her son was a bastard. When Henry had his mental collapse during her pregnancy, she battled the Duke of York for supremacy; Henry's recovery in January 1455 ended York's Protectorate, but a few months later, the recurrence of Henry's illness led to York again being Protector. Margaret was outraged. When Henry again regained his sanity, he was anxious for peace and stability and wanted York to continue as his chief councillor, but Margaret insisted on his removal. A reconciliation in 1458 was short-lived; Margaret managed to get the Council to condemn the Yorkist faction the following year, leading to civil war between the house of York and the house of Lancaster, later known as the Wars of the Roses. Margaret was successful at labeling York as a rebel and de-stroying him, but this policy eventually led to the downfall of the house of Lancaster.

York, expelled from power, finally did claim that he had a better right to the English throne than Henry. He wanted to rule as regent until Henry's death and then be king. But this would have disinher-ited Margaret's son, and it was strong-willed Margaret, rather than Henry, who led the defense of the rights of the house of Lancaster to the Crown. York took up arms to support his claim, but Margaret's army defeated the Yorkists at the battle of Wakefield in 1460, where the duke himself was killed. Margaret's army looted Yorkist towns as they moved south after the battle. The leaders of the city of London were so appalled that they agreed not to allow the queen and her army into the city. London's support of York's son, Edward, allowed him to seize the throne in March 1461 as Edward IV, and with the help of his uncle, the Earl of Warwick, he secured his position by defeating Margaret's army at Towton. Margaret, Henry, and their son fled to Scotland.

In 1463, Henry VI was captured, and Margaret, with her son, made her way to France. She was never to see her husband again. Margaret did not stop trying to regain the throne for her husband and to protect her son's interests. Contemporaries asserted she did nothing in France but teach her son about making war and getting revenge on one's enemies. In a startling changeover, in 1470 she arranged for her son to marry Anne Neville, the daughter of one of her greatest enemies, the Earl of Warwick, after he quarreled with Edward.

Warwick returned to England with an army and was able to briefly restore Henry VI, who had been lodged in the Tower, to the throne. Henry by this time was again suffering mental illness. In February 1471 Henry had urged his wife and son to join him, but Margaret delayed in France. On March 24 she and Edward attempted to cross into England, but the winds made the channel crossing impossible. It was not until April 13 that she was able to set sail, landing the next day, Easter Sunday, at Weymouth. That same day Edward IV had a stunning victory at the battle of Barnet. Warwick was killed and Henry soon after died a prisoner in the Tower. Although the Yorkists claimed he died of "pure displeasure and melancholy," he was actually murdered on their order. Margaret, deeply distressed by the turn of events, still raised an army, which was defeated at Tewksbury on May 4. Margaret's son Edward was killed in the battle, and Margaret was taken prisoner. In 1475 she returned to France after an agreement between Edward IV and Louis XI, but she was forced to renounce her rights as Queen Consort of England, including her dower rights. She lived the last years of her life in extreme poverty and isolation and died in August 1482. Shakespeare characterized her as both powerful and cruel in his history plays. In her last appearance in *Richard III*, having lost everything she cared about, she prophesied similar losses to the women of the Yorkist cause.

BIBLIOGRAPHY

Bagley, J. J. *Margaret of Anjou, Queen of England.* London: H. Jenkins, 1948.

Erlanger, Philippe. *Margaret of Anjou, Queen of England.* Trans. Edward Hyams. London: Elek Books, 1970.

Haswell, Jock. *The Ardent Queen: Margaret of Anjou and the Lancastrian Heritage.* London: Peter Davies, 1976.

Lee, P. A. "Reflections of Power: Margaret of Anjou and the Dark Side of Queenship." *Renaissance Quarterly* 39, 2 (1986): 183–217.

Carole Levin

MARGARET OF AUSTRIA
(1480–1530)
Austria
Political Leader

Margaret was the granddaughter of the powerful and ambitious Duke of Burgundy in northeast France, also known as "Charles the Bold," who ruled from 1467 to 1477. His territories comprised not only French lands but much of the Low Countries as well, including the prosperous Flemish cities and the Northern Netherlands. Charles was married three times, but there was no male heir to the Burgundian lands, only one daughter from his second marriage. It was thus important that the duke seek a favorable marriage alliance for his daughter, Mary of Burgundy. The result was a union in 1477 (which Charles didn't live to see) between Mary and Archduke Maximilian of Austria, son of the Holy Roman Emperor Frederick III. However, when Charles the Bold was killed in 1477 while fighting against the Swiss near the town of Nancy, the duchy of Burgundy was claimed by the King of France, Louis XI. Mary of Burgundy found herself facing opposition from every side: the French king, disgruntled town councils, and Dutch nobles who had deeply resented her father's heavy-handed rule.

The revolt by local notables in the provinces of Flanders and Brabant, especially by leading townsmen in the city of Ghent, forced Mary to concede a special charter called the *Grand Privilege of 1477.* This document gave the States General, the legislative body of the territories of the French-speaking Burgundian Netherlands the right to assemble on their own initiative and curbed the power of the ruler to raise taxes or gather troops without the consent of the constituent provinces. Later that same year, Mary was obliged to grant a similar charter to the Dutch-speaking northern provinces of Holland and Zeeland.

Margaret of Austria was born in the midst of these political difficulties. When her mother Mary died at the age of twenty-four in 1482, her father Maximilian served as regent for her young brother

Philip I of Hapsburg. The following year Maximilian was elected to succeed his father as Holy Roman Emperor. Eight-year-old Philip was proclaimed ruler of the Hapsburg Netherlands by the legislative body of the territories, the States General. The great landed magnates of Flanders and Brabant supported the Hapsburgs in their efforts to consolidate power and in their conflict against the French, but urban resistance to Hapsburg control continued throughout the provinces until 1492. Margaret's earliest years were thus filled with political turmoil and upheaval in the land of her birth, as the process of Hapsburg centralization clashed with the interests of localism and urban autonomy. Her brother Philip was able to rescind the *Grand Privilege of 1477*, but resentment at the resurgence of imperial power continued, especially in the cities of Ghent, Bruges, Brussels, and Louvain.

Philip's regime continued until his death in 1506. In the meantime, his sister Margaret had married Don Juan of Spain, son of King Ferdinand of Aragon and Queen Isabella of Castile. But Don Juan and their infant son died within months of each other only one year after the marriage in 1498, and the following year, Margaret married Philibert, Duke of Savoy, in Italy. Three years of happiness ensued, but this second marriage would also end abruptly with the death of Margaret's husband in 1504, leaving her twice widowed by the age of twenty-four. She pledged never to marry again, instead dedicating herself to supervising the education and upbringing of her nephew and godchild Charles of Burgundy, the future Holy Roman Emperor and King of Spain, Charles V. The sudden death of the child's father, Philip, in 1506, together with the tragic mental instability of his mother, **Juana of Castile** (Juana the Mad), daughter of Ferdinand II and Isabella I, thrust the entire responsibility for the child's upbringing—along with that of Charles's five siblings—on his childless and widowed twenty-six-year-old godmother.

As a native-born Netherlander, Margaret's tenure as regent of the Netherlands from 1506 to 1515, and again from 1517 until her death in 1530, was a period of relative stability, although not without its challenges. The lands under her control were not a kingdom in the traditional sense but rather seventeen loosely federated provinces and a number of prosperous city–states. Some of these lands owed allegiance to France, others to the Holy Roman Empire. Different languages and dialects, distinct cultural traditions, varied levels of economic development—these variables tested the skill of the regent on every occasion. Margaret established her court not in the large cities of Flanders, but at Malines (now called Mechelen) in the northern Flemish part of Belgium, where she occupied a palace devoid of the excess and luxury characteristic of other royal residences of the period.

In politics, she pursued close relations with Tudor England, mindful of the fact that the commercial interests of the Flemish cities depended upon the English wool trade. One of her first successes in this area was the conclusion of a new trade agreement with England, one that promoted the interests of her subjects as equal partners with their foreign neighbors. Margaret was pressured by her father Maximilian to consider marrying the widowed English King Henry VII, but she was adamant in her refusal. In 1508, however, Margaret proposed a marriage between her nephew Charles and Princess Mary, daughter of England's Henry VIII, but in the end the negotiations, which continued for several years, were unsuccessful. The regent also attempted to maintain good relations with the Valois kings of France, a policy applauded by her Burgundian nobility. Her frequent role as intermediary between France, England, and the Holy Roman Empire was testimony to her place as a key political figure during the first quarter of the sixteenth century.

After 1517, Margaret's regency was reconfirmed by her nephew, the future Holy Roman Emperor Charles V. In that year, Charles left the Netherlands to claim his inheritance to the Spanish throne. Margaret was a strong advocate for her nephew's claims and, more important, Charles's efforts to succeed his grandfather Maximilian as emperor after the latter's death in 1519. Margaret was very influential in persuading the imperial electors—the German princes and bishops who chose the Holy Roman Emperor—to elevate her nephew to the office. Once this goal was secured, she turned her attention again to the Low Countries. Of particular concern at this juncture was the spread of Protestant principles in the wake of the reformer Martin Luther's break with the Roman Church. Margaret had already expressed concerns regarding abuses in the Church, and she was not convinced that the papacy was endowed with any special mystique. She remained an opponent of Luther, but she harbored deep reservations about the extensive use of force being employed by Catholic Inquisitors against Protestants in her lands. She recommended the appointment of a number of prelates whose attitudes toward Protestant heresy were deemed too soft by her nephew the emperor. Under her regency the full force of the Inquisition was blunted; after her death Charles would pursue a policy of stern persecution.

During the later years of her regency, she ruled in an authoritarian style that was very much disliked by the high nobility, but she retained the support of her nephew throughout, who by 1530 was at the high point of his power. Victorious in war over archrival France, King of Spain, master of a growing American empire, and at peace with the Church in Rome, the man who had been educated under Margaret of Austria's direction was unquestionably Europe's most powerful ruler. During the final year of her life, the regent longed for release from the duties of high office. Religious quarrels continued to divide her subjects. She hoped to spend her final years residing in a convent in the city of Bruges, but after a brief illness, Margaret died on 1 December 1530. With her death Emperor Charles V lost a lifelong adviser and unwavering supporter.

BIBLIOGRAPHY

Bonner, Shirley Harrold. "Margaret of Austria: Her Life and Learning in Europe's High Renaissance." Ph.D. dissertation, University of Pittsburgh, 1981.

de Iongh, Jane. *Margaret of Austria: Regent of the Netherlands.* New York: W. W. Norton, 1953.

Israel, Jonathan. *The Dutch Republic.* Oxford: Clarendon Press, 1995.

W. M. Spellman

MARGUERITE DE VALOIS
(1553–1615)
France
Queen and Writer of Memoirs

Praised by many for her beauty, intelligence, courage, and joie de vivre but vilified by others for her scandalous behavior, the colorful Marguerite de Valois was a member of the controversial Valois monarchy of sixteenth-century France. Although her father, three of her brothers, and her husband all reigned as kings of France, Marguerite never ruled as her country's queen, but she had a marked influence on the Valois dynasty. Marguerite recorded events from her tumultuous life in one of the first memoirs ever written by a woman; *Les Memoires de la Reine Marguerite* are admired for their literary as well as their historical value.

Known throughout her life as Margot, Marguerite de Valois was the third daughter of King Henry II of France and his dauntless queen, Catherine de' Medici. Marguerite was said to be a lovely, affectionate, and intelligent child, but like many royal children, she lived apart from her parents during her early childhood. When she was six years old, her father was accidentally killed in a jousting accident. Her brother, François II, succeeded the throne, but he died only four years later, leaving the kingship to the next brother in line, Charles IX. Nine years later, Charles died and yet a third brother became king, Henry III. During the reigns of her sons, the Queen Mother Catherine assumed a great deal of power. In spite of her aptitude for politics, Catherine was unsuccessful at promoting bonds of affection and loyalty among her children. Marguerite was never able to fully trust any of her brothers, although she remained closest to her youngest brother, the Duc d'Alençon.

As a royal princess, Marguerite was destined to be a pawn in the game of political marriages. When she was seventeen she was betrothed to Henry of Navarre, a Protestant Huguenot prince of Navarre, a small but strategically significant kingdom in southwest France on the Spanish border. The Queen Mother and King Charles claimed that the alliance would stabilize tensions between the religious and political factions in France, particularly the Catholics and the Huguenots. As a loyal Catholic, however, Marguerite resisted this marriage, nor was Navarre eager for the match. Their mutual reluctance was well founded, for the marriage began in disaster. Instead of being an occasion of reconciliation between Protestants and Catholics, the grand wedding celebration in August 1572 was an occasion of destruction when thousands of Protestants were slaughtered in Paris, a tragedy now referred to as the St. Bartholomew's Day Massacre.

A particularly grisly incident occurred on Marguerite's wedding night: While Navarre was conferring with his entourage, Marguerite lay sleeping alone. One of her husband's servants suddenly burst into the room, clutching at Marguerite and screaming for help. He flung himself onto Marguerite's bed, bleeding copiously from his injuries. Marguerite summoned the composure to attend to his injuries, but her gruesome, bloodstained chamber presaged the terror and chaos that was to follow in the next several days. Throughout the massacres, Marguerite was caught in a precarious position between her Catholic family and her Protestant husband, but she proved to be loyal to Navarre as well as compassionate and courageous, pleading for the lives of some of the Huguenots who were still present in the palace.

In the aftermath of the massacres, Navarre and Marguerite both became virtual prisoners at court. Navarre converted to Catholicism, but the conversion was only a public gesture of self-preservation. He finally managed to escape in 1576; King Henry III was furious and refused to allow Marguerite to join her husband. It was with this third brother that Marguerite had the most antagonistic relationship. Marguerite finally rejoined her husband in 1578, thrilled to escape the oppressive tyranny of both her brother and her mother.

Although Marguerite and Navarre were never in love, they were initially loyal to each other. Marguerite worked to establish a culturally and intellectually brilliant court at Navarre; the court was so well known that Shakespeare would later use it as a setting for an early comedy, *Love's Labour's Lost*. The atmosphere at court, however, was not entirely cerebral; contemporary chroniclers also referred to the prevailing atmosphere as one of sensuality and decadence. Indeed, Marguerite and Navarre's ability to live together harmoniousy was predicated on their acceptance of each other's adulterous relationships.

Both Marguerite and her husband enjoyed a series of affairs that they made no attempt to conduct secretly; Marguerite, however, received far more criticism for her liaisons than her husband. In time, however, their mutual tolerance broke down amidst arguments over religion, political alliances, and infidelity. Their personal relationship deteriorated, and they were increasingly subject to political pressures from external France; the fact that Marguerite had not been able to provide Henry with an heir did not further the stability of their marriage. In the winter of 1582 Marguerite finally left Navarre and returned to Paris, but her relationship with the King and the Queen Mother was still antagonistic. In 1584 she returned to Navarre, but as she was of less political use to her husband, he was not very enthusiastic about her presence. In June of 1584, Marguerite's youngest brother—the Duc d'Alençon and the last Valois heir—died, leaving Navarre next in line to the throne, since French law excluded women from the line of succession.

This occasion did not improve Marguerite's marriage, however, and eventually she found her situation in Navarre so intolerable that she left for Agen, a nearby Catholic city that she owned as one of her dowry properties. The people of Agen were at first optimistic about their new mistress until she attempted to help the Catholic cause by launching an expensive and unsuccessful attack on some of the neighboring Huguenot areas, leaving the town devastated and impoverished. In 1585 Marguerite was forced to seek refuge at another of her properties, the remote castle of Carlat in the Auvergne, where she would spend the next year. From Carlat, King Henry ordered Marguerite to remove to another obscure castle, the Château of Usson. She remained at Usson for the next eighteen years, sustained in these years of isolation by her religious faith, a passion for reading, and some brief love affairs. It was during this time that she also wrote her memoirs, although she only wrote about events until 1582. The wars between the Catholics and the Protestants continued throughout France, so her relatively quiet life at least provided a refuge from the ongoing strife.

In 1589, Catherine died, followed a few months later by the assassination of Henry III, the last Valois king. Marguerite's estranged husband, Henry of Navarre, became the next king of France, Henry IV, beginning the Bourbon dynasty. He again agreed to convert to Catholicism (the sardonic comment "Paris is worth a Mass" is attributed to him), but he asked Marguerite for a divorce so he could remarry and provide a legitimate heir to the throne. After prolonged negotiations, Marguerite agreed to dissolve the marriage on the condition that she would be well provided for financially. The papal dispensation was granted, and in 1600 Henry married Marie de' Medici.

After her many years at Usson, Marguerite decided she missed the life of court society, so in 1605 she returned Paris. She reestablished a relatively friendly relationship with Navarre: He appreciated her willingness to yield her place to his new queen, and she was grateful for his financial support, particularly since she was known for her extravagant spending and generosity to the poor. Marguerite and the new queen, Marie, eventually became good friends as well. In matters of etiquette, court entertainment, and social protocol, both the king and queen turned to Marguerite for advice. In 1610, Henry IV was assassinated, and Marie found Marguerite to be a valuable friend and adviser; Marguerite was also very kind to Marie's children, caring for them as if they were her own.

Marguerite, "*la reine Margot,*" died on 27 March 1615. She was criticized by many for her lax, immoral behavior, but she was also beloved and admired for her generous spirit, her glamour, her intelligence, and her courage. She was extremely ill used by both her family and her husband in the complicated political machinations of sixteenth-century France; Cardinal Richelieu, statesman during the reign of Louis XIII, wrote that Marguerite was a "toy of fortune." But she did not abandon herself to bitterness or despair, for she had great courage and a zest for life. She was a survivor, the last in the great dynasty of the Valois.

BIBLIOGRAPHY

Chamberlin, E. R. *Marguerite of Navarre.* New York: Dial Press, 1974.
Strage, Mark. *Women of Power: The Life and Times of Catherine de' Medici.* New York: Harcourt, Brace, Jovanovich, 1976.

Jo Eldridge Carney

MARY OF HUNGARY
(1505–1558)
Hungary
Queen and Regent

Given her illustrious family connections, it is not surprising that Mary would be thrust into the political world of Renaissance Europe, but she became more than just a queen by virtue of a political marriage; she became an important ruler in her own right.

As the daughter of **Juana, Queen of Castile**, and Philip of Burgundy, the only son of Maximilian I, the Holy Roman Emperor, Mary was born into the most powerful dynasty of the Renaissance. Her parents, better known by their nicknames, Juana the Mad and Philip the Handsome, had five other children who would also play important roles on the European political stage. As was customary for daughters of royalty, important political marriages were arranged for Mary and her three sisters. When she was only an infant, Mary was promised in marriage to the yet unborn heir to the throne of Hungary and Bohemia. The expected male heir arrived, though prematurely, so his physicians put him in an incubator of freshly killed pigs to keep him warm. The young prince, Lajos, or Louis, survived, and when Mary was ten years old and Louis of Hungary was nine, they were officially betrothed. This union between the Hapsburgs and the Hungarian and Bohemian Crown was further cemented with a marriage between Mary's brother Ferdinand and Louis's sister Anna. Politically advantageous marriages were also arranged for Mary's three sisters: Isabel was married to Christian II of Denmark; Eleanor was the queen of Francis I of France; and Catherine was the bride of John III of Portugal. Mary's two brothers were destined for even greater positions of power: Ferdinand as the Archduke of Austria and Charles as Europe's most powerful leader, the Holy Roman Emperor Charles V.

Mary was only a few months old when her father Philip died suddenly of an illness, and her mother, in precarious mental health, spent the rest of her life in Spain. Mary grew up in the Netherlands under the care of her aunt, **Margaret of Austria**, who became the regent of the Netherlands upon her brother Philip's death. When Mary was eight, Emperor Maximilian sent for her to live with him in Austria where she and her young sister-in-law, Anna, continued their education. During her years in Austria, Mary developed two of the passions in which she would indulge throughout her life: hunting and music.

Maximilian died in 1519, and Mary's brother, Charles, succeeded to the imperial throne. A few years later, Mary was considered of appropriate age to join her husband, and she began the arduous journey to Hungary. As she neared her new kingdom, she was informed that the country was being attacked by the Turkish ruler Süleyman and that she should wait at the border until her safety could be guaranteed. Mary, showing the resolve that would mark her future years as a ruler, refused to wait and demanded that she be allowed to join her new husband.

Mary found her new country to be suffering from extreme poverty and internal dissent as well as the ever-present threat of Turkish invasions. Mary was fond of her young husband, who returned her affection, but he was too young and inexperienced to be a competent ruler. Mary tried to assist Louis in establishing some stability in their kingdom, but Hungary had too long been prey to starvation, floods, pestilence, civil unrest, and attacks by the Ottoman Turks. The Hungarian nobles resented the presence of this determined Hapsburg queen, and Mary received little support from her brothers. To make matters worse, she and Louis spent much of their time pursuing their beloved pastime of hunting wild boar and emptying their already depleted coffers for court festivities, behavior that did not endear them to their subjects.

In 1526, after just four years of happy marriage, Louis was killed trying to defend his country against yet another invasion by the Turks. Mary was devastated by the loss of her husband, but in the ensuing chaos, she exerted what control she could until her brother Ferdinand arrived to claim the title of the next King of Hungary. Overcome by grief and suffering from poverty, Mary spent the next couple of years traveling around the country, moving from one castle to another and hunting strenuously for days at a time.

When Ferdinand decided that he could not reside permanently in Hungary, he offered Mary the position of regent, but, still grieving over Louis's death, she refused her brother's request, although she assisted him in his attempts to unify the warring nobles. She also rejected another offer from Ferdinand when he proposed that she marry King James V of Scotland for political gain, vowing never to remarry. Mary was devoted to her brothers and the interests of the Hapsburg empire, but regarding decisions about her specific role, she could also be strong-willed.

The next proposal for Mary's future came from her brother Charles, and this time she did not refuse. When their aunt Margaret, regent of the Netherlands, died in 1530, Charles proposed that Mary should be her successor. Charles displayed complete confidence in his sister's abilities as ruler, but he objected to her religious views; at the Hungarian court, Mary and Louis had become sympathetic to the ideas of religious reformer Martin Luther. When Louis died, Luther had sent Mary a letter of consolation and dedicated to her four sermons on the Psalms. The more moderate humanist Erasmus had also dedicated a work to her, *Concerning the Christian Widow*. The staunchly Catholic Charles made it clear that Mary's Lutheran tendencies would not be acceptable in the Netherlands and that any Lutherans among Mary's entourage or council should be dismissed. Although she did not entirely disguise her interest in reformist ideas, Mary agreed to accept the regency of the Netherlands, and in 1531, she returned to her native country, which she had left seventeen years earlier.

For the next twenty-five years, Mary worked tirelessly to promote the Hapsburg interests in the Netherlands. Lacking the personal warmth and charm of her predecessor, Mary was at first greeted with suspicion and mockery, but she soon proved herself worthy of her position. Her regency was marked by her aim to unify the various provinces of the Low Countries under one centralized government. She was also faced with the task of suppressing the extreme religious reform movements in accordance with Charles's wishes. Mary has been criticized for compromising her own religious beliefs in promoting her brother's ideological purposes, but scholars have pointed out that Mary was never as zealous in her persecution of the heretics as Charles had hoped and that she often acted decisively to protect them. Mary's greatest charge as regent was to support Charles's military efforts to expand and secure his empire, a task that she always fulfilled, though at great cost to herself and her people. During a war between France and the Netherlands, Mary donned armor and went to the front herself, but her council would not allow her to enter the battle. The English ambassador noted with admiration the queen's fighting spirit. Mary was also admired as an enthusiastic patron of musicians and artists.

Although Mary was not loved by the Dutch, she was respected, especially when it became evident how much Charles depended on his sister, not only as regent but as a councillor. During a famous quarrel between Charles and Ferdinand about the Hapsburg succession, Mary acted as mediator between the two brothers. In 1556 Charles proclaimed his abdication; Mary announced her resignation as well, in spite of Charles's and his son Philip of Spain's desire that she continue her regency. In 1556, Charles, Mary, and their sister Eleanor, the widowed Queen of France, retired to Spain for a life of peaceful seclusion, but their retirement was short-lived: All three of them died in 1558. In 1574, Philip of Spain gathered the remains of members of the Hapsburg family for burial in his grand monastery, the Escorial. Mary of Hungary is buried next to her brother Charles V; her sister, Eleanor of France; her mother, Juana the Mad; and several other princes of the greatest political dynasty in sixteenth-century Europe.

BIBLIOGRAPHY

de Iongh, Jane. *Mary of Hungary: Second Regent of the Netherlands.* Trans. M. D. Herter. Norton. London: Faber and Faber, 1958.

Spruyt, B. J. " 'En bruit d'estre bonne luterienne': Mary of Hungary (1505–58) and Religious Reform." *English Historical Review* (April 1994): 275–307.

Thompson, Glenda. "Mary of Hungary and Music Patronage." *Sixteenth Century Journal* 15 (1984): 401–418.

Jo Eldridge Carney

MECHTHILD OF MAGDEBURG
(ca. 1207/1212–ca. 1282/1297)
Germany
Christian Mystic and Writer

In thirteenth-century Europe, a number of Christian women had mystical experiences and left written accounts of these moments, either in their own words or as dictated to others. Historians generally agree that at this time in Christian history women were more likely than men to have ecstatic or visionary experiences and to acquire reputations as mystics. Scholars suggest that such experience allowed women personal contact with divinity at a time when they were increasingly excluded from direct participation in the liturgy and sacraments. One of these women was Mechthild of Magdeburg, whose book *The Flowing Light of the Godhead* records more than fifteen years of her visionary experience. Mechthild wrote on loose sheets of paper, using the dialect of Low German that she spoke rather than Latin. She is the first German mystic, male or female, to write in her native vernacular, a choice that probably made her work more accessible to a secular audience. (When Mechthild claimed ignorance of Latin in *The Flowing Light*, many scholars believe she meant theology, as her work indicates familiarity with the Latin liturgy and Psalms.)

Heinrich of Halle, a Dominican friend of Mechthild, organized her writings into six books or chapters; he is most likely the confessor mentioned in *The Flowing Light* who in 1250 urged her to record her mystical experiences. Readers can find recurring themes, concerns, and images in *The Flowing Light*, but given Heinrich's role, it is not possible to trace their development. Although the original manuscript has been lost, Latin translations made soon after Mechthild's death have survived. Sometime after Heinrich's death, a seventh book was added; it contains some early material as well as writings during Mechthild's later years at a Cistercian convent at Helfta. In the fourteenth century, *The Flowing Light* was translated into a form of High German and circulated widely throughout southern Germany. Although some scholars once speculated that the Matelda mentioned by Dante in his *Purgatorio* is Mechthild, this view is no longer accepted. Mechthild wrote her book—she referred to it this way at several points—in prose and verse; it is a remarkable mixture of visions and revelations, sometimes in allegorical or dialogue form, advice, reflections, criticism, and prayers.

Most of our information about Mechthild's life derives from *The Flowing Light*. She was probably born near Magdeburg in Lower Saxony, sometime between 1207 and 1212. References in her book to the courtly love genre (in German, *Minnesing*), court etiquette, and the rich clothing of close friends and relations suggest that her family, if not noble, was well born and presumably wealthy. She mentioned one brother named Baldwin, who entered the Dominican order and eventually became an assistant prior at Halle. When she was twelve, Mechthild was "greeted" by the Holy Spirit for the first time; from that moment forward, she stated, she could never commit any "great daily sin" and desired to lead a spiritual life. Mechthild described herself at this point as having only a simple notion of a spiritual life, with little knowledge of God beyond basic Christian beliefs, and as ignorant of evil and the hypocrisy of some outwardly pious people. She continued to have daily greetings or visions for the next thirty-one years.

At the age of twenty-three, Mechthild left her family for Magdeburg, relinquishing material comfort and social privilege in order to devote herself to God without distraction. There she joined a community of Beguines (a beguinage) where she stayed for forty years. Beguines were women who lived together and pursued a devout, celibate life but who did not live in cloisters or take religious vows. Established mainly in urban areas, Beguines lived austerely, supporting themselves through their labor, and dedicated themselves to serving the poor and needy; in this respect, their beliefs were compatible with Dominican and Franciscan friars who also embraced poverty and service to others. (Magdeburg's Beguine community seems to have had a close relationship with the Dominicans, a situation that created friction with the local clergy.) Thus, like nuns, Beguines rejected marriage and secular pursuits for a life dedicated to God, yet unlike nuns, they did not reside in convents and had a more ambiguous place in the hierarchical organization of the Church. Beguines were periodically accused of heresy by various church authorities who suspected these self-sufficient, relatively autonomous communities of women of being doctrinal nonconformists as well. In fact, one reason scholars are certain that portions of *The Flowing Light* circulated during Mechthild's time in Magdeburg are its repeated references to hostile enemies, including a threat to burn her writings. Persistent harassment and accusations of heresy against Mechthild may explain why she eventually left Magdeburg for the Cistercian convent at Helfta around 1270. A preface to *The Flowing Light* describes Mechthild as "suffering oppression and scorn" for over forty years.

As a Beguine, Mechthild had daily visions and mystical experiences for two decades. She also practiced an extremely rigorous program of physical self-denial that left her always sick, weak, and tired. Her self-inflicted bodily pain was not a sign of self-hatred, however, but a means to identify more closely with Christ's suffering and to achieve a purer union with God. Like many in the medieval period, Mechthild viewed her body as an obstacle to achieving oneness with God. After a particularly lengthy illness, Mechthild revealed her mystical experiences to her confessor, who then instructed her to "go joyfully forward" and record them without fear. As mentioned above, most scholars believe her confessor was a Dominican friar named Heinrich, from nearby Halle. Several passages of *The Flowing Light* speak favorably of his order. Scholars have suggested that Heinrich and/or her brother Baldwin, who was also a Dominican, either arranged for or encouraged Mechthild's move to more secure surroundings at Helfta.

In 1250, at about the age of forty-three, Mechthild began to write down her spiritual experiences. Her writings from this period, her roughly fifteen-year stay at Magdeburg, comprise the first six books of *The Flowing Light*. One of the most striking features of her work is the passionate, erotic language with which she describes the soul's desired union with God. Religious writings of the time, by both men and women, used sexual imagery to convey the intimate, ecstatic fusion of human and divine. Mechthild's language expresses an especially ardent, earnest desire for and experience of communion with God. In a famous allegorical passage, Christ is a "beautiful youth" who leads his courtly mistress (Mechthild's soul) in a dance that ends with her seduction and "two-fold intercourse" that is "Love eternal." Elsewhere God and Mechthild's soul are lovers "who could not be closer" and who "are fused in one." The reciprocal nature of this love, as Frances Beer points out, differentiates Mechthild's spiritual use of courtly love conventions from secular writings, where the parties typically feel love in unequal degrees. Other instances of Mechthild's beautiful and intense erotic language appear throughout *The Flowing Light*. These visions are part of a trend in the twelfth and thirteenth centuries that emphasized Christ's humanity, the individual's likeness to Christ, and a more approachable God. Historians suggest that mystical union with God helped to satisfy the desire some women felt for direct contact with God, at a time when women were increasingly barred from exercising clerical authority, especially performing the sacraments.

Mechthild's writings frequently portrayed God as Love, and she positioned herself most often as his unworthy but passionate lover. She presented herself with great humility, as a sinner who did not deserve the visions she received, and she insisted that she never asked for them. This claim not only demonstrated her piety and obedience to God but also may have been intended to counter accusations that her visions were not genuine. Mechthild's feelings of unworthiness were informed by medieval beliefs both about humankind's natural imperfection and about women's inferiority to men, and her writings display ambivalence about women's nature. At times she described herself as a "poor despised little woman," an "unworthy bride," and "unworthy soil" to receive divine communication. Yet she was also acutely aware that she was more vulnerable to persecution for her visions and writings than a man would have been. At one point, she prayed to God after being told that her book should be burned, and God reassured her that no human can burn truth. She then lamented that if she were a "learned priest," God would instead have garnered praise for his revelations. God explained that he deliberately chose Mechthild to receive his "special grace" rather than learned men *because* of her humility. Moreover, God continued, the Church is strengthened when "unlearned lips" teach his words to "learned tongues." Other sections show Mechthild's firm belief that she had both the authority and the duty to communicate her experiences. In her words, she "must glorify God" both in speaking and in writing her book, and her preface states that she "send[s] it forth as a messenger" to all "spiritual people."

Some portions of *The Flowing Light* deliver harsh criticism of religious individuals whose conduct did not demonstrate genuine piety. Speaking for God, she advised the Canon of Magdeburg to live a less lavish and comfortable life, and she called the local clergy "goats" because "they reek of impurity regarding Eternal Truth." She condemned a priesthood corrupted by unchastity, gluttony, pride, and

hypocrisy that acted contrary to God and his true servants and promised divine punishment. Beguines who took communion out of
"blind habit" rather than awe and awareness were also rebuked. "My
Pharisee" was Mechthild's name for the person (perhaps a cleric) who
objected to her vision of John the Baptist performing communion
because he was a layman. Mechthild defended her vision by reminding her accuser of the enormous divide between divine truth and
man's ability to express it in human language and warning not to
interpret her words literally. She argued further that as a man who
actually touched Christ, heard God's voice, and preached his truth,
John the Baptist was no layman and that no earthly pope, bishop, or
priest could imitate him except in spirit. Who then, she concluded
ironically, was really the one in need of religious instruction?

The Flowing Light contains recurring references to adversaries hostile to Mechthild and her writings, and she often equated her suffering and persecution with Christ's experience at the hands of
unbelievers. Near the end of the sixth book, she compared herself to
a "post or target" at whom people had thrown stones or shot and
"long assailed" her character with their "evil cunning." Tired and
approximately sixty years old, Mechthild moved to the Cistercian convent at Helfta sometime around 1270. There she was welcomed and
honored as an important spiritual person. Beginning in the mid-
thirteenth century, the Helfta convent was famous for the learning
and piety of its nuns, thanks to the leadership of its abbess Gertrude
of Hackeborn. It also gained a reputation as a spiritual center, for
two other mystics: Gertrude the Great and Mechthild of Hackeborn
also lived there during Mechthild of Magdeburg's stay. The two
younger women later became influential, central figures in the development of German mysticism. Mechthild was the first of the three
female mystics directly to experience a vision of the sacred heart, a
vision whose symbolic importance Gertrude and Mechthild of Hackeborn elaborated in later years. Shortly after Mechthild's arrival, she
became seriously ill and lost her sight. Although deeply grateful for
the care and respect she was given, Mechthild worried about her
uselessness until God told her to teach and enlighten those around
her. Perhaps in response, the seventh book of *The Flowing Light*,
dictated to a nun at Helfta, contains fewer visions and more general
prayers and advice. Mechthild died at Helfta in 1282 or 1297.

BIBLIOGRAPHY

Beer, Frances. *Women and Mystical Experience in the Middle Ages.* Suffolk, UK: Boydell Press, 1992.

Bynum, Carolyn Walker. *Jesus as Mother: Studies in the Spirituality of the High Middle Ages.* Berkeley: University of California Press, 1982.

Menzies, Lucy, ed. *The Revelations of Mechthild of Magdeburg or The Flowing Light of the Godhead.* London: Longmans, 1953.

Wilson, Katharina. *Medieval Women Writers.* Athens: University of Georgia Press, 1984.

Gwynne Kennedy

MELISENDE, QUEEN OF JERUSALEM
(ca. 1102–1161)
Middle East
Queen Regent and Patron of the Arts and the Church

Melisende, the eldest daughter of King Baldwin II (ruled 1118–1131) and his wife Queen Morphia, governed the Latin Kingdom of Jerusalem, a kingdom established during the First Crusade (ca. 1099), for a period of approximately thirty years. A capable administrator, as well as an influential patron of the arts and of the Church, Melisende, Queen of Jerusalem, received acclaim from contemporary figures, such as William of Tyre (ca. 1130–1186), the historian of the Latin East.

Queen Morphia, in bearing four daughters—Melisende, Alice, Hodierna, and Joveta—to her husband instead of the desired male heir, might have been regarded as having failed to secure the succession to the throne. Lacking a male heir, King Baldwin II arranged a suitable marriage for his eldest daughter and acknowledged heir, Melisende, in 1129 with Fulk V, Count of Anjou. When Melisende gave birth to the future king, Baldwin III (ca. 1130–1163), the question of the future succession was secured.

Baldwin II's public recognition of both Melisende and Fulk as his kingdom's joint heirs, named along with their son Baldwin III, suggests his confidence in his eldest daughter's capacity to rule. Shortly after her father died in 1131, King Fulk and Queen Melisende were jointly crowned in the Church of the Holy Sepulchre. Once crowned, King Fulk appears to have tried to exclude Melisende from wielding any real power. A period of five years elapsed without Fulk's associating Melisende's name with his in any public act. By eliminating Melisende from her share in governing the kingdom, Fulk kept her from being able to exercise the patronage necessary to maintain and to increase her own group of loyal supporters.

As Baldwin II's legal heir, Queen Melisende already had a loyal following of supporters, and these individuals soon clashed with those who favored King Fulk. A natural leader on behalf of the queen and her party would have been Melisende's second cousin, Hugh II of Le Puiset, Count of Jaffa. The details surrounding Hugh's revolt (ca. 1132) against King Fulk remain obscure. Some historians have suggested the existence of a romantic liaison between Hugh and Queen Melisende; however, others find no evidence to validate this theory. Whichever account one accepts, upon the failure of Hugh's uprising against the king, Melisende, backed by her supporters, succeeded in negotiating lenient terms for the rebel, with Fulk agreeing to send Hugh into temporary exile. Hugh's subsequent murder (d. ca. 1132) so incensed Queen Melisende that her ire extended both to Hugh's enemies and to her husband, all of whom feared for their lives. King Fulk recognized that if he were to rule with any success, he would have to assuage Melisende's anger by publicly recognizing her as his coregent and by permitting her to participate in governing her birthright, the Latin Kingdom of Jerusalem. In spite of King Fulk's attempt to reign supreme, he failed to gather enough followers to supplant Queen Melisende.

Fulk and Melisende appear to have reconciled their differences after the birth of their second son, Amalric (ca. 1136–1174; ruled 1163–1174). Their reconciliation finally allowed Queen Melisende to demonstrate her skill as a ruler during the remaining years of King Fulk's reign. For a woman living in the twelfth century, Melisende held unparalleled power.

A hunting accident in 1143 that prematurely killed Fulk left Queen Melisende with an underage son and a kingdom exposed to many potential enemies. Queen Melisende took the only course of action open to her. Since the kingdom's barons could not conceive of a woman governing alone, Melisende had herself and her young son, Baldwin III, jointly crowned on Christmas Day in 1143. Officially, Queen Melisende was newly installed as regent for and coruler with Baldwin III, the kingdom's heir; however, Queen Melisende soon began exercising direct authority as a queen regnant, reigning under her own name and authority. To protect her kingdom, Melisende appointed as her military commander and adviser Manasses of Hierges, the son of Baldwin II's sister, Hodierna of Rethel. The kingdom's leading men evidently viewed Queen Melisende's abilities to govern her birthright with approval since no one challenged her authority.

During Melisende's regency, an event of unparalleled splendor occurred when Queen Melisende and her son King Baldwin III received and lavishly entertained the leaders of the Second Crusade (ca. 1148). Among those in attendance were King Conrad III of Germany (1093–1152; ruled 1138–1152) and the leader of the Crusade, Louis VII of France (1120–1180; ruled 1137–1180), with his wife Eleanor of Aquitaine.

Queen Melisende fully understood the value of rewarding her throne's supporters with appointments and land, and she secured the goodwill of the ecclesiastical authorities by establishing herself as a prominent patron of the Church. One of her most significant charitable contributions, which she founded on behalf of her sister Joveta, is the Convent of St. Lazarus in Bethany, located at the site of Lazarus's tomb.

At the height of her power (ca. 1140–1150), Queen Melisende's support of the arts helped stimulate a period of prosperity for Crusader art. Her husband, Fulk, is credited with having commissioned an extraordinary work known as the *Psalter of Melisende*, which is currently housed in the British Museum. The *Psalter of Melisende* is an ancient manuscript text in book form. Its illuminations are particularly noteworthy for the manner in which they blend artistic styles from the East and the West. In addition, the *Psalter*'s exquisite cover is a wonderful example of Romanesque ivory carving.

With the support of many loyal friends, including the ecclesiastical authorities, Queen Melisende governed capably for many years. Even though Queen Melisende had built up a powerful group of supporters intent on securing her power and on supporting her throne, her contemporaries still viewed her subsequent refusal to relinquish rule to her son Baldwin III—the throne's legal heir—when he came of age (ca. 1145) with great surprise.

A breach between mother and son occurred around 1150, and a period of disorder ensued. Baldwin, who pleaded his case before an assembly of the kingdom's lords and churchmen, formally accused his mother of not permitting him to rule. Queen Melisende, however, still possessed enormous power. A compromise proposed by the churchmen divided the kingdom, with Queen Melisende retaining sway over Jerusalem and Nablus, while Baldwin III was given authority over the lands in the north. Queen Melisende also retained sovereignty over the County of Jaffa, which she held in the name of her younger son, Amalric, the kingdom's next heir-apparent after Baldwin III. The solution of dividing the kingdom proved ineffective almost immediately. Baldwin III invaded his mother's territory, laid siege to her tower fortress in Jerusalem, and ultimately gained his victory; however, he did not succeed in wresting power from his mother until 1152.

In spite of Baldwin's eventual military triumph over his mother in 1152, Queen Melisende, supported by her powerful allies, managed to retain considerable power. She ruled, for example, over Nablus and its neighborhood, which she had been allowed to retain as her dower. Baldwin eventually recognized his own need of the support of his mother's influential relatives and allies, because he once more began associating her name with his in public acts from 1154 on. Queen Melisende once more helped her son rule Jerusalem. When military affairs required his absence, she presided over councils, and she even initiated an important military action. Queen Melisende also remained an important patron of the Church throughout her life.

Queen Melisende ruled as her male ancestors had, with princely excellence and magnificence. A remarkable woman, Melisende enjoyed an unprecedented position of authority in a kingdom where no woman had previously held public office. As Queen of the Latin Kingdom of Jerusalem, Melisende exercised her authority for a period of approximately thirty years, as coruler, as queen regent, and, for a period of approximately seven years, as queen regnant. An incapacitating stroke in 1161 so disabled Queen Melisende that she could no longer exercise her authority. Upon her death a few months later, the twelfth century witnessed the passing of a striking personality.

BIBLIOGRAPHY

Folda, Jaroslav. "Images of Queen Melisende in Manuscripts of William of Tyre's *History of Outremer: 1250–1300.*" *Gesta* 32.2 (1993): 97–112.

Folda, Jaroslav. "A Twelfth-Century Prayer Book for the Queen of Jerusalem." In *Medieval Perspectives.* Proceedings of the Eighteenth Annual Conference of the Southeastern Medieval Association, 1992, Williamsburg, VA. Richmond, KY: Southeastern Medieval Association, 1993. 1–14.

Hamilton, Bernard. "Women in the Crusader States: The Queens of Jerusalem (1100–1190)." In Derek Baker, ed., *Medieval Women.* Oxford: Blackwell, 1978. 143–174.

Riley-Smith, Jonathan, ed. *The Oxford Illustrated History of the Crusades.* Oxford: Oxford University Press, 1995.

Runciman, Steven. *A History of the Crusades: The Kingdom of Jerusalem and the Frankish East, 1100–1187.* Vol. 2. Cambridge: Cambridge University Press, 1951.

Debra Barrett-Graves

ELEANOR DE MONTFORT
(1215–1275)
Britain
Royal Rebel

Born the youngest daughter of King John of England in 1215, Eleanor was sister to the future King Henry III, whose long and troublesome reign (1216–1272) spanned the greater part of the thirteenth century. The turbulent relationship between King Henry and his sister Eleanor would provide the backdrop to some of the most important political developments in England at the midpoint of the century.

When Henry III succeeded to the throne upon the death of his father in 1216, England was in the midst of a baronial revolt against the crown. Henry was but nine years old when he acceded. A regency was established, the Magna Carta, a charter guaranteeing justice issued in 1215, was reissued, and a measure of political unity was restored under the able leadership of dedicated servants of the Crown. In 1224, one of the king's chief vassals, William Marshal II, second Earl of Pembroke, negotiated a marriage contract with the monarch's counselors for the hand of the nine-year-old Eleanor. The king, who was still three years away from declaring himself of age to govern without his regency council, settled a dowry of ten manors and an income of £200 a year on his sister, but when her husband died suddenly in 1231, the sixteen-year-old widow was denied any portion of her husband's considerable estates in England, Wales, and Ireland. In particular, the Irish lands had been dowered to Eleanor, but William's older brother Richard claimed the inheritance and sold the widow's property in order to pay off her husband's debts. This action was in violation of the law that entitled widows to one third of their husband's estate. Although King Henry, as his sister's guardian, attempted to force compliance with the requirements of the law, Eleanor was never satisfied with the outcome, and her claims against her late husband's land became a lifelong enterprise. The episode revealed something of the young Eleanor's strong, and perhaps avaricious, personality, for throughout her adult life, she would remain keen to advantage both herself and her offspring in the area of land aggrandizement.

Soon after the death of her husband, Eleanor was convinced by her governess, Cecily de Sandford (who was also recently widowed), to take a vow of lifelong chastity. There had been no children from the marriage with William Marshal, and Eleanor agreed to take this vow in the presence of the Archbishop of Canterbury, Edmund Rich. By 1236, however, the young woman met twenty-eight-year-old Simon de Montfort, Earl of Leicester. The two were privately married in the king's chapel at Westminster. Eleanor's repudiation of her previous vow of chastity alienated some clergy who felt that the Archbishop of Canterbury had been deceived, whereas Simon was viewed by many of the English barons as a meddling foreigner (Simon was born and raised in France) who had ingratiated himself with the court. Complaints of royal favoritism toward outsiders had long been voiced by the king's closest English advisers, including Eleanor's brother Richard, Earl of Cornwall. For these powerful men, the marriage of Eleanor to Simon de Montfort had been undertaken in direct violation of a previous royal promise to do nothing of consequence without the counsel of the barons. But in the end the new Countess of Leicester and her husband could rely on the support of her brother the king, who soothed the anger of the barons by keeping Simon off the king's council.

In an effort to counter those English churchmen who questioned the validity of the marriage in light of Eleanor's previous vow of chastity, Simon traveled to the Holy See in Rome. After considerable payments to papal authorities, Pope Gregory IX granted a dispensation for the marriage, in effect overriding the validity of the previous vow. In January 1239 the king ordered Eleanor's dowry to be paid to Earl Simon, signaling the start of a series of royal favors bestowed on the powerful couple. When Henry III's first son, the future Edward I, was born in June of that same year, Montfort was made one of the nine godfathers to the infant prince.

Unfortunately for both Eleanor and her husband, royal favor was a voluble commodity, for in August 1239 the king turned on Simon and accused the earl of having seduced Eleanor before the marriage. He also upbraided the earl for having named the king as his security in promising money to the papal court at Rome. Fearful that the king's anger might compromise their safety, the couple sailed for

France, temporarily leaving an infant son behind at Kenilworth castle. Between 1239 and 1244 the couple lived at the Montfort family castle. During this exile, two more sons were born, and Simon attempted to repair his relationship with the king by joining Richard, Earl of Cornwall, on crusade. By 1244 the king, whose resolve was never firm irrespective of the issue, allowed his sister and her husband to return to England. During the years that followed, Simon attempted to position himself as a mediating force between an increasingly restive baronage and a monarch who repeatedly offended his most powerful magnates with requests for additional revenue in the form of tax levies. Eleanor continued to be the recipient of royal largess, as lands and estates and outright monetary grants were made to the couple by the Crown. Eleanor enjoyed a household staff of over sixty servants at mid-century and lived a life of ease and ostentation.

The turning point in Eleanor's relationship with her brother Henry occurred when in 1254 the king entered into an agreement with the Pope whereby Henry's second son, Edmund, was offered the crown of the Norman kingdom of Sicily in return for an English expedition against the current Norman ruler whom the Pope wished to oust. The expedition was a fiasco, and the exorbitant cost of the whole affair led to fiscal crisis. Turning once again to his barons for assistance, the king was forced to surrender much of his prerogative powers. Simon de Montfort was one of the barons who in 1258 reached an agreement with Henry III known as the Provisions of Oxford. Under this humiliating document the king agreed to meet with a great council of the realm three times each year. Moreover, a small advisory council of fifteen barons was imposed on Henry, and this body came to dominate every aspect of royal administration, from exchequer to justice to chancellor's duties.

Under the Provisions of Oxford, the king was reduced to political equality with his greater magnates, including Simon de Montfort, who now for the first time took up a leadership role in the struggle against the king. But when, over the course of the following four years, the barons fell to quarreling among themselves over executive matters, Henry abolished the provisions and returned to his practice of government under the advice of royal favorites. Failing to prevent this reversion to old habits, the barons took up arms against the king in 1264. The military opposition to the Crown was led by Simon, whereas King Henry's cause was taken up by his eldest son Lord

Edward. After defeating Edward in May 1264 at the battle of Lewes, near the Channel coast, Simon de Montfort became the de facto ruler of England, governing in the king's name for the next fifteen months.

Simon held Lord Edward captive during this period in order to assure the king's cooperation with his government. The Montforts celebrated Christmas 1264 at their castle at Kenilworth, hosting doubtful allies and their royal captives alike. Eleanor's husband attempted to rule according to the Provisions of Oxford, sharing authority with the Earl of Gloucester and the Bishop of Chichester, but the permanent executive council of fifteen barons could not agree on a common set of policies. Gradually support for de Montfort evaporated, and when Lord Edward escaped from imprisonment and began to raise an army in 1265, Simon's allies began to defect. In June 1265 Eleanor moved to the great castle at Dover, entertaining local dignitaries and hoping to rally the support of the Channel coast towns in her husband's cause. At the battle of Evesham in August 1265, however, Edward's forces routed the rebel army, and Simon de Montfort was killed. Eleanor's son Henry was killed alongside his father. Her sons Richard and Simon wished to continue fighting, but it was now clear that the baronial cause was lost.

Eleanor was in possession of a large sum of money entrusted to her at Dover by the rebel barons, but in October 1265, the fortress was attacked by Prince Edward, and Eleanor was obliged to surrender. Eleanor and her children were sentenced to banishment and confiscation of their considerable estates. She left England in October and settled at the Dominican convent of Montargis, just south of Paris. During her remaining years, she continued her legal battles for rights to lands in France, and the French King Louis IX attempted, unsuccessfully, to intervene on her behalf with the aged Henry III. Lord Edward succeeded to his father's throne in 1272, rejecting the restrictions placed upon royal prerogative mandated by the Provisions of Oxford but, unlike his father, eager to work in concert with his leading magnates.

In addition, the new king undertook a reconciliation with his aunt. Eleanor was at last allowed to plead her case for rights to lands in England. Edward restored her English dower lands and even ordered the Marshal family to compensate his aunt for claims against them made decades earlier. When she died in 1275 at the age of sixty, Eleanor was still living in exile, and her hopes for Montfort power within the ranks of the English aristocracy were shattered. Having supported her husband's ambitions even to the point of opposition to her brother the king, Eleanor de Montfort suffered something of the fate of all unsuccessful rebels.

BIBLIOGRAPHY

Bemont, Charles. *Simon de Montfort, Earl of Leicester.* Oxford: Clarendon Press, 1930.

Gies, Francis, and Joseph Gies. *Women in the Middle Ages.* New York: Crowell, 1978. 120–142.

W. M. Spellman

MURASAKI SHIKIBU
(ca. 973–ca. 1030)
Japan
Author

Murasaki Shikibu is the name traditionally given to the female author of *The Tale of Genji*, one of the classics of Japanese literature. Written in the early eleventh century, its status in Japanese literary history and culture is analogous to that of Homer's and Vergil's epics or Shakespeare's plays in many Western countries. Today, most Japanese have read at least part of the *Genji* and are familiar with its main events and characters, and it remains an important source, as it has for many centuries, of literary allusions, plots, and imagery. It is probably the work of Japanese literature best known to non-Japanese readers. A recent translation into modern English by Edward Seidensticker has made the *Genji* more accessible to an English-speaking public. The *Genji* is a *monogatari*, loosely translated in English as narrative or tale, with a romance structure and many features of a novel. It includes more than prose; there are also numerous poems throughout the work, composed by various characters. In later centuries, readers copying the tale onto scrolls for their own use often drew illustrations to accompany the narrative, and thus surviving scrolls have created a visual as well as verbal dimension to the *Genji*. In addition to the tale, we also have the author's diary (known as *The Murasaki Shikibu Diary*) covering the years 1008 to 1010 and her poetic memoirs.

About the author, we have little information, not even her actual name. It was not considered polite to refer publicly by name to court women other than consorts or concubines. *Shikibu* refers to a title (Bureau of Ceremonial) held for a time by her father, Tametoki. *Murasaki* is a principal female character in the tale who marries Genji and experiences both his deep love and his infidelities; Genji dies soon after Murasaki. According to her diary, a male courtier once jokingly referred to the author as Murasaki. His remark both links the author with her tale and indicates that the *Genji* was known in court circles during her time there.

The woman we know as Murasaki Shikibu was born sometime around 970 into a lesser branch of the dominant clan in the Heian period, the Fujiwara. At this time, the Fujiwara were the most powerful political family in Japan. They did not rule directly but exercised power through their control over a succession of young, weak emperors whose consorts, mothers, or other female kin were related by blood or marriage to Fujiwara men. Murasaki Shikibu's great-grandfather and grandfather had several of their poems chosen for inclusion in prestigious imperial anthologies. Her father, Tametoki, also wrote poetry throughout his lifetime and studied Chinese classics before pursuing a political career. As a government official, he held several court positions and was twice a provincial governor. This was a lucrative post, though lacking in prestige because of its distance from the capital, Heiankyō, the center of cultural and political life. Tradition has it that after Tametoki wrote a poetic complaint to Emperor Ichijō about his appointment to a province far from the capital, he was awarded a more distinguished one! Nothing is known about her mother.

While an education in Chinese classics and literature was necessary for a successful political career, women of Murasaki Shikibu's background were expected to have a casual, rather than scholarly, knowledge of such material. Yet she appears to have studied alongside her brother, Nobunori, for the diary records Tametoki's lament that his daughter was a better student of Chinese classics than was his son; Tametoki apparently wished that she had been born a boy. The *Genji* also demonstrates its author's familiarity with Japanese literature (especially diaries, poetry, and *monogatari*) and history. According to the diary, the Emperor Ichijō, after hearing the *Genji* read aloud, remarked that the author was certainly learned and familiar with *The Chronicles of Japan*. His comment caused others to call Murasaki Shikibu "the lady of the chronicles," a mocking reference to her erudition. Nonetheless, she secretly taught the empress classics of Chinese poetry for several years; this action suggests that while choosing not to display or defend her learning in public, Murasaki Shikibu continued privately to use and value it. The diary also reveals her considerable knowledge of Buddhist scriptures, also unusual for women at this time.

In 996, Murasaki Shikibu accompanied her father to Echizen when he became provincial governor there. She apparently returned to the capital two years later to wed Fujiwara no Nobutaka; this was an arranged marriage to a man nearly her father's age who had several other wives. A daughter, Kenshi, was born in 999, but the union was a short one. Nobutaka died in 1001, probably during an epidemic. Soon after her husband's death, Murasaki Shikibu began writing the *Genji*, perhaps in 1002 or 1003. She came to the imperial court as a tutor and companion to the empress, Akiko or Shōshi, somewhere around 1005 or 1006. The diary implies that a sizable portion of *Genji* was already written by this time, and many scholars speculate that the tale itself was responsible for Murasaki Shikibu's employment. The work may have brought her to the attention of Fujiwara Michinaga, the most powerful man at court, who hired her for his daughter Shōshi's entourage. As a private employee of Michinaga, Murasaki Shikibu did not have a specific title or role, as did other ladies serving Shōshi, and this made her position rather anomalous in the intricate hierarchies of rank that governed court social life. A woman's title affected where she lodged, what garments she wore, and where she sat at various formal and informal gatherings; the diary reveals its author's attempts to negotiate this elaborate social network as someone with privileged access to the empress but no clearly defined place in the hierarchy. Some scholars have suggested that Murasaki Shikibu was Michinaga's concubine, but there is no clear evidence for this, and the diary's references to him are allusive and discreet, as one would expect, given his great power and Murasaki Shikibu's dependence on him for her position.

The *Genji* was one of several major literary works by women in the early eleventh century; others include **Sei Shōnagon**'s *Pillow Book* and several diaries (*The Murasaki Shikibu Diary, The Gossamer Years, The Izumi Shikibu Diary* [see **Izumi Shikibu**], and *The Sarashina Diary*). It differs from male-authored literature in one essential respect: its script. For several hundred years before the *Genji*, written Chinese was the language of law, politics, and serious literature. It was a male domain, much like Latin during the European Middle Ages, to which women were denied access, except as light readers, as mentioned above. Female authors, including Murasaki Shikibu, wrote instead in a phonetic script called *kana*, which recorded the Japanese language as actually spoken. Disparaged as inferior to written Chinese, *kana* was often referred to as a "private" language or "women's" language. The Japanese syllabary (table of syllables) was called "the woman's hand," whereas Chinese characters were known as "men's letters." This gendering of written language may have made

writing itself more accessible and acceptable to privileged women like
Murasaki Shikibu or Sei Shōnagon. Morever, Chinese classics formed
the standard against which Japanese male writers measured their
works. The Chinese preference for poetry may have influenced
women's decisions to write diaries (which have plots and characters)
and *monogatari*, though the two women mentioned above wrote
verse as well. As a result, women's works from this time provide most
information we now have about early eleventh-century court culture.

The *Genji* is a massive work with fifty-four chapters and over 400
characters. It recounts the life and loves of "the shining Genji," a
prince demoted to common status by his father, the emperor, and
those of his children and grandchildren. Set roughly seventy-five years
before Murasaki Shikibu's time, the tale has a nostalgic and historical
quality; several scholars see it as implicitly critical of contemporary
court politics. Genji, the son of the emperor and his favorite concubine, is raised at court but precluded from succeeding his father on
the throne. He and the brother of his first wife have numerous affairs
and adventures, while the ties among related characters grow increasingly complex. Genji eventually builds a large house for the women
who are important to him, including Murasaki, the main love of his
life. Sexual and romantic relationships in the tale, frequently extra-
marital, are characterized by absence; men wander and have affairs,
while women remain fixed, secluded in their residences behind
screens and walls. Much of the narrative describes waiting for visits,
chance meetings, accidental glimpses of women through screens or
curtains, and the exchange of poems and letters. Both male and female characters display great concern for detail and grace; for instance, the type of handwriting, paper, and ink often symbolize the
writer's state of mind or situation. Yet there is considerable dynamic
action, too: betrayals, vengeful women, violent storms, political intrigues, incest, cases of mistaken identity, and other staples of romance. After Genji's death, the remaining chapters continue the
adventures of his children, younger brother, and other characters.

There is no single authoritative version of the *Genji*; nor is there
any consensus about the order or number of its chapters. Sections of
the tale circulated in manuscript during Murasaki Shikibu's lifetime
and were copied by admiring readers; and according to the diary,
there were at least two versions early on—one for public readership
and another for the author's private use. Michinaga apparently took
the latter copy from Murasaki's rooms without permission, and the

diarist worries about the impact its circulation might have on her reputation. (This remark suggests that there were key differences between the two copies.) The female author of *The Sarashina Diary* relates her considerable difficulties (and extreme joy) in obtaining a complete *Genji* to read in 1021 or 1022, though previously she had read bits and pieces. No manuscript in Murasaki Shikibu's handwriting has survived; the earliest copy is an illustrated scroll from the early to mid-twelfth century. The tale gained its reputation as a masterpiece in the late twelfth century, when scholars began to construct authoritative versions of the work. Hundreds of commentaries on the *Genji* have been written over the centuries.

There is little information about Murasaki Shikibu's later years and death. She could have died as early as 1014, when her father suddenly left his provincial post and moved to Heiankyō, then retired away from the capital the following year. Several scholars argue instead that references in her poetic memoirs and other contemporary documents indicate that Murasaki Shikibu served Shōshi as late as 1025. Because a list of Shōshi's attendants in 1031 does not mention her, there is general agreement that she died between 1025 and 1031. Murasaki Shikibu's daughter, Kenshi, became a prominent figure at court, serving as wet nurse to the future emperor Goreizei and principal handmaid. Also known as Echigo no Ben, Kenshi was a skilled poet; thirty-seven of her poems were selected for imperial anthologies, and her own poetry collection has survived.

BIBLIOGRAPHY

Bowring, Richard. *Murasaki Shikibu: The Tale of Genji*. Landmarks of World Literature Series. Cambridge: Cambridge University Press, 1988.

Bowring, Richard, trans. *Murasaki Shikibu: Her Diary and Poetic Memoirs*. Princeton, NJ: Princeton University Press, 1982.

Murasaki, Shikibu. *The Tale of Genji*. Ed. Edward Seidensticker. New York: Knopf, 1976.

Gwynne Kennedy

NZINGA, QUEEN OF ANGOLA
(ca. 1580–1663)
Angola
Queen and Military Leader

In the early seventeenth century, through a combination of ruthlessness and cleverness, Queen Nzinga was able to consolidate power in
the Kimbundu territory of Ndongo and Matamba (what is now Angola) in Northwest Africa. Although often perceived as an outsider
by Africans as well as Europeans because of her gender, she was able
to manipulate her enemies and gather other outsiders around her to
gain support to rule effectively. At times she supported the slave trade
from Africa to the Americas, but she also sometimes protected escaped slaves, who would then be loyal to her. She was a consummate
politician and warrior queen so greatly beloved she was known as the
"Black Mother."

Before she became queen, she negotiated with the Portuguese on
behalf of her brother, who was King of Ndongo, and then later ruled
in her own name and with the aid of the Dutch and African allies
revolted against the Portuguese, who were ruling this part of Africa
as a province in the seventeenth century. Through her shifting alliances with the Portuguese, the Dutch, and other African tribes, she
was able to consolidate her power to become successively the monarch of Ndongo and Matamba. She ruled in one part or another of
the Kimbundu territory from 1624 to 1663. Both friends and enemies perceived her as a shrewd negotiator and a fierce warrior, and
she was able to provide her people the Ndongo with a degree of
political unity. The Portuguese referred to the people of the region
as "Jingas," after her name.

Nzinga was the emissary of her brother, or possibly half brother,
Ngola Mbandi, King of Ndongo, who had sent her to negotiate with
the Portuguese governor in Luanda after being defeated in battle.
One of the ways Portuguese officials attempted to assert their authority and superiority was that when the governor received an African ruler or diplomat, he sat but did not furnish a chair for his

Nzinga, Queen of Angola. From Kevin Shillington, *A History of Africa*. Copyright © Kevin Shillington. Reprinted with permission of Macmillan Press Ltd. and St. Martin's Press, Incorporated.

African counterpart, who was expected to stand. Nzinga, however, refused to stand while the governor sat. She ordered one of her female servants to kneel down on all fours so that she could sit on her servant's back for the length of the interview. While this must have been hard on the servant, it was a clear demonstration of Nzinga's sense of pride and self-value, and also her ingenuity, and the action serves as a metaphor for Nzinga's entire career. There are several drawings memorializing this incident.

Nzinga was a skilled negotiator. She persuaded the governor to recognize Ndongo as an independent monarchy owing no allegiance to Portugal despite the fact that the Portuguese had defeated Ngola Mbandi in battle. Nzinga also persuaded the governor to promise to help the Ngola in fighting the Imbangala, invaders from the east who were causing serious trouble. Nzinga was not able to win on her third objective, however. She wanted the Portuguese to vacate and destroy the fort they had built in the heart of the Mbundu territory at Mbaka.

Despite Nzinga's great skill as a negotiator, the Portuguese did little to help Mbandi rebuild his kingdom. In 1624 Nzinga succeeded to the throne of Ndongo after her brother died in what some called suspicious circumstances. The Imbangala, once her enemy, became her supporters. The Imbangala chief, or *kaza ka hango*, had been driven out of Ndongo in 1621 by Portuguese. He had fled to the south, where he had a firm base of support to plot against the Portuguese, and he had supported Ngola Mbandi when he opposed the Portuguese in Ndongo. After Ngola's death he then aided Nzinga in her political maneuvering. The *kaza* had agreed to support Ngola's heir in his struggles with the Portuguese, who referred to the heir as Ngola's son. Some scholars now suggest that Ngola and his heir may not have been related, and calling him the son was a Portuguese effort to impose their beliefs of hereditary rule. The *kaza* broke his promise and instead turned the heir over to Nzinga, who seemed more able to withstand the Portuguese, and she had the heir killed to consolidate her rule. According to the Portuguese, she had thus killed her own nephew, which added to horrific tales they told of her. Nzinga then bolstered her position by a symbolic marriage to the *kaza*. Her alliance with the Imbangala would provide Nzinga with a safe haven when the Portuguese drove her out.

That same year as her brother's death, Fernão de Sousa became governor of the Portuguese colony, and he realized that for the slave trade to operate effectively, Portugal must have an African trading partner, and Nzinga enticed him. She converted to Christianity and was baptized as Ana de Sousa, though many historians believe the conversion was a political move on her part and that she at this time in her life did not accept the theological beliefs of Catholicism. When it was no longer politically useful, she for awhile abandoned the faith. Her so-called conversion was part of her negotiations with the Portuguese, and she agreed to allow slave traders, missionaries, and Portuguese officials to come to the central marketplace near her capital if in return the Portuguese would withdraw from a fortress they had constructed near the historic capital of her kingdom. De Sousa recommended to his superiors in Portugal that the fort at Mkaka be withdrawn, but Lisbon did not support this policy, and Nzinga's relations with the Portuguese worsened once she started offering asylum to slaves who fled the Portuguese plantations on the coast.

De Sousa reconsidered policy; he wanted to expel Nzinga and her followers and replace her with a monarch who would be subservient to the needs and wishes of the Portuguese. The Portuguese were able to force her off her throne and replace her with a puppet ruler, Ari Kiluanji. Nzinga fled to her former enemies-turned-allies, the Imbangala. Nzinga worked to convince her followers to destroy this usurper's rule and to expel the Portuguese who had maintained him in power. She moved north to the ancient kingdom of Matamba only after she recognized that her strategy of taking refuge with the Imbangala did not protect her position in Ndongo. Her alliance with the Imbangala deteriorated. Yet Nzinga's warriors were able to close the newly revived trade routes developed by the Portuguese. In 1630 the governor de Sousa left the colony in defeat.

Nzinga rallied her supporters in her exile on the eastern marches of Ndongo. She knew she needed her following to be loyal and fierce and adopted some of the ritual and training of her enemies the Imbangala. She allowed no children to be raised in the camps and introduced her people to a ritualistic form of cannibalism, again to the horror and fascination of the Portuguese. Unable to win Ndongo from the Portuguese, Nzinga decided to conquer the kingdom of Matamba to the northeast.

Matamba was one of the few places in the southern Konga and northern Kimbundu that had a history of women ruling. Matamba was the principal African slave-trading state in the Luanda region. Once in control there, Nzinga realized she needed allies against the Portuguese and worked to develop strong ties with the Dutch to use against the Portuguese. She was interested in allying herself with the Dutch for commercial as well as political reasons, but her alliance was only to serve her own ends. Her goal was to remove the Portuguese altogether from Angola and have the Dutch as the European trading power on the coast. She believed she could negotiate better commercial relations with them and have them trade to her people higher-quality goods.

Matamba dominated the whole Kimbundu region, and after successfully fighting the Portuguese, Nzinga turned on her Dutch allies and defeated them as well. She then had a new alliance with the Portuguese so that she could export the slaves she had captured in war or received from her vassals. In 1656 she signed a peace treaty with the Portuguese governor of Angola and reconverted to Catholicism. She was able to keep the peace until her death at approximately eighty-one in 1663. Nzinga died a Catholic, and her deathbed was surrounded by the missionary advisers she had valued in the last eight years of her life. Through her clever manipulations of the Portuguese, the Imbangala, and the Dutch, Nzinga was able to dominate Kimbundu politics for forty years.

BIBLIOGRAPHY

Birmingham, David. *The Portuguese Conquest of Angola*. London: Oxford University Press, 1965.

Henderson, Lawrence W. *Angola: Five Centuries of Conflict*. Ithaca, NY: Cornell University Press, 1979.

Miller, Joseph C. *Kings and Kinsmen: Early Mbundu States in Angola*. Oxford: Clarendon Press, 1976.

Miller, Joseph C. "Nzinga of Matamba in a New Perspective." *Journal of African History* 16, 2 (1975): 201–216.

Wheeler, Douglas L., and René Pélissier. *Angola*. Westport, CT: Greenwood, 1971.

Carole Levin

ONO NO KOMACHI
(ca. 830/835–899)
Japan
Waka Poet and Rokkasen

Ono no Komachi's status as one of Japan's most highly regarded poetic geniuses represents a singular accomplishment. A remarkable woman, Ono no Komachi was intensely passionate and devout, as well as being an immensely gifted poet. Her surviving poems have secured her a permanent place in the history of women, and her legendary life has provided inspiration for numerous works of outstanding literary achievement.

Ono no Komachi's father is presumed to have been the governor of Dewa Province. If, as is reported, her father was Ono no Yoshizane, then Komachi may have inherited her poetic aptitude from her paternal grandfather, Ono no Takamura (802–852), a distinguished poet versed in both Chinese and Japanese letters. Scholarly consensus about the details of Komachi's life is limited. Supposedly born in Dewa, as a member of the Ono clan, Komachi is said to have been connected in some manner with the imperial court in Heiankyō (modern-day Kyōto), during which time she engaged in a number of intimate relationships with men. Her specific role at the imperial court is uncertain, although she may have been a lady-in-waiting. Komachi also had an older sister, who probably spent time at the imperial court along with Komachi. A poem that appears in a later royal anthology, one attributed to "Komachi's grandchild," suggests that Komachi had at least one child.

What else is known about Ono no Komachi has necessarily been reconstructed from the circumstances surrounding her literary output and from the content of her poems. Approximate dates for her birth (ca. 830–835), for the time she spent at the imperial court (ca. 850–869), and for her death (ca. 899) have been derived from her poems. The poems Komachi is known to have exchanged with men about whom some historical information still exists have been especially helpful to scholars in reconstructing the details of her life.

More information exists about the period during which Ono no Komachi lived than can be known with certainty about her life. The Heian period (794–1192) is particularly noteworthy because of the high quality of literary works its writers produced. Toward the end of the eighth century, the development of a new phonetic writing system known as *kana* came into use. Since women generally did not receive instruction in Chinese, they now had an opportunity to express themselves in writing. When Ono no Komachi began writing her poems, around the middle of the ninth century, the unique Heian culture had begun to flourish.

The influence of two continental cultures—China and Korea—had created a climate that fostered creative output. Poets of the period knew of and had reference to earlier Chinese and Japanese models. Throughout the Heian period, men still contributed the majority of works with significant literary status; therefore, the achievement of the accomplished *waka* poet Ono no Komachi is worthy of great respect.

The dominant poetic form in the Japanese language from approximately the ninth century on was the *waka*, or "Japanese poem." *Waka* contained thirty-one syllables, presented in five lines, which consisted of five, seven, five, seven, and seven syllables, respectively. Royally commissioned imperial *waka* collections, or *shū*, begin with the *Kokin[waka]shū* (*Collection of Old and New Japanese Poetry*, ca. 905–920), an anthology that brought together the best works of Japanese poets, both old and new, male and female. Ki no Tsurayuki (ca. 868/872–945), in his preface to the *Kokinshū*, identifies six poetic sages, known as the *rokkasen*. As the only woman to be included among the *rokkasen*, Ono no Komachi's place in the history of Japanese literature is unique. The other *rokkasen* named by Ki no Tsurayuki are the priest Kisen (fl. ca. 810–823), Bishop Henjō (816–890), Ariwara no Narihira (825–880), Ōtomo no Kuronushi (fl. ca. 860), and Bun'ya no Yashuide (fl. ca. 870). Ki no Tsurayuki's identification of Komachi as one of the *rokkasen* constitutes a public acknowledgment of her creative genius.

Particularly striking aspects of Komachi's poetic canon are its relative scarcity and its exceptional quality. Komachi's poems appear in several sections of the *utamonogatari* ("tales of poems") known as the *Ise monogatari* (*Tales of Ise*, ca. 905–920), although she is never mentioned by name as their author. A personal collection of her poetry, entitled the *Komachi Shū* (the *Komachi Collection*), consists of a hundred or so poems. The *Kokinshū* contains eighteen of Komachi's poems, thirteen of which focus on love. When compared with the number of surviving poems that have been attributed to the Heian poet **Izumi Shikibu** (ca. 966/979–1030?), the number of poems that can be positively attributed to Komachi remains relatively small; however, the passionate intensity of Komachi's poetry more than compensates for the limited number of poems that have survived.

A central concern of Komachi's poems, and of *Kokinshū* poems in general, is unrequited or unfulfilled love. Komachi's poetry also affirms her deep religious faith and her familiarity with Amidist, or Pure Land, Buddhist beliefs. The genius of Komachi's poetry stems partially from her ability to absorb and to use the literary traditions of China and Japan. One striking trademark of Komachi's verse is her impressive use of language. Komachi's poems often attain a high degree of sophistication through her inclusion of a pivot word (*kakekotoba*), a literary device that relies on a series of sounds to suggest two meanings.

Shortly after she died, the Komachi legend began inspiring literary works in a variety of genres, including short stories and plays. Japan's Nō repertory still contains five of seven Komachi-inspired Nō plays: *Komachi Clears Her Name* (*Sōshi Arai Komachi*); *The Nightly Courting of Komachi* (*Kayoi Komachi*); *Komachi's Parrot-Answer Poem* (*Ōmu Komachi*); *Komachi on the Stupa* (*Sotoba Komachi*); and *Komachi at Seki Temple* (*Sekidera Komachi*). The Komachi legend highlights those aspects of Ono no Komachi's life—as a passionate woman of extraordinary beauty, as a religious woman of deep faith, and as an exemplary poet of immense skill—that proved especially captivating. Artists today still draw upon the extraordinary life of this engaging ninth century poetic genius when creating works of contemporary theater and fiction.

BIBLIOGRAPHY

Fischer, Felice. "Ono no Komachi." In Chieko I. Mulhern, ed., *Japanese Women Writers: A Bio-Critical Sourcebook*. Westport, CT: Greenwood, 1994. 302–311.

Hirshfield, Jane, and Mariko Aratani, trans. *The Ink Dark Moon: Love Poems by Ono no Komachi and Izumi Shikibu*. New York: Vintage, 1990.

Miner, Earl, Hiroko Odagiri, and Robert E. Morrell. *The Princeton Com-*

panion to Classical Japanese Literature. Princeton, NJ: Princeton University Press, 1985.

Teele, Roy E., Nicholas J. Teele, and H. Rebecca Teele, trans. *Ono no Komachi: Poems, Stories, Nō Plays.* New York: Garland, 1993.

Debra Barrett-Graves

CARITAS PIRCKHEIMER
(1467–1532)
Germany
Abbess, Defender of Her Faith, and Humanist
Scholar

In the early years of the Reformation, Caritas (or Charitas) Pirckheimer, German abbess of the convent of Saint Clare in Nuremberg, courageously resisted efforts by city officials, religious leaders, and citizens with Protestant sympathies to close her convent. She used her reputation as a pious and exceptionally learned woman to defend the religious beliefs and practices of her Catholic community. In doing so, Caritas deployed her impressive humanist training in a more public way than European humanist teachers or writers, almost all of them men, considered appropriate for women.

As an intellectual movement, humanism looked to classical Greece and Rome, particularly its philosophy and literature, as models for contemporary Europe, and it emphasized the study of classical writings as the best means to produce educated, virtuous men for service to the state. Hence, many debated the value of such intellectual training for women, who were barred from nearly all public offices or careers because of their sex. Yet some, including perhaps Caritas's father, felt that humanist studies were appropriate for women, because they furthered personal virtue, even if women had little practical outlet for their studies. Caritas Pirckheimer, however, did put her learning to public use as she defended her institution from its earliest opponents and left a remarkable written history of that crisis.

Caritas was born in 1467 into an affluent and powerful Bavarian family with a commitment to humanist learning, for both daughters and sons received an impressive education. Her father, Johannes Pirckheimer, served as legal advisor to the Nuremberg city council. The oldest child, Caritas entered the convent of Saint Clare at age twelve. The convent was highly regarded throughout Germany for both its learning and piety; a wealthy institution, it boasted an impressive library and a strong community of literate nuns, many of them the daughters of elite Nuremberg families. Several of Caritas's younger sisters also took religious vows, and three (Klara, Sabina, and Eufemia) became abbesses of their convents. Her brother, Willibald, was a famous figure in international humanist circles. Among his friends and correspondents were the great Dutch philosopher Desiderius Erasmus and the artist Albrecht Dürer. Willibald appears to have encouraged his sister's intellectual pursuits by refining her command of Latin and supplying her with books by important classical and Christian authors. He dedicated three of his own works to her, each with a preface that praised her learning. In this way, Caritas's intellectual accomplishments came to the attention of important male humanists throughout northern Europe; several of them also dedicated works to her or corresponded with her directly. In this period, letters were a key means of circulating scholarly opinions and materials. They were not necessarily seen as private or personal, as we might think of them today, but instead, they were often intended to be read by larger audiences than their initial recipients. Letters were occasionally published, as were three by Caritas to her brother and two to Conrad Celtis, a renowned scholar and poet laureate of Nuremberg, in 1515; the printer's preface specifically acclaims Caritas as a "special ornament" of her sex and her city.

Although Caritas's communication with leading European intellectuals testifies to her impressive learning and intelligence, she was nonetheless viewed as an exception to her sex, as a *"special"* case rather than an example of women's innate potential. There was also the popular perception that a woman's participation in the public exchange of ideas compromised her reputation and raised doubts about her character. Indeed, the Italian humanist scholar Isotta Nogarola was accused of being a whore, because of her erudition and desire to participate in male intellectual conversations as an equal. Caritas carefully negotiated the tension between appropriate feminine self-effacement and justified pride in her accomplishments, as can be seen in her letters to Celtis. Thanking him for dedicating to her his edition of writings by **Hrotsvit of Gandersheim**, a tenth-century nun who wrote Latin plays, Caritas first denied her worthiness to receive such an honor and then asserted that God grants wisdom not only to men but also to women. In this way, she continued, a "wise virgin" testifies to God's use of weakness (i.e., women) to confound or humble (male) strength. A later letter to Celtis, thanking him for a dedicatory ode of praise, again began modestly; she described herself as an "insignificant woman" and Celtis's "unworthy" though "enthusiastic" disciple. The majority of the letter, however, strongly urged Celtis to renounce his interest in secular and classical pagan subjects and to direct his scholarly gifts toward divine matters instead. It is vanity, she argued, to pursue worldly rather than spiritual knowledge; his choice put his soul at risk, because the more one knows, the more severe God's judgment. Perhaps sensing that Celtis would take offense at such bold instruction by a woman, Caritas claimed to act only as God and her brother commanded her by answering him. She further justified her authority by reminding him that her name (which means "charity") is a vital dimension of one's spiritual learning and love of God. It appears that her correspondence with Celtis ceased with this letter.

As her arguments suggest, Caritas was able to reconcile her intellectual pursuits and religious devotion, seeing the first as both necessary to and furthering the second. To her, learning and piety were inextricably linked, a position decidedly at odds with the prevailing view of women's intellectual activity mentioned above. She edited a chronicle of the early history of her religious order and its Nuremberg convent, in both Latin and German versions. In 1503, Caritas became abbess of Saint Clare. She continued to write Latin letters and to receive praise in humanist circles.

The Protestant Reformation posed a grave threat to women like Caritas who had chosen convent life. Its emphasis on marriage and motherhood as the proper, natural course for women was at odds with Catholic nuns' vows of virginity and renunciation of marriage. Their way of life was also at stake, for one of the first actions by Reformers across Europe was to close monasteries and convents. Convents responded in various ways: by accepting Protestant doctrine, by relinquishing their property in exchange for pensions for their nuns, and by resistance. Caritas chose to fight efforts to close or seize control of the Saint Clare convent. She oversaw the production of a record of the convent's dealings with its Protestant adversaries between 1524 and 1528 (entitled *Denkwürdigkeiten*). It is a compilation of documents, some by Caritas herself, that sets forth her view of events; of the surviving manuscript copies, one has editorial comments and instructions in her handwriting.

Nuremberg was one of the earliest cities to accept Lutheran reforms. According to the record, the city council ordered the closure

of monasteries and convents in late 1524 and 1525 and strongly discouraged Catholic beliefs and practices. Priests were replaced by reforming pastors in convents including Saint Clare, where they
preached Protestant sermons several times a week and attacked the
nuns' religious convictions. The nuns were denied confessors and forbidden to take Catholic communion; church services were conducted
in German instead of Latin. Other aspects of their religious worship,
including prayers to female saints, were prohibited. With the support
of Protestant clergy, townspeople harassed the convent. Some refused
to sell food or other supplies to the convent; they sang obscene songs
and shouted threats when the nuns sang; they threatened to burn the
convent and threw rocks through its windows. Rumors were spread
of scandalous, immoral practices behind the convent walls. The city
council refused to protect the convent or condemn its assailants. In
March 1525, it insisted that the convent comply with additional demands that meant the end of its communal religious life. The council
ordered nuns to wear secular dress and commanded the abbess to
free the sisters of their religious vows. Nuns were allowed to leave
the convent, and their parents received permission to remove them.
The convent was also required to install a window (relinquishing its
enclosed, cloistered condition) so that the nuns would be visible to
visitors.

Caritas forcefully protested the council's efforts to exert its authority over the convent and its spiritual affairs. She tried to have
Franciscan priests reinstated even after the council removed them. She
insisted that only God could free her nuns of their religious vows and
asked reformers to extend their own belief in the supremacy of individual conscience to her nuns. Caritas argued that it would be impossible to clothe her nuns in secular attire in the short time allotted
(four weeks), since the sisters made their own clothes. After a meeting
of the convent, the sisters agreed to a window but decided that they
would not speak to visitors alone but have another sister present as
witness to prevent false accusations. Caritas worked with her brother
Willibald, initially a strong champion of reforming policies, to prepare
a defense of the nuns in Latin for presentation to the council. Often
attributed to Willibald, recent scholarship suggests Caritas's authorship, because it contains many points she makes elsewhere and is
written in a plural feminine voice.

Caritas's reputation as a learned, pious woman (Nuremberg's "special ornament") lent considerable weight to her opinions. A city

council emissary remarked to Caritas that not only her own convent but all the surrounding convents followed her lead so that if she converted, the "entire land" would as well. On another occasion, Caritas refused to let the mothers of four nuns enter the convent, despite their claim to act with the council's authority. The women then slandered Caritas before the council, but after talking with the abbess, its representatives sided with her and determined the mothers were lying.

Chapter thirty-four of the record contains possibly the most chilling and painful episode in the convent's dealings with hostile Protestants. It relates the forcible removal from the convent of three sisters (Margaret Tetzel, Katharina Ebner, and Klara Nutzel), taken against their will by their mothers and the mothers' friends. It is clear from Caritas's account that the sisters, who had spent six (and in one case, nine) years at the convent, did not want to leave their religious life or break their vows. Their despair and agony are intensely moving. As fellow nuns removed their veils and gave them headdresses and other secular attire to wear, the three sisters wept profusely. Barred by council policy from preventing their removal, Caritas nonetheless made it difficult for the family members to act contrary to their daughters' wishes. She refused to allow them entry through the back gate, away from the crowds who had assembled to watch, but insisted that they take their daughters in plain sight, at the chapel door where they had first entered religious life. There was no need for secrecy or shame, Caritas stated, if the mothers (whom Caritas called "she-wolves") were acting rightly. The abbess insisted that she would not order her nuns to leave the chapel, thus requiring the mothers and their accomplices to take the sisters away. Alternately threatened and cajoled, the three young women defiantly refused to go or relinquish their vows, claiming a higher obedience to God; according to some in the chapel, Katharina Ebner defended her actions eloquently for an entire hour. With no resolution in sight and fearing violence to the convent, the men in the mothers' party asked Caritas to return to the chapel to show the mothers that she was not responsible for their children's resistance. There, Caritas again refused to absolve her nuns of their vows. The mothers cursed, scolded, and in one case, struck their defiant children. Despite the daughters' pleas to remain, they were pulled and dragged from the chapel by force; four people were necessary to remove each sister. As the nuns left in wagons, they protested their unwilling removal to the crowds. The young women apparently generated sympathy among onlookers, some of whom remarked that if they had not feared a riot and the city's soldiers, they would have helped the daughters.

After that event, Caritas continued to reject Lutheran doctrine, and tensions between the council and the convent remained high. A meeting in November 1525 between the abbess and the Protestant leader Philip Melanchthon ended the immediate crisis. Alerted to the convent's situation by Willibald, Melanchthon engaged Caritas in a lengthy discussion of doctrine, during which they discovered many points of agreement. He strongly criticized the forcible removal of nuns, believing instead that convents like Saint Clare should neither lose nor be given anything, and he expressed his views to the council. As a result of that meeting, all convents in Nuremberg territory were allowed to continue, though only temporarily, since they were forbidden to accept new novices. Only one nun left the convent of Saint Clare and converted. Caritas died in her sixties in 1532. The Saint Clare convent closed in 1590, after the death of the last remaining sister.

BIBLIOGRAPHY

Barker, Paula Datsko. "Caritas Pirckheimer: A Female Humanist Confronts the Reformation." *Sixteenth Century Journal* 26, 2 (Summer 1995): 259–272.

McNamara, Jo Ann. *Sisters in Arms: Catholic Nuns through Two Millennia.* Cambridge, MA: Harvard University Press, 1996.

Wilson, Katharina, ed. *Women Writers of the Renaissance and Reformation.* Athens: University of Georgia Press, 1987.

Gwynne Kennedy

DIANE DE POITIERS
(1499–1566)
France
Royal Adviser

Born into a noble family and married at age sixteen to fifty-six-year-old Louis de Breze, leader of the French province of Normandy, Diane de Poitiers was the mother of two girls at the time of her husband's death in 1531. Louis de Breze was a close ally and loyal subject of the King of France, Francis I. Diane first met Francis I's second son, Prince Henry of Orleans, in 1530, when the future king of France was only eleven. Soon after the death of her husband, Diane began an association with eleven-year-old Henry that was viewed by most observers as strictly maternal in nature, especially given their differences in age. In 1543 Prince Henry was married to Catherine de' Medici, cousin of Pope Clement VII. But Henry never grew to love his wife, and it seems likely that the relationship between the Dauphin and Diane de Poitiers had become sexual by the mid- to late 1530s. Despite being twenty years his senior, Diane remained Henry's mistress until his death in 1559. Queen Catherine appears to have suffered this relationship in silence, remaining at all times polite and deferential to the older woman.

Diane's importance at the French royal court was enhanced considerably in 1536 when Henry's older brother and heir apparent Francis died unexpectedly. Henry succeeded to the French throne after the death of his father in 1547, and according to more than one contemporary observer, Diane played a key role in the appointment of the king's advisers. The king created a new title for his mistress, Duchess of Valentinos, and he bestowed upon her the royal jewels. Henry then levied a special tax on all the churches in France and turned the receipts over to Diane for her personal use. The king would normally share a noon meal with his informal adviser, and Diane became very adept at balancing the many factions and interest groups at court.

The personal impact of her influence on the new king was imme-

Diane de Poitiers (*A Lady in her Bath* by François Clouet). Samuel H. Kress Collection, Photograph © 1999 Board of Trustees, National Gallery of Art, Washington. Reprinted with permission.

diate: Diane's son-in-law Robert de La Marck was made a marshall of France, whereas three of her nephews were elevated to bishoprics during the first few years of the new reign. In addition, the king's mistress was granted a number of valuable properties, some of which had been seized from his late father's mistress Anne de Pisseleu. Diane's ambitious nature was noted by jealous courtiers in Paris, many of whom deeply resented the fact that she had become one of the key recipients of the king's patronage. Even the king's children were placed under the educational supervision of Diane; one of her cousins was made tutor to the children of the king and queen.

Throughout the years of her relationship with the king, Diane was a strong benefactor of the arts and literature. She supported poets, artists, and architects on a regular basis. She is also thought to be responsible for the dissemination of one of the last medieval romances, *Amadis de Gaul*, which was first translated into French in 1540. King Henry II was eager to restore the tournament to court life, even personally participating in a number of jousts, and the romantic tales of knight-errantry contained in *Amadis de Gaul* appealed to both king and mistress. Indeed, Henry's fondness for the tour-

nament turned fatal in 1559 when, at festivities celebrating the marriage of his daughter to the King Philip II of Spain, the king was
killed in a mishap while jousting.

Henry dedicated most of his energies as king to frustrating the
territorial ambitions of his arch rival, the Holy Roman Emperor
Charles V. Despite the fact that both monarchs were staunch Roman
Catholics and faced emerging Protestant movements within their re-
spective realms, Henry was not reluctant in offering military support
to Protestant enemies of Charles V. Such cynicism in foreign relations, however, did little to settle domestic difficulties. For one of the
most troublesome features of the reign of King Henry II was the rise
of the Protestant faith in France. All of the king's closest advisers,
including Diane de Poitiers, were very conservative Roman Catholics,
and the king was committed to stamping out Protestant ideas in his
own kingdom. In 1558 the papal nuncio to France reported that
Diane was steadfast in her desire to see French Protestants punished
severely. It is not surprising, given the fact that a substantial portion
of the estates and property of convicted heretics was given by royal
mandate to the duchess. Both king and mistress worked tirelessly to
intensify the prosecution and punishment of Protestants throughout
the realm. Just before the king's death, for example, an investigation
of the Parlement of Paris, the main judicial body in the capital, was
undertaken by officers of the Crown with the aim of rooting out all
Protestant sympathizers.

Henry and Diane's efforts to stamp out Protestantism in France
had clearly failed by the time of the king's sudden death in 1559.
The debt accumulated by the Crown amounted to two and a half
times the monarchy's annual revenue, and religious divisions were
spreading rapidly. Diane de Poitiers lived for another six years, but
she was excluded from all further influence at court by Catherine,
Henry's widow.

BIBLIOGRAPHY

Baumgartner, Frederic J. *Henry II: King of France*. Durham, NC: Duke
       University Press, 1988.
Strage, Mark. *Women of Power*. New York: Harcourt Brace, 1976.

W. M. Spellman

MARGUERITE PORETE
(ca. 1250–1310)
France
Spiritual Director, Martyr, and Author

We possess very little biographical information on the woman who became the victim of the first auto-da-fé—burning at the stake—on record in Paris. Most likely born in Hainaut, a region south of Flanders and Brabant, Marguerite Porete was a member of the Beguine movement, female and male lay followers of the apostolic life who committed themselves to poverty and abstinence in imitation of Christ. A label of contempt and derision bestowed upon them by their many enemies, by the middle of the thirteenth century the word *Beguine* had come to be applied to a wide variety of individuals, most of whom were women, who lived a religious life outside of the established orders. In 1946 Marguerite Porete was conclusively identified as the author of *The Mirror of Simple Souls*, a spiritual treatise and handbook designed to assist others in their search for the divine. True to the message contained in that work, and to the Beguine emphasis on personal spirituality, the author lived and died in the conviction that the soul's union with God was attainable in this life without the mediation or direction of ecclesiastical authorities.

Composed sometime between 1296 and 1307, *The Mirror of Simple Souls* is written in the form of a dialogue between the allegorical figures of love, reason, and the soul. Interspersed with this are verses and examples that comment on the dialogue, the main focus of which is the relation of the human to the divine and the ascent of the soul to God. Seven stages of grace are treated, each leading the soul up to final union with its Maker. In the final state the human soul no longer has needs, desires, or indeed a will separate from God. Fully liberated, the soul is not obliged to answer to mere human authority. Intermediaries on the road to salvation are redundant; masses, penance, prayers, and fasts are so many distractions. It is these purified souls alone who constitute the genuine Holy Church of Christ and, in this condition, may forego the spiritual ministrations of the institutional Church. Marguerite acknowledged that her work was aimed at an esoteric audience who had achieved a form of understanding beyond mere formal education and the ways of reason. In this her efforts remained within a wider mystical tradition whose appeal was to the contemplative initiate and not to a more general audience.

The Beguine movement with which Marguerite Porete was associated was unique in the Western Church for a number of reasons. Emerging during the late twelfth century, it was largely a women's movement; it maintained no definite rule of life, claimed no saintly founder, sought no patrons, refused to impose vows over a lifetime, and—perhaps most disturbingly—functioned without authorization from Rome. Some Beguines lived in self-supporting communal houses called *beguinages*, some remained at home with their families, whereas others followed a mendicant (beggar) lifestyle as solitaries. Marguerite may have been one of these independent, itinerant Beguines, for at the close of *The Mirror of Simple Souls*, she anticipates that Beguines, along with "priests, clerics, and Preachers, Augustinians, Carmelites, and the Friars Minor" would take offense at her work.

Despite their unofficial status within the Church, the Beguines were not without their admirers and powerful patrons. Robert Grosseteste (ca. 1168–1253), the great English Franciscan and Bishop of Lincoln, informed members of his own order that there was a higher kind of poverty than that practiced by the Franciscan fathers, and this was to live by one's own labor like the Beguines. In addition, Godfrey of Fontaines (ca. 1250–ca. 1305), a respected scholastic philosopher of the University of Paris, approved of Marguerite's *The Mirror of Simple Souls*, although he recognized that it did not provide an appropriate model of Christian discipline for the majority of believers. However, there were others within the Church establishment who attacked the movement. The Fourth Lateran Council of 1216 forbade the founding of new religious orders, and churchmen like William of Saint-Amour (ca. 1200–1272) insisted that Beguine communities were in violation of this mandate. The Second Council of Lyons (1274) reaffirmed the decision of the Fourth Lateran Council, and Beguine houses were targeted for dissolution. Finally, one year after the execution of Marguerite of Porete, the Council of Vienna (1311–1312) condemned the status of Beguine and associated the movement with the heretical claim that one could reach perfection or union with God before bodily death while simultaneously avoiding sin in the present life. This heresy of the

"Free Spirit," it was alleged, defied the authority of the Church and all obedience to human laws. For the delegates at Vienna, the Beguines represented a serious threat to the hierarchical discipline of the Roman Church.

It seems clear that Marguerite of Porete must have received some form of education, for *The Mirror of Simple Souls* demonstrates a familiarity with theological issues and with contemporary court literature. The book was written in vernacular French, a factor that the Church leadership may have found particularly disquieting. It was later translated into Latin, Italian, and Middle English—more often than not in monastic houses—indicating that not all of the ideas contained in the book were taken to be pernicious by subsequent generations of churchmen. Sometime between 1296 and 1306, however, the Bishop of Cabrai, Guy II, condemned *The Mirror of Simple Souls* and ordered the work to be burned in the presence of the author. It was a book that allegedly endorsed pantheism (many gods) and antinomianism, the belief not only that the soul can become one with God but that the individual in consequence is no longer bound by moral law. Then, in 1308, after the author continued to send copies of her condemned work to important churchmen, she was detained once again. After being held in prison for almost a year and a half, the Dominican inquisitor William of Paris gathered five professors of law and eleven theological regents of the University of Paris to reach a decision respecting the heretical import of certain articles in *The Mirror of Simple Souls.*

Marguerite refused to cooperate with this inquiry, declining even to take the vows necessary for her examination. She was condemned as a lapsed heretic on 31 May 1310, turned over to the secular authorities, and burned at the stake on 1 June 1310. The ecclesiastical-political situation at the time of her imprisonment probably contributed to this end. King Philip IV was at the same moment engaged in a controversial struggle to dissolve the military-religious order of Templars. Eager to solidify his own authority in France, Philip used his commitment to orthodoxy as a mechanism whereby the French clergy were allied to the royal program of administrative consolidation. William of Paris was not only the inquisitor responsible for Marguerite's imprisonment and death; in addition, he served as the king's confessor and the man in charge of the campaign against the Templars beginning in 1307. The king cultivated the image of activist defender of the faith and won the support of the French clergy in his actions against the Templars and their considerable properties. The prosecution of Marguerite provided an additional opportunity to demonstrate one's orthodox credentials.

In spite of the official condemnation of *The Mirror* at the start of the fourteenth century, the book was copied and distributed quite widely. There are a number of fifteenth-century Latin and Italian translations, together with three Middle English versions. In 1927, before the book had been conclusively identified as the work of a condemned heretic, a modern English translation was published by the Downside Benedictines. More recently the Paulist Press has issued a critical edition as part of its "Classics of Western Spirituality" series, rightly placing Porete's work within the larger ambit of a mystical Christian tradition. In providing her readers with an alternative vision of Christian perfection separate from the official Church, her work contributed to reform tradition that has both challenged and broadened the mandate of the wider Christian community of believers.

BIBLIOGRAPHY

Bryant, Gwendolyn. "The French Heretic Beguine: Marguerite Porete." In Katharina M. Wilson, ed., *Medieval Women Writers*. Athens: University of Georgia Press, 1984. 204–226.

Lerner, Robert. *The Heresy of the Free Spirit in the Later Middle Ages*. Los Angeles: University of California Press, 1972.

Porete, Marguerite. *The Mirror of Simple Souls*. Trans. and intro. Ellen L. Babinsky. New York: Paulist Press, 1993.

Southern, R. W. *Western Society and the Church in the Middle Ages*. Harmondsworth: Penguin, 1975. 319–322.

W. M. Spellman

RAZIYA, THE SULTAN
(also Raziyya, Razia, Radiyya)
(no dates)
India
Muslim Queen

Sultan Raziya ruled in northern India from 1236 to 1240 as a Muslim ruler, the fifth in the first Muslim dynasty, known as the Slave Kings. Islamic Turks had conquered territory in northern India in the late twelfth century and established a Sultanate of Delhi. Raziya's father chose her as his heir instead of her brothers because she was most able. The author of *Tabakat-i Nasiri*, the only contemporary authority for the period, describes her as wise, fair, generous, and brave. She protected her people, dispensed justice, and led her armies. She dressed as a man and rode at the head of her troops on an elephant. She did all she could to break the power of the Muslim nobles. But despite all her gifts, the fact that she was a woman made her unacceptable to too many of her subjects, and she was able to rule for only four years. She was imprisoned and later killed. Because of the horror so many felt over having a woman ruler, Raziya's rule was ignored or slandered by many historians.

Raziya's father Iltutmish Kutb-ud-Din ascended the throne of Delhi in 1210 or 1211 and immediately fought to keep his rivals from taking over his territory. Most of his reign was spent fighting both Hindu and other Muslim chiefs in an attempt to consolidate his empire and make his throne secure. He was successful and by the end of the reign ruled much of northern India. He was not only a brave warrior but also a shrewd and talented ruler who worked to keep his empire independent and to encourage its economy. He built up the city of Delhi so that it was beautiful and a center of learning and culture. He was also intensely religious and always spent part of each night in prayer and meditation.

In 1229 his oldest son and heir, Mahmud, died. Raziya, daughter of Iltutmish's chief wife, Turkan Khatun, lived in the chief royal pal-

ace. Although most females were kept sheltered, her father early recognized her bravery and skill, and after the death of her oldest
brother, he gave her the authority to rule, as regent, while he was
away. In 1229, when he returned from a military campaign, he decided to make her his heir. His counselors were appalled, especially
as the king had other adult sons. They asked him why he would bring
such disrepute to his kingdom by making a woman his heir. The king
told his advisers that his sons were addicted to pleasure and not competent to rule. None of them would be able to manage the affairs of
the country, whereas Raziya was completely worthy to be his heir and
would bring great honor to his realm. The sultan claimed that though
Raziya was a woman, she had both a man's head and a man's heart
and was worth more than twenty useless sons.

Six years later, while on campaign, he became ill and returned to
Delhi carried on a litter. He died on 29 April 1236, having ruled for
over twenty-five years. Iltutmish's second son, Rukn-ud-Din Firuz,
had been with him on his last campaign. Rukn-ud-Din Firuz's
mother, Shah Turkan, in the meantime was doing all she could to
charm the nobles. Possibly Iltutmish, as he was dying, changed his
mind about who should be his heir—or more probably those around
him simply claimed that he did. The important men of the kingdom
supported Firuz as the next heir, and he ascended the throne. The
nobles had done all they could to ensure a masculine succession, but
once Firuz was sultan, he did as his father had feared: He took his
father's treasury to spend on luxury and devoted himself to pleasure.
The new sultan would drunkenly ride his elephant through the streets
of Delhi, scattering wealth. People were appalled by his dissipation
and debauchery. The sultan's mother, in the meantime, was reveling
in the power her position gave her and avenged herself on other
women in Iltutmish's harem. She had a number of them murdered.
Worried that a younger son of Iltutmish might someday be a rival to
his half brother, the queen mother conspired with her son to have
the child blinded and then murdered. Raziya feared with justification
that she would be next.

Nobles throughout the realm almost immediately rebelled. The
sultan left Delhi with an army but found many of his supporters were
deserting him. During this chaotic time, Raziya openly expressed her
hostility toward the queen mother and accused her of conspiring to
have her murdered. She appeared before the people gathered at the
mosque for Friday prayers, dressed in red, the color of one aggrieved,
and appealed for help against her stepmother. She asked the people

to support her, to give her a chance to prove herself, and stated that if she were not better at governing than her brother, they should then cut off her head. Raziya so roused the people's support that they stormed the royal palace and seized her stepmother Shah Turkan. When the sultan returned to the capital, he found the city in revolt and his mother in prison. People flocked to Delhi to support Raziya, and in November 1236 she assumed the throne and the title of "Sultan" with the royal suffix Duniya wa-ud-Din added to her name. Her brother was taken, imprisoned, and soon after murdered. His reign had lasted less than seven months. Raziya did all she could to restore order to her realm. The fact that she had come to power via the support of the people instead of the nobility upset some of the most powerful men in the realm.

Almost immediately Raziya herself also faced a rebellion, led by dissident Muslims. Raziya left Delhi to establish camp and support her soldiers. The rebellion was soon suppressed, and peace was restored to the kingdom. Raziya did all she could to take care of her subjects. She was a patron of the arts. She was a devout Muslim who read the Koran, the Muslim book of sacred writings, but she attempted to treat her Hindu subjects fairly and insisted that all her people were treated justly. The nobles came to Delhi to swear their loyalty to her and pay homage, but some may well have supported her because they thought as a woman she could be easily manipulated, and they would be able to retain power. They also did not like her toleration of Hindus. Raziya worked to have loyal and intelligent men help her, and one she chose was Malik Jamal-ud-Din Yakut, who was known as the Ethiopian, as that was his place of origin. She gave him the important position of Master of the Horse. The nobles were envious and angry to see someone not of their group receive favor, and rumors spread that he was her lover. Although many later chroniclers repeated the story, in part because they could not accept that an unmarried woman would rule alone, scholars today argue that there is no evidence of impropriety and that this was slander to discredit Raziya. At the same time, Raziya decided that she must show everyone that she was indeed in charge and rode through the streets unveiled and in a male costume so that all could see her. Raziya had visually underscored that she would defy the expectations for women's behavior. She refused to be a figurehead.

Just as her father had had to constantly deal with unrest, so too did Raziya. Raziya, herself at the head of her army, led her forces into the Punjab against rebels and forced their submission. Raziya returned in triumph to Delhi, but the peace was again short-lived. Malik Ikhtiyar-ud-Din Altuniya, who had received his first fief from Raziya herself when she had ascended the throne, rebelled with the secret aid of some of the court nobles. Raziya again set out herself to confront the new rebel, but at Tabarhindah the faithful Yakut was killed, and she was imprisoned.

When news of the debacle reached Delhi, her brother Muiz-ud-Din Bahram Shah assumed power, and the nobles who had betrayed Raziya returned to Delhi and paid homage to the new sultan. Bahram was, however, as weak as his brother, and soon several of the nobles had taken control and ruled in his name. Bahram eventually had two of the nobles murdered.

Raziya had not given up, however. In a move that must have surprised many, she married her erstwhile enemy, Altuniya, and the two headed an army to go regain her throne. A number of the nobles flocked to join them. Bahram Shah left Delhi at the head of his troops. In October 1240, Raziya's forces were defeated, and she and her husband were subsequently killed. There are a number of versions of her death. They were possibly murdered by Hindus to whom Raziya and her husband had turned for support. Or possibly they were killed by a peasant after fleeing the battlefield. Another version suggests they were killed by soldiers. Whatever the manner of her death, it was the violent end of a brief reign. She had been queen for only three and a half years.

Although Raziya's reign was a short and turbulent one, she was the only woman ever to rule India in her own right. She was not sultana but sultan, not queen but crowned king. Though she was her father's heir, the nobles had ignored her claim. Raziya had refused to accept this and gained power by appealing to the people—the first time in the history of the Delhi Sultanate that the people of Delhi, not the nobles, had decided the succession. Raziya maintained the support of the people in Delhi itself. It was only when she left the capital that she lost power. She was indeed the best of the children of Iltutmish.

BIBLIOGRAPHY

Allan, J. A., T. W. Haig, and H. H. Dodwell. *Cambridge Shorter History of India*. Cambridge: Cambridge University Press, 1934.

Brijbhushan, Jamila. *Sultan Raziya. Her Life and Times: A Reappraisal*. New Delhi: Manohar Publications, 1990.

Carole Levin

RENÉE OF FERRARA
(1510–1574)
France
Protestant Reformer and Political Leader

Renée was the second daughter of King Louis XII of France and his wife Anne de Bretagne. Renée's father and mother died when she was four years old, and her earliest education took place within the court of her brother-in-law, King Francis I. Her closest companion during the years at court seems to have been the king's sister Marguerite. Although Marguerite was some eighteen years older than Renée, her attachment to a form of Christian humanism that focused on inner spiritual reform may have had a lasting impact on Renée. The spread of new ideas hostile to the Roman Catholic Church hierarchy, and Marguerite's protection of the advocates of reform within the Church, cannot have been unknown to Renée, and her own actions in later years testify to the importance of this early friendship.

In 1528 Renée married Ercole d'Este, eldest son of Alfonso I, Duke of Ferrara, Italy. It must have been difficult, at age eighteen, to be removed from the exciting life of a major European court and relocated to a minor Italian duchy against her will. The marriage had been arranged by the king as part of an ongoing diplomatic effort to expand French influence in Italy. Renée left France with great reluctance, and once in Ferrara, she surrounded herself with French courtiers, much to the disappointment of her husband. The following year the alliance between Ferrara and France that had occasioned the marriage was repudiated, making Renée's "exile" all the more painful.

When King Francis I of France began a campaign against religious dissent in 1534, a number of recent converts to the Reformed faith, including the youthful John Calvin, fled the country. And although we do not know the nature of her own religious opinions at the time, Renée allowed a number of these refugees to take up residence in Ferrara. By 1536 Renée's court had become known as a refuge for French religious reformers. Her husband, now eager to secure an alliance with the papacy, had some of these Frenchmen arrested and prosecuted for heresy. Renée managed to secure their release and safe passage to Venice, but her husband was outraged by these efforts, understandably associating his wife with Protestant Reformers. Her private secretary, Lyon Jamet, was a known dissenter from the Roman Catholic Church, whereas another French heretic named Clement Marot also spent upwards of a year at court under Renée's protection.

In 1536 Calvin himself was a visitor at the duchess's court, and although the author of the *Institutes of the Christian Religion* ultimately settled in Geneva, Calvin and Renée maintained a lifelong correspondence. Calvin was eager to recruit noblewomen to the Protestant cause because he knew the success of the movement depended in no small part on the support of the aristocracy; securing the public conversion of a French Princess of the Blood would have been an important accomplishment from Calvin's perspective. It is a significant fact that the Protestant theologian Theodore Beza dedicated the first edition of Calvin's collected *Works* to Renée of Ferrara in 1566. Calvin and Renée never met again after that first encounter in 1536, but his brief presence at her court signaled the key nature of her work in assisting those Frenchmen who were persecuted at home for their religious convictions.

In 1547 Renée intervened with her husband on behalf of an Italian Protestant named Fanino Fanini, but her appeals were in vain, and Fanini was executed. She had already been examined by the Italian inquisition in 1543, and ten years later, King Henry II of France sent Mattieu Ory, Inquisitor-General and Prior of the Dominicans of Paris, to Ferrara in order to convince Renée of her need for repentance. The Roman Catholic Counter-Reformation was now under way, and these activities were supported by Ignatius of Loyola, head of the Society of Jesus (Jesuits) and, like Calvin, a man eager to enlist noblewomen in the struggle against the enemy.

After enormous pressure, including imprisonment and a threat by her husband to remove their children from her care, Renée capitulated and publicly returned to the Roman Catholic fold in 1555. Calvin had gone so far as to send an ally, François Morel, to Ferrara in order to persuade Renée not to bend to Roman Catholic intimidation. When this effort failed, Calvin wrote to a number of other Protestant leaders expressing disappointment at Renée's submission. Despite the public return to Rome, however, it is clear that Renée continued to support Protestants financially during the remainder of her years in Italy. Circumspect about her own beliefs, she was unwilling to abandon those who embraced the Reformed faith.

Returning to France upon the death of her husband and establishing her court at Montargis, east of Orleans, in 1560, Renée extended her earlier efforts in support of Protestant Reformers. Religious civil war was about to begin in France, and Renée decided to remain in the background during these conflicts. She befriended Gaspard II de Coligny, head of the Huguenot Protestant army in France, but she was also mother-in-law to Francis, Duke of Guise, leader of the Catholic forces. Although she attempted to maintain neutrality during the long conflict, the patronage of women like Renée was key to the survival of the Reformed cause during these wars of religion (1562–1589). She was joined in this work by a number of powerful noblewomen, including Marguerite de France, sister of King Henry II. Calvin sent spiritual advisers from Geneva, but they quarreled with Renée because she wanted to attend meetings of the synod or council of church elders.

Renée's work of granting refuge and repose to those who suffered during the decades of religious conflict was part of a larger movement by aristocratic women to forward the cause of the Protestant Reformers. Of the thirty-seven women arrested at a Protestant demonstration in Paris in 1557, half were of noble birth. In Renée's case, it is probably fair to say that her religious views were of a highly personal nature. Unwilling to openly embrace the teachings of the major Protestant Reformers, she extended her sympathy to victims of intolerance across the Catholic and Protestant religious divide.

BIBLIOGRAPHY

Bainton, Roland H. *Women of the Reformation in Germany and Italy.* Minneapolis: Augsburg Publishing House, 1971.

Jenkins-Blaisdell, Charmarie. "Renée de France between Reform and Counter-Reform." *Archiv für Reformations-geschicte* 63 (1972): 196–226.

W. M. Spellman

MARGARET MORE ROPER
(ca. 1505–1544)
Britain
Humanist and Classical Scholar

The children of Sir Thomas More (1478–1535), chancellor of England from 1529 to 1532, and his first wife Jane Colt (d. 1511) received an excellent humanist education, a remarkable event for the time. As a result of her training, More's eldest daughter, Margaret, enjoys a place in the history of women as an accomplished female scholar. Margaret More Roper's status as an English humanist, a classical scholar, and a woman of letters represents a singular accomplishment, one that the humanist Desiderius Erasmus (1466–1536) acknowledged by referring to Margaret as the "ornament of Britain."

More's decision to provide training in humanist studies for all his children—Margaret, her sisters Elizabeth and Cecily, her brother John, and others attached to the More household, such as More's adopted daughter **Margaret Giggs Clement**—was truly unique. The students' classical education included instruction in grammar, rhetoric, and logic. The children learned to master Greek and Latin. Other subjects included theology, philosophy, astronomy, and medicine. To achieve his educational aim, More employed numerous tutors, including John Clement, the Greek scholar and physician, and Nicholas Kratzer, the astronomer, both of whom served at the Tudor court of King Henry VIII of England (ruled 1509–1547).

By the time Juan Luis Vivés (1492–1540) published his *Instruction of a Christian Woman* (1523), in which he praised More's daughters for their learning, the girls had already become accomplished scholars. Their fame continued to grow, and even Henry VIII was curious enough about the girls' learning to invite Margaret and at least one of her sisters to dispute before him.

Whether or not women should receive such training was frequently debated at the time More chose to provide his children, irrespective of gender, with a humanist education. In a letter written to William Gonnell, one of his children's tutors, More states his reasons for ex-

Margaret More Roper by Hans Holbein the Younger. Courtesy of The Metropolitan Museum of Art, Rogers Fund, 1950 (50.69.2). Reprinted with permission.

tending instruction on "humane letters and liberal studies" to his daughters. More argued for the practical uses of such an education. An educated woman would be pious, charitable, and humble. Her husband would profit from her company, while her children would benefit from their mother's learned guidance and instruction. Such a woman would enjoy an ideal union with her husband. Through his daughters' education, Sir Thomas More hoped to effect these goals.

In Tudor England, the Ropers' household, along with More's, could be counted as being among the most literate. Margaret More married William Roper (ca. 1498–1578) in 1521. After her marriage, her father encouraged his brilliant daughter to continue her training in sacred literature and medical science, along with her training in liberal studies.

In addition to continuing her own studies, Margaret More Roper arranged for her children—three girls and two boys—to receive a humanist education similar to her own. At one point, Margaret tried to employ Roger Ascham, a leading humanist educator who eventually worked for the future Queen Elizabeth I (ruled 1558–1603), as her children's tutor. Although her attempt failed, Margaret clearly wished to educate her children as she had been educated; and in doing so, Margaret was fulfilling one of the humanist goals for a well-educated woman. She also assured the transmission of her father's educational system to another generation of young women who could reap the benefits of having received training in humanist studies. Mary Clarke Basset (fl. 1553–1558) proved to be the most gifted of Margaret's daughters. Basset translated one of Sir Thomas More's incomplete works (*Treatise on the Passion*) from Latin to English, a translation that later appeared in the published 1557 edition of More's works.

Margaret More Roper's most important surviving work is her translation of Erasmus's commentary on the Lord's Prayer entitled *Precatio dominica in septem portiones distributa* (Basle 1523). Her skillful translation of its Latin meanings into English provides evidence for her high level of scholarly achievement. Although a young woman, and only the daughter of a knight, Margaret's extraordinary abilities so impressed European intellects that her *Devout Treatise upon the Paternoster* was printed, and by the early 1530s, the work had gone into three editions. Margaret's translation secured her place among sixteenth-century humanist scholars.

Margaret's connections with Erasmus and his humanist network were probably well established by 1524. Erasmus had dedicated one of his works, a hymn by Prudentius, to Margaret in 1523, upon the birth of her child. Erasmus also accepted Margaret's emendation of a corrupt passage from St. Cyprian, and he paid her a supreme compliment when he chose to include it in his edition of St. Cyprian's works. Margaret's ability to emend this corrupt passage further demonstrates her capable scholarship.

Along with Margaret's published translation of Erasmus's treatise, important letters that her father wrote to her while he was being held in the Tower on charges of treason have also survived. More wrote eight of thirteen surviving prison letters to Margaret. Three of these hold particular significance because they record the details of several of More's interrogations. More apparently hoped that the letters he wrote would be circulated, with the result of justifying his position.

Perhaps the most significant letter still extant is the letter of reply to Lady Alice Allington, which Margaret and her father may have written together. In the form of a reply to Lady Allington, More presents a sophisticated dialogue in which he analyzes his "case of conscience."

Additional works written by Margaret that have not survived include epistles and orations in Latin and a work her father thought to be better written than his own attempt on the same subject, a treatise on the *Four Last Things* (hell and heaven, death and judgment) (ca. 1522). Margaret is also credited with having written poetry. While scholars may view the loss of Margaret's works with regret, Margaret herself seems to have had little interest in gaining widespread literary fame. When she learned that a bishop had been attempting a translation from Greek to Latin of the early Church historian Eusebius's (ca. fourth century) *Ecclesiastical History*, with characteristic humility Margaret set aside her own translation of the same work.

After More's execution in 1535, Margaret, along with More's adopted daughter, Margaret Giggs Clement, lovingly oversaw the interment of his corpse at the Chapel of St. Peter ad Vincula in the Tower. Later, Margaret would bribe a guard to receive her father's head, which she then preserved. Family members continued to protect the head until its final interment in the Roper family vault in St. Dunstan's, Canterbury.

In the troubled years that followed More's death, religious tensions continued to plague England. Margaret More Roper and Margaret Giggs Clement, along with other members of their families, found themselves being watched and persecuted. These two brave women remained loyal to More's memory even after his execution for treason, and both of them heroically endured an interrogation by Henry VIII's ministers.

An esteemed scholar, and a devoted daughter, wife, and mother, Margaret More Roper represents the ideal female humanist of her father's aspirations. Published or not, Margaret More Roper's literary output clearly anticipates the future contributions of the exceptionally gifted women writers who would be born to succeeding generations and who would distinguish themselves by producing impressive literary works of their own.

BIBLIOGRAPHY

Beilin, Elaine V. "Learning and Virtue: Margaret More Roper." In *Redeeming Eve: Women Writers of the English Renaissance*. Princeton, NJ: Princeton University Press, 1987. 3–28.

King, Margaret L. *Women of the Renaissance.* Women in Culture and Society. Chicago: University of Chicago Press, 1991.

McCutcheon, Elizabeth. "Education of Thomas More's Daughters: Concepts and Praxis." In Roger L. Hadlich and J. D. Ellsworth, eds.,
East Meets West: Homage to Edgar C. Knowlton, Jr. Honolulu: De-
partment of European Languages and Literature, 1988. 193–207.

Reynolds, E. E. *Margaret Roper: Eldest Daughter of St. Thomas More.* New
York: Kennedy, 1960.

Warnicke, Retha M. *Women of the English Renaissance and Reformation.*
Contributions in Women's Studies, No. 38. Westport, CT: Greenwood, 1983.

Debra Barrett-Graves

MARIA DE SALINAS
(d. 1539)
Spain
Friend and Supporter of Catherine of Aragon

Maria de Salinas, Lady Willoughby, was the closest friend of the English king Henry VIII's first wife, Catherine of Aragon. She managed to be with her when she died even though Henry VIII forbade it, a daring and courageous act for a sixteenth-century woman. Maria was the daughter of Don Martin de Salinas and Dona Josepha Gonzales de Salas of Spain. As a young girl, she replaced her cousin Maria de Rojas in the retinue of Catherine of Aragon during the reign of Henry VII of England after the cousin returned to Spain to be married. Maria may well have been attractive by the lights of her age because in 1501, at the time of the marriage of Catherine and Arthur, Henry VII's eldest son, Henry insisted that the ladies who served Catherine should be good looking. This was not for his own pleasure but for the pragmatic reason he thought it would be easier to find them husbands and so relieve him of the cost of a large suite of retainers for Catherine.

Maria came during a hard time for Catherine, since she was the widow of Henry VII's eldest son, Prince Arthur, who had died in the spring of 1502 only five months after the wedding, and there were grave doubts about her future. By 1507 the people around Catherine recognized that she considered Maria to be her closest friend. The years of Catherine's widowhood in the reign of Henry VII were very difficult for Catherine and her suite. Her father Ferdinand of Aragon refused to send her money since he expected Henry to take care of her, whereas Henry VII said Ferdinand, rather than he, was responsible for Catherine's household expenses. While Catherine hoped to marry Arthur's younger brother Henry, his father the king kept his options open for the marriage of his only remaining son, and no one knew what Catherine's fate would be. Maria was one of the few who was thoroughly loyal to Catherine, and the bond forged between them was never broken. Catherine wrote to her father about Maria

Maria de Salinas. Courtesy of the Peterborough Museum
and Art Gallery. Reprinted with permission.

that she always faithfully served her, and when things were difficult
for Catherine, she would always have comfort from Maria.

When Henry VII died in 1509, the new young king, Henry VIII,
made the decision to marry Catherine. Maria was her favorite lady-
in-waiting and one of the few Spaniards who remained with Catherine. The Spanish ambassador was, in fact, upset by Maria's influence
on Catherine, especially her encouraging the queen to support English interests over Spain and to do whatever she could to gain the
love of her husband and her new people. Maria had a great deal of
influence, reported Luis Caroz in 1514, because Catherine loved her
more than any other. Catherine did not want Maria to return to Spain
and helped to find her an English husband.

In June 1514, after becoming a naturalized English citizen, Maria
married William, 10th Baron Willoughby d'Eresby, becoming his second wife. Henry and Catherine were in attendance. They were in
such favor with Catherine and Henry that the king and queen lent
them Greenwich Palace for their honeymoon and presented them

with the manor of Grimsthorpe in Lincolnshire as a wedding present. Henry also named one of his ships the *Mary Willoughby*. In June 1520, the Willoughbys accompanied the king and queen as part of Catherine's entourage when they went to France to the lavish meeting with Francis I known as the Field of the Cloth of Gold, held outside Calais. Willoughby was Henry's Master of the Royal Hart Hounds until his death in 1526. Even though she was married, Maria often returned to court to serve the queen. Maria was one of a very select group who had a room provided for her at court near Catherine's. Maria became more and more concerned for her queen in the late 1520s as Henry sought to annul his marriage since he and Catherine had no living sons, only their daughter Mary, born in 1516.

Like her mistress, Maria also had trouble providing her husband with an heir. Her two sons, Henry and Francis, died as infants. In 1520 she had a daughter, **Catherine (Willoughby)**, named for the queen. After her husband's death she fought with her husband's brother Christopher to protect her daughter's position and holdings. They disputed what Willoughby had left to his heirs male (thus his brother) and what to his heirs general (his daughter). Two years after her father's death, Catherine became the ward of Charles Brandon, the Duke of Suffolk, and he intervened in the family quarrel on the side of Maria and her daughter. Suffolk was a close friend and brother-in-law of Henry VIII, having married his younger sister Mary. Catherine and her mother Maria were among the chief mourners at Mary's funeral in 1533.

Only a few months after the death of his wife, the Duke of Suffolk married his ward. Maria approved of the marriage in part because she saw it as a way to have Charles Brandon be more sympathetic to her old friend Queen Catherine. By this time Henry had broken with the Catholic Church, and Thomas Cranmer, Archbishop of Canterbury, had declared the marriage of Henry and Catherine null and void, and Henry had announced his marriage to Anne Boleyn. Catherine, however, refused to accept that she had never been the true wife of Henry, that her daughter Mary was illegitimate, and that she should accept the title of princess dowager. At that point Maria was dividing her time between her home in Suffolk and her London house. The last time she saw Catherine was 1532, since as punishment for refusing to accept the divorce Henry was isolating Catherine and refused Maria's request that she could go to her. Maria, however, continued to receive news of her beloved mistress.

When Maria heard that Catherine was dying in December 1535, she begged Thomas Cromwell, Henry's Principal Secretary, to intercede with the king and allow her to visit Catherine. But no such permission was forthcoming. Undaunted, Maria made her way to Kimbolton Castle; it was a dangerous and difficult trip on horseback for a no longer young woman. She left before dawn with a small retinue of servants and rode through a bleak and barren countryside, knowing she was at risk of being intercepted by bandits. After riding all day, she arrived in the evening at the beginning of the new year. Sir Edmund Bedingfield, whom Henry VIII had put in charge of Catherine, shouted from across the moat that he could not admit her since she had no permission from the king. Maria told him he did not have a choice. She stated that it was a foul night and the roads were terrible. Moreover, she had fallen from her horse. She did not care what orders Bedingfield had; she was not going away. At his wits' end, Bedingfield finally allowed her to enter, and she went straight to Catherine's rooms and stayed with Catherine until the end. Catherine died in the arms of her oldest friend on 7 January 1536.

For the last years of Maria's life she lived with her daughter and the duke, dying three years after her beloved mistress. Although she was not punished for disobeying the king to be with the dying Catherine of Aragon, as she might well have been, when Maria herself died one might have expected her to have a formal and ceremonial funeral as befitted the mother of the second-ranking duchess in the realm. There is, however, no record of her funeral, and in this way Henry may well have been taking his revenge. We do not know Maria de Salinas's final resting place, but legend has it she was buried near Catherine as was her request.

BIBLIOGRAPHY

Claremont, Francesca. *Catherine of Aragon*. London: Robert Hale, 1939.
Goff, Cecilie. *A Woman of the Tudor Age*. London: John Murray, 1930.
Mattingly, Garrett. *Catherine of Aragon*. Boston: Little, Brown, 1941.
Read, Evelyn. *My Lady Suffolk, a Portrait of Catherine Willoughby, Duchess of Suffolk*. New York: Knopf, 1963.

Carole Levin

SEI SHŌNAGON
(ca. 965?–?)
Japan
Heian Diarist and Waka Poet

Sei Shōnagon merits recognition for her singular role as one of Japan's greatest prose writers. Historians esteem *The Pillow Book* (*Makura no sōshi*) as an invaluable compendium of court events and customs, making it one of the most important documents to have survived from the Heian period (794–1192). In addition to *The Pillow Book*, Shōnagon has left behind a small collection (*shū*) of poems entitled the *Sei Shōnagon shū*. The exceptional quality of Shōnagon's prose writing, rather than her surviving *waka* ("Japanese poem" with thirty-one syllables), ranks her among the best poets of her time.

When the acknowledged poetic genius **Ono no Komachi** (ca. 830/835–899) began writing her poems, the unique cultural advances associated with the Heian period had started to flourish, having been initially influenced by two continental cultures: China and Korea. During the late tenth and early eleventh centuries, at the acknowledged height of the Heian culture's amazing literary achievements, a group of uniquely gifted female authors produced works of exceptionally high quality, some in poetry and others in prose.

The appearance of these impressive literary masterpieces, which were written around the turn of the century (ca. 1000), is partially attributed to the existence of a phonetic writing system known as *kana*. The existence of *kana* gave women the means to express themselves in writing. Additionally, court ladies-in-waiting enjoyed a stimulating social environment and had adequate leisure time in which to write, along with access to paper, all of which facilitated the production of their literary works.

Two prose works that depict life in the Heian court around the turn of the tenth century represent historically important documents of the highest significance, and many people also regard them as being among the greatest contributions to Japanese literature. Lady **Murasaki Shikibu**'s *The Tale of Genji* (*Genji monogatari*), seen as the world's oldest novel, is also valued for its historical content. *Genji* definitely constitutes a preeminent contribution to Japanese literature. Because *The Tale of Genji* (ca. 1010) remains primarily a work of fiction, others consider *The Pillow Book* by Sei Shōnagon to hold even greater historical significance and to be worthy of the esteem in which it, too, is held.

The name of *The Pillow Book*'s author—"Sei"—reflects a Sino-Japanese rendering of the first character—"Kiyo"—in her surname—"Kiyowara." The remainder of her name—"Shōnagon" ("Minor Counselor")—is thought to designate her court rank. New information reveals that her name may have been Nagiko. Shōnagon's birthdate has been placed sometime around 965.

While the identity of Shōnagon's mother has eluded discovery, Shōnagon's lineage on the paternal side discloses an impressive list of scholars and writers. The founder of the Kiyowara clan is Prince Toneri, who helped compile the *Nihongi*, or "Chronicles of Japan" (ca. 720). Natsuno (d. ca. 837), another ancestor, authored a significant work entitled *Commentary on the Penal Code*. Verses attributed to Fukayabu (fl. ca. 905–930), yet another distinguished ancestor, appeared in the first of the royally commissioned imperial *waka* collections (*shū*), the *Kokin[waka]shū* (*Collection of Old and New Japanese Poetry*, ca. 905–920), an anthology that brought together the best works of Japanese poets. A scholar, bureaucrat, and poet, Kiyowara no Motosuke (908–990), Shōnagon's presumed father, was one of the Five Gentlemen of the Pear Chamber who compiled the second imperial anthology of *waka* poetry known as the *Gosen[waka]shū* (*Later Collection*, ca. 951).

The only tangible information available about the unique personality known as Sei Shōnagon, other than what can be gleaned from *The Pillow Book* itself, comes from a comment by her contemporary Murasaki Shikibu. In her diary, Murasaki Shikibu discloses her distaste for Shōnagon, declaring her intolerance of Shōnagon's "knowing look." What *The Pillow Book* provides is a character sketch of a personable woman with an engaging intellect.

While Shōnagon probably received some formal training in *waka* and had familiarity with fragments of Chinese literature, she always earned the highest praise for her remarkable readiness of wit. Shōnagon attended at court as a high-ranking lady-in-waiting, serving the Empress Fujiwara no Teishi (Sadako) (ca. 976–1000) for a period of approximately seven to ten years at the imperial court of Heiankyō (ca. 990/993–1000). Sadako was the royal consort of the Emperor Ichijō Tennō (980–1011; ruled 986–1011), as well as the daughter of the powerful head of the Fujiwara clan: Fujiwara no Michitaka (d. 993). When Empress Sadako died, accounts indicate that Shōnagon married Fujiwara no Muneyo (fl. ca. 995–999), with whom she is believed to have had a daughter, Koma no Myōbu. What her life was like after her service to Sadako ended remains a mystery. Traditional accounts paint a bleak end for Shōnagon, relating that she died lonely and impoverished.

At first glance, Shōnagon's *Pillow Book* appears to represent a haphazard arrangement of various topics. Many see it as constituting a hybrid genre: part miscellany, part diary, and part essay. It contains numerous lists, which name flowers and trees, among other entries. Both factual and fictional, *The Pillow Book* records events and impressions of Heian life over a period of approximately ten years. *The Pillow Book* has been called the first true *zuihitsu* (miscellany), although the term *zuihitsu* did not exist in Shōnagon's day. Some scholars suggest that *The Pillow Book* anticipated the genre known as *zuihitsu*, a term loosely defined as meaning "to follow the brush." Other scholars choose to classify *The Pillow Book* as a diary (*nikki*) of the variety being written during the tenth and eleventh centuries, even though its official title lacks the word *nikki*, because *The Pillow Book* recreates portions of Shōnagon's life. While the date of *The Pillow Book* is uncertain (ca. 990–1010), the members of the court knew of its existence, whether complete or not, by circa 996.

The Pillow Book's sections, or chapters, are generally agreed to constitute more than a mere collection of facts. One reason for its seemingly informal character is the result of its uncertain textual history. The earliest manuscripts did not appear until many years after Shōnagon's death. Over the centuries, copyists and scholars are believed to have altered the original manuscript through a series of unintentional mistakes and intentional improvements. Two different versions of *The Pillow Book* have come down to posterity: manuscripts organized according to the miscellaneous tradition and manuscripts organized according to the classified tradition, with modern texts following for the most part a miscellaneous format.

Given its detailed account of customs and events at the Heian court, scholars revere *The Pillow Book* for the important historical information it has preserved. *The Pillow Book* also provides readers today with insight into the consciousness of a woman who comments on the highborn women of the Heian period, who provides a detailed look at their world, and who discloses her own engaging personality. *The Pillow Book,* either directly or indirectly, has inspired many traditional Japanese classics, earning it a distinguished place in the history of Japanese literature.

BIBLIOGRAPHY

Fischer, Felice. "Sei Shōnagon." In Chieko I. Mulhern, ed., *Japanese Women Writers: A Bio-Critical Sourcebook.* Westport, CT: Greenwood, 1994. 339–345.

Jin'ichi Konishi. *A History of Japanese Literature: The Early Middle Ages.* Vol. 2. Trans. Aileen Gatten. Ed. Earl Miner. Princeton, NJ: Princeton University Press, 1986.

McCullough, Helen Craig, ed. *Classical Japanese Prose: An Anthology.* Stanford: Stanford University Press, 1990.

Morris, Ivan. *The World of the Shining Prince: Court Life in Ancient Japan.* New York: Kodansha, 1994.

Morris, Ivan, trans. *The Pillow Book of Sei Shōnagon.* New York: Columbia University Press, 1991.

Shuichi Kato. *A History of Japanese Literature: The First Thousand Years.* Trans. David Chibett. Tokyo: Kodansha, 1979.

Waley, Arthur, trans. *The Pillow Book of Sei Shōnagon.* Boston: Houghton Mifflin, 1929.

Debra Barrett-Graves

CATERINA SFORZA
(1462–1509)
Italy
Territorial Ruler

Although the circumstances of her birth were far from glorious, Caterina Sforza became one of the most powerful women in fifteenth-century Italy. She was born in 1462, the illegitimate daughter of the powerful Galeazzo Maria Sforza, the second Sforza Duke of Milan. At the time of her birth, however, her father was not yet the duke; he was a lively prince of eighteen who had become enamored with Lucrezia Landriani, the wife of a close friend; Lucrezia would eventually bear Galeazzo three other children in addition to Caterina.

When Caterina was four her father became Duke of Milan. He assumed responsibility for his children; their illegitimacy did not prevent him from providing them with an aristocratic upbringing. At age ten, Caterina was betrothed to Girolamo Riaro, a man of simple origins who rose to immense power as the nephew of Pope Sixtus IV. Galeazzo intended the marriage to secure an alliance between his family in Milan and the papacy in Rome. Girolamo came to Milan to confirm the betrothal with magnificent gifts for his future bride; he then returned to Rome, leaving Caterina behind to mature and continue her education. For the next few years, Girolamo increased his political power in Rome and gained control over Imola, a small but politically and strategically important town in the Romagna area of northeast Italy.

Plans for Caterina's future were accelerated in 1476 when her father was brutally assassinated by political enemies. In order to preserve the planned alliance between Milan and Rome, Caterina was hastily married to Girolamo; she was just fourteen. In 1478, their first child was born; Caterina would eventually give birth to nine children. She grew up quickly from a shy young girl to a beautiful, confident wife and mother. One of her favorite pastimes was hunting; she owned several beloved hunting dogs and horses. She also had an avid interest in collecting and experimenting with recipes for cosmetics

Portrait of Caterina Sforza. Credit: Alinari/Art Resource, NY. Reprinted with permission.

and medicines, and she compiled a massive collection of her findings. Her ambitious husband, meanwhile, was occupied with increasing their landholdings in northern Italy, acquiring the town of Forli near their territory of Imola.

For the next several years, their marriage was marked by travel between their Imola and Forli estates and their residences in Rome; wherever they lived, turbulence followed. In Imola and Forli, rebellious families threatened their power, and in Rome, Girolamo was embroiled in the wars between various Italian factions. In spite of Caterina's continuous pregnancies, she became increasingly involved in the management of their territories. She was a courageous and capable leader, but she was also severe and often cunning.

Girolamo's powerful foothold in Rome was lost when his protector, Pope Sixtus, died in 1484. Those angry at Sixtus's reign took revenge by looting palaces and attacking his supporters. In the ensuing chaos, Girolamo was ordered to stay outside the city, but Caterina, seven months pregnant, ignored the orders and rode into Rome, taking possession of their castle and refusing to yield until a compromise was reached with the new Pope. Girolamo was granted the position of governor of Imola and Forli in exchange for their voluntary exile from Rome.

Forli now became their permanent residence, and they established themselves as rulers of the Romagna area; however, they were faced with a number of problems: earthquakes, droughts, famine, poverty, plague, and endless uprisings from rival families. Caterina and Girolamo were stern leaders, and their marriage was often strained, largely because of financial concerns; Caterina had to pawn her jewelry because they had lost so much of their property when Pope Sixtus died.

In early 1487 Caterina returned to Milan, her first visit since her marriage, but after a few weeks, she received news that Girolamo was ill. She rushed back to Forli to care for him, bringing her mother, Lucrezia, and her sisters with her. Girolamo survived the illness but never fully recovered, so Caterina assumed full rule. She decided to fortify the area against external threats by ensuring the security of their most important fortress, Ravaldino. Though heavily pregnant, she rode to the fortress one night and demanded its surrender, but when its controller refused, she arranged his murder and took over the castle; shortly afterward she gave birth to her seventh child.

The rival factions persisted, however, and on 14 April 1488 Girolamo was assassinated. Caterina resisted, but she and her family were taken prisoner. The palace was savagely looted, and Girolamo's corpse was mutilated by the mobs. Caterina, her six children, Girolamo's illegitimate son, their nurses, Caterina's mother, and her two sisters were all imprisoned in a small room of the tower gatehouse. The crowded, miserable conditions of captivity were intended to force Caterina to order her fortress keepers to surrender, but she steadfastly refused. One guard insisted that if he could speak directly with Caterina, he would convince her to persuade her forces to surrender. Her captors decided that it was safe to permit her to enter the fortress for negotiations, since they held her family hostage.

What followed has now become the material of legend. The drawbridge to the fortress was lowered, she walked across, and then she turned and hurled insults at her enemies, claiming that she had no intention of surrendering her castle. Her attackers threatened to murder her children, but she ignored them; for the next several days, they waited for her to yield, but she outlasted them. Eventually the rebels' support and resolve weakened and Caterina prevailed.

On 30 April 1488, she reassumed control of Forli and Imola, ordering the restoration of all looted property and the severe punishment of all rebels. The vengeance exacted against the traitors was grisly and deliberately public so the people could witness the consequences of disloyalty. Then, in an equally public ceremony designed to strengthen her image as a ruler, she ordered all of the men of Forli to appear before her to proclaim a pledge of loyalty.

In the following years, Caterina had various love affairs; one of the most serious was with Giacomo Feo, a captain in Caterina's army. As Caterina became increasingly enamored with Feo, she elevated him with various honors and positions of power. The people became increasingly displeased by his arrogance, and their dissatisfaction increased when she gave birth to his son. Poverty and bad crops added to the unrest of the people, which Caterina tried to mitigate by reinstituting city councils, reducing taxes, and restricting soldier activity.

Caterina was also beset by the external turmoil between Naples and Milan. Although she tried to remain neutral, she was pulled into the wars; many of her people survived because they took refuge in Caterina's fortresses, but their property and countryside suffered much ruin. Soon after, Feo was brutally murdered, and Caterina again ordered severe punishments for the assassins, just as she had when her husband was murdered.

Caterina turned to restoration and repair of her community; she also turned, once again, to love when she married Giovanni de' Medici from the powerful Florentine family in 1497. In 1498 she gave birth to a son; soon after, Giovanni died of a fever. In spite of her grief, Caterina remained an active ruler. The contentious political climate grew worse when Cesare Borgia, the ruthless son of Pope Alexander VI, joined with France to drive out the ruling families of northern Italy, especially the Sforza. A papal bull granted Cesare Borgia possession of Imola and Forli. Rulers in the surrounding areas fled from Borgia's imminent takeover, and Caterina was advised to seek refuge in Florence, but passive strategy was not her style. Determined to resist, she fortified the city walls, laid in supplies, and destroyed all of the homes and trees outside of the wall that might provide enemy cover, including the beautiful parks that she had established.

Realizing that much of Cesare Borgia's power derived from his father, the Pope, she hatched another plan; she sent letters to the pontiff that were allegedly tainted with poison or covered in cloth that had touched plague victims. The plot was discovered, which added to Borgia's desire to conquer Caterina's territories. With thousands of troops, he first marched on Imola, which surrendered immediately. He then turned to Forli where Caterina held fast in the fortress of Ravaldino. The people of the outer city "gave themselves up like whores," wrote one chronicler, though the rape, murder, and pillage that followed led them to regret their disloyalty to Caterina.

On Christmas morning, Cesare Borgia rode out to Ravaldino. From beyond the moat, he called out to Caterina, offering peace in exchange for surrender. She refused; he tried again the next day, and again she refused. The Pope sent an envoy and still she refused to yield. An enraged Borgia began his attack, which, to his surprise and dismay, lasted several days, with Caterina and her soldiers fighting valiantly. The constant bombardment eventually created a gap in the walls, and Borgia's men stormed the fortress. Caterina resisted even when her own men yielded, but she was eventually captured, and according to some historians, she was repeatedly raped by Borgia.

Cesare Borgia then returned to Rome with his famous captive. The Pope demanded Caterina's concession to her properties in writing, but she refused, so she was imprisoned in a dungeon for over a year, suffering enormously from the horrific conditions. She was finally released in 1501 after agreeing to relinquish rights to her property and was granted safety in Florence. Although weakened and aged by her imprisonment, she still maneuvered to regain her territories, but she finally had to accept the end of her political career. Her remaining days were spent attending to the future careers of her children, and she was successful in placing many of them in high offices. Her son by Giovanni de' Medici grew up to become Giovanni della Bande Nere, one of Italy's most famous *condottiere*, or military heroes. Caterina Sforza died at the age of forty-six of a liver ailment. Although she was more universally feared than loved, she was admired by many who were in awe of her courage, ambition, and political power.

BIBLIOGRAPHY

Bradford, Sara. *Cesare Borgia.* New York: Macmillan, 1976.
Breisach, Ernest. *Caterina Sforza: A Renaissance Virago.* Chicago: University of Chicago Press, 1967.

Jo Eldridge Carney

GASPARA STAMPA
(1523–1554)
Italy
Poet and Virtuosa

Although Gaspara Stampa is known as a famous poet and virtuosa singer from Venice, she was actually born in Padua. Her family was not of the aristocracy, but Gaspara's father, a wealthy jeweler, was able to provide his family with a comfortable living. Gaspara, her sister Cassandra, and her brother Baldassare were fortunate enough to receive the type of education usually reserved for aristocrats that included Latin, poetry, history, art, and music. Before Gaspara was ten years old, her father died, so Gaspara's mother, Cecilia, moved her family to her native Venice where they continued their studies.

In the middle of the sixteenth century, the population of Venice was about 160,000, making it the second largest city in Italy. Cecilia Stampa may have decided to take her children to Venice because of the musical atmosphere that was so much a part of Venetian culture. *Virtuosi*, or professional singers and accompanists, were in high demand for both private entertainment and public events. Both Gaspara and her sister were particularly talented in singing and instrumental music; Gaspara sang the poems of the late medieval poet Petrarch to her own accompaniment along with a variety of other musical compositions. There are many contemporary testimonies to the angelic qualities of Gaspara's singing as well as to her intellectual gifts.

In Venice, the Stampa home was also a *ridotti*, or salon, where writers, musicians, artists, and intellectuals gathered and in this glittering world of art and music Gaspara grew up. Such famous writers as Sperone Speroni, Domenico Venier, and Giovanni della Casa frequented the Stampa salon. Gaspara's brother, Baldassare, was also a scholar and a gifted poet whose talents were praised by a number of contemporary authors. Tragically, this admired and talented young man died prematurely in 1544 while he was a student at the University of Padua.

In 1548, Stampa fell in love with Count Collaltino de Collalto, a courtier from a prestigious aristocratic family who had earned an impressive reputation as a noble warrior and a patron of the arts. He was said to be particularly fond of *virtuosi*, which may have led to his initial attraction to Gaspara. They were lovers for three years, although Gaspara's love for Collaltino was a far more consuming passion than what he returned to her. Though Stampa's feelings for the count were only partially requited, her love for him did inspire her to begin writing; she adopted the pseudonym Anaxilla, in reference to a river on the count's property, and she became associated with the intellectual coterie, the Accademia dei Dubbiosi. The events of their love affair resulted in some 200 poems. Stampa sent this collection of poems, along with a letter of dedication, to Collaltino. The amorous poems of longing, praise, and despair were appreciated more by Stampa's literary circle, however, than by Collaltino, the muse and recipient. By 1551, the count ended their relationship. That year was one of deep depression and ill health for Stampa, but she eventually recovered.

Stampa fell in love once more with a member of a prominent patrician family, Bartolomeo Zen. This affair also inspired some sonnets, but otherwise little is known about their relationship. On 23 April 1554, Stampa died of an illness, possibly appendicitis. Numerous tributes followed her death, praising her beauty, her divine singing voice, and her poetry. Many of these writers persuaded Stampa's grief-stricken sister Cassandra to gather her works together for publication; only three of her poems had been published in her lifetime.

Cassandra dedicated her sister's book of poetry, *Rime*, to the writer Giovanni della Casa, a friend of the family. *Rime* included Stampa's own poetry as well as the many sonnets written in her honor. Most of the poems deal with the torments of love, but there are also several occasional poems written to various friends and a few of a religious nature. As well known as Stampa was while she circulated in the Venetian literary world, her reputation faded in the years following her death. Collaltino de Collalto, who had inspired most of Stampa's literary creations, also died an early death.

After 200 years in virtual oblivion, however, Stampa's reputation was resurrected by a descendant of the Collalto family, Antonio Rambaldo. In 1738, Rambaldo decided to reprint her *Rime*, along with poems by Collalto himself. While the republication of Stampa's poetry was valuable, Rambaldo's brief biography of Stampa gave rise to many myths about her life. The biography was highly romanticized; Rambaldo even suggested that in despair for Collalto's love, Stampa poisoned herself. This apocryphal account gave rise to further highly romantic novels and plays about Gaspara Stampa in the eighteenth and nineteenth centuries.

Twentieth-century scholars and critics have turned their attention to the question of whether or not Stampa was a *cortegiana onesta*, or honored courtesan, as was the Venetian poet **Veronica Franco**. The *cortegiana onesta* occupied a unique place in Renaissance Venice, enjoying a status well above the ordinary prostitute; she was an unmarried woman who offered intellectual, cultural, and sexual gifts and who received some financial security and patronage in return. While married women lived more secluded and restricted lives, the *cortegiane oneste* were active participants in the social, intellectual, and cultural milieu of sixteenth-century Venice. Gaspara Stampa was indeed unmarried and beautiful, and her intellectual, musical, and poetic accomplishments were very impressive, but evidence for her status as a *cortegiana onesta* is not conclusive, and the question may never be resolved.

Fortunately, more critical attention is now focused on Stampa's literary production. Like most of her contemporaries, her works owe a great debt in form and content to the lyric poetry of Petrarch. Stampa, however, imbues her poetry with a specifically female voice, charting the emotional fluctations of love that is often tortuous but empowering as well. The twentieth-century German poet Rainer Maria Rilke celebrated Gaspara Stampa in his own works as a woman who, through her art, turns the torment of her unrequited love into a "bitter, icy magnificence."

BIBLIOGRAPHY

Bassanese, Fiora A. *Gaspara Stampa*. Boston: Twayne Publishers, 1982.
Jones, Ann Rosalind. *The Currency of Eros: Women's Love Lyric in Europe, 1540–1620*. Bloomington: Indiana University Press, 1990.

Jo Eldridge Carney

ARBELLA STUART
(1575–1615)
Britain
Scholar and Courtier

At the end of the sixteenth century in England, the last Tudor monarch Elizabeth I's childlessness and refusal to name an heir created both problems and possibilities for a variety of people related to her. For Arbella Stuart, great-granddaughter of Henry VIII's older sister Margaret through her father Charles Stuart, the problems were all too severe. Although Arbella did all she could to fight against the restrictions placed on her and create a life that was satisfying, including a secret marriage, though she crafted much admired letters that demonstrate her literary prowess, her nearness to the throne made her life a tragedy.

In 1574 Lady Margaret Douglas Stuart, Dowager Countess of Lennox, and **Elizabeth Hardwick** (Bess of Hardwick), Countess of Shrewsbury, secretly arranged a marriage between her son, Charles Stuart, Earl of Lennox, and Elizabeth Cavendish, Bess's daughter by her second husband. At the time of the marriage, Charles was his mother's only surviving child; his older brother, Henry Stuart, Lord Darnley, the second husband of Mary Queen of Scots, had been murdered in mysterious circumstances a decade earlier. The mothers deliberately brought the young people together—Charles was nineteen and Elizabeth twenty—and they fell so deeply in love they refused to be parted. The mothers were successful at keeping the arrangement from Queen Elizabeth until after the marriage. The queen was seriously upset when those close to the Crown married, and Margaret Douglas spent some time in the Tower for her part in the plot.

Arbella, born the year following the marriage, was the couple's only child. She was not only a somewhat distant cousin to Elizabeth but through her father the first cousin of James VI of Scotland, who hoped to succeed Elizabeth. Since Arbella was born in England and also related to Elizabeth, some saw her as an alternate heir to the English throne. Arbella was still an infant when her father died in April 1576 of tuberculosis, or consumption as it was then called. Less

Lady Arbella Stuart. Hope Collection, HP 2736. Copyright Ashmolean Museum, Oxford. Reproduced by permission of the Ashmolean.

than six years later, Arbella's mother died after a short illness. She was raised by her maternal grandmother, Bess of Hardwick, Countess of Shrewsbury, who saw to it that Arbella received a thorough classical education. Arbella was fluent in Latin and French and also read Hebrew and Greek. She was a talented musician and skilled at needlework. Throughout her life, she cared deeply about her studies. Also in the household when Arbella was a small child was her aunt Mary Stuart, Mary Queen of Scots. The Earl of Shrewsbury had her in charge, and the strain of controlling the Scottish queen was so great that the earl and the countess separated soon after the death of Arbella's mother. It is probable that Mary Stuart's trial and subsequent execution in 1587 was a frightening reminder to Arbella of the dangers of being too near the throne.

The countess had worked for the marriage in the hopes that she would one day be grandmother to the ruler of England, but Elizabeth did not confer any special recognition on Arbella nor grant her the pension the countess was sure she deserved due to her status. In fact, Elizabeth and James between them absorbed her entire inheritance in England and Scotland, and Arbella never had the financial resources her position dictated. During her childhood her grandmother doted on Arbella and was sure she was a future queen, but Elizabeth was not welcoming of the idea. She was highly suspicious of any plans to have Arbella married and insisted she be kept under close watch. Elizabeth's favorite, Robert Dudley, the Earl of Leceister, attempted to arrange a marriage between Arbella and his infant son, but the boy died at the age of four in 1584. In 1587 and 1588 Elizabeth invited the young Arbella to court, and many were impressed by her learning. Three years later Elizabeth again invited the young Arbella to court to show her off, as there was talk of marrying Arbella to Rainutio, the son of the Duke of Parma, but the negotiations did not work out, and after eight months, Arbella went back to her grandmother. There was some suggestion that Arbella had presumed upon her position and angered the aging queen. After 1592 Arbella was not invited back to Elizabeth's court for the rest of the queen's reign, more than a decade. Although there was other talk of arranging a marriage for her, it came to nothing. For Arbella, as for Elizabeth herself when younger, the queen preferred negotiations to an actual marriage. During the last decade of Elizabeth's reign, a plot was uncovered to kidnap Arbella and force her to marry a Catholic noble. Bess of Hardwick promised Elizabeth's government she would keep Arbella very strictly so that no one could get at her. This resulted in a hard time for the bright, educated young woman.

By the summer of 1602, Arbella was feeling desperate. She and her grandmother, thwarted in her dreams for Arbella, did not get along. Arbella wanted to leave her grandmother's house and to have one of her own. But the prospect of a marriage being arranged for her was slim. She wrote to the Earl of Hertford and suggested that she marry his grandson, Edward Seymour, as he was one of the few men of England of an appropriate rank. Hertford, however, was the last one to look favorably on a clandestine marriage with a potential heiress to the throne. In 1560 he had secretly married Catherine, the younger sister of Lady Jane Grey, Queen of England for nine days, and granddaughter of Henry VIII's younger sister Mary and thus another cousin of Elizabeth. Elizabeth had been furious, and Hertford and Catherine had both ended up in the Tower. It had been years after Catherine's death in 1568 before Hertford had reestablished his place at court. A marriage between a Seymour and a Stuart would have fused two different claims, and, no doubt, would have deeply troubled Elizabeth. Hertford informed Elizabeth's chief adviser, Robert Cecil, who promptly informed the queen. Elizabeth immediately dispatched an official to Hardwick Hall to investigate. Arbella was soon in tears. Bess of Hardwick protested she knew nothing about the plan. Both Elizabeth and Bess of Hardwick were infuriated by Arbella's initiative. Bess begged to have Arbella removed from her keeping, but Elizabeth refused.

For Arbella, it seemed that she had fewer options than ever. In a desperate attempt to force Elizabeth to make some arrangement for her, Arbella created a fantasy lover she hinted about in letters. She hoped this would cause Elizabeth to arrange a real marriage for her. Arbella was clever and well-read; these letters read as if they were a novel. But the ailing queen and her advisers soon realized it was indeed a fantasy and refused to do anything for Arbella, dismissing her as hysterical. When Elizabeth died the next March, Arbella was invited to be the principal state mourner, but she refused, stating that since Elizabeth had not wanted to see her when she was alive, it was not seemly for Arbella to push herself on the queen now that Elizabeth was dead. She added that she refused to be brought on stage as a public spectacle.

When James I ascended the throne in March 1603, he invited Arbella to court. There were suggestions that Arbella was involved in treasonable plots against James with Sir Walter Raleigh and Lord Cobham, but Arbella swore she was innocent, a statement that James accepted. At the men's trial, Robert Cecil, James's most trusted adviser, specifically cleared her name of all involvement. But Arbella was all too aware of the danger and fragility of her position even if she was completely loyal to the new king, her cousin.

James did not believe Arbella conspired against him, but he did not treat Arbella with the generosity for which she had hoped; so generous with others, he was parsimonious with her, although he insisted that Arbella must stay at court where he could keep an eye on her. Though at first Arbella was delighted to be at court, she did not have the financial resources she needed for court life. James did not restore to her the estates that had been confiscated in both Scotland and England, saying that she would have them on her marriage, except that he, too, refused to arrange a marriage for her. Arbella decided to again take the initiative and was again attracted to the idea of marrying a grandson of the Earl of Hertford. But this time she had gotten to know his younger grandson, William Seymour, a scholarly young man a dozen years younger than she, and the two had grown to care deeply for each other. They secretly wed on 22 June 1610. Arbella apparently was the one who most decisively wanted to marry. By July 8 the marriage was known to the court. The Privy Council summoned William and then sent him to the Tower of London. Arbella was placed under the care of Sir Thomas Perry. Both James's wife, Anne of Denmark, and his son, Prince Henry, begged James to be merciful, which Robert Cecil also counseled. Indeed, most of the court expected James to forgive his cousin; instead, he was adamant. Seymour was sent to the Tower, and Arbella was under house arrest. But many were sympathetic to the couple, and Arbella was able to sneak into the Tower to be with her husband. By September she was convinced she was pregnant. Unfortunately for her hopes, if this were the case, she soon miscarried. James was furious and condemned Seymour to life imprisonment, while he ordered Arbella to be sent to the North so that they could never see each other. Arbella claimed to be too ill to travel, and with the help of her aunt Mary Talbot, she and William planned a daring escape.

Arbella disguised herself as a boy so that she could travel, and William bribed his way out of the Tower on the pretext of going to say farewell to his wife before her trip north. They were to meet and take a ship together for France. But William was delayed, and Arbella postponed her departure, finally leaving it too late. Ironically, William managed to get to France, but Arbella was captured. This time it was Arbella who was lodged in the Tower, as was her aunt who had tried to help the couple. Though there were rumors at the time that Arbella once in the Tower suffered from insanity, there is no suggestion of it in the official records. Arbella finally refused all sustenance and died on 25 September 1615. In a sense, this was an act of suicide, though given her options, it is difficult to label this an irrational act. Certainly it was a tragic one. Arbella had bravely tried to take control of her life and had been severely punished for it. After her death, James finally allowed William to return to England. He eventually married a second time—to a daughter of the Earl of Essex. They named one of their daughters Arbella.

BIBLIOGRAPHY

Durant, David N. *Arbella Stuart*. London: Weidenfeld and Nicolson, 1978.
McInnes, Ian. *Arabella: The Life and Times of Lady Arabella Seymour. 1575–1615*. London: W. H. Allen, 1968.
Steen, Sara Jayne, ed. *The Letters of Lady Arbella Stuart*. New York and Oxford: Oxford University Press, 1994.

Carole Levin

LEVINA TEERLINC
(ca. 1510–1576)
Belgium
Artist

Levina Bening Teerlinc was born in Bruges, the eldest of five daughters. Her father, Simon Bening, and her grandfather, Alexander Bening, were both famous miniaturists of international standing, and Levina, trained by her father, followed in his footsteps. Another sister, Alexandra, became an art dealer. Levina studied in Bruges with her father and by the 1530s was becoming well known for her skill. By 1545 she had married George Teerlinc; when the English King Henry VIII, who had heard of Teerlinc's gifts as an artist, invited Levina to join his court as official painter, the couple moved to England. At the same time he made her husband a Gentleman Pensioner of the Royal Household. Henry had been in great dismay when his earlier court artist, Hans Holbein, had died in 1543. The invitation to Teerlinc was part of Henry's attempt to bring in artists and musicians from abroad who would add to the glamour and splendor at court, but it is remarkable that a woman was to hold such an important position as court artist in sixteenth-century England. Anne, Countess of Pembroke, the sister of Henry VIII's last wife Katherine Parr, was also a patron of Teerlinc, and Teerlinc probably painted a miniature of the Queen Katherine.

In 1546 Levina was granted £40 per annum as a court painter, the most a court artist would receive in England until the end of the century, and she was paid considerably more than Hans Holbein had been, today a far more famous artist. Teerlinc was a court painter in the reigns of Henry VIII and all three of his children, Edward VI, Mary I, and Elizabeth I. Around 1550, Teerlinc painted a portrait of Elizabeth as a young girl. Records from the Privy Council show a warrant was given to pay George Teerlinc £10 to take his wife to Elizabeth at Hatfield so that Teerlinc could paint the princess's picture. This was a large amount, as the usual fee for miniatures was between £3 and £4, and some scholars hypothesize that this was a full-scale portrait. There is a scholarly dispute, however, as to exactly which portrait this might be, though some people believe it is the famous one of Elizabeth as a young girl dressed in red and holding a book.

During Mary's reign, she did miniatures of the queen at prayer, of Mary blessing rings to cure pregnant women of cramp, and of Mary touching to cure someone afflicted with scrofula, known as the king's evil and believed to be cured by the monarch's touch. She also presented Mary with a small picture of the Trinity. Teerlinc as well did portraits of other noblewomen, such as Mary's cousin, Lady Catherine Grey. Upon becoming queen in 1558, Elizabeth confirmed the patent granted by her father to Teerlinc, as she greatly valued Teerlinc's work. When one of her courtiers was wearing a Teerlinc miniature, Elizabeth liked it so much she asked to have it given to her. Teerlinc not only painted individual portraits of Elizabeth but also portraits of Elizabeth as part of groups showing her on progress, with her Knights of the Garter, and participating in various religious ceremonies such as washing the feet of poor women on Maundy Thursday as part of the Easter rituals. Elizabeth's first great seal was done from a design by Teerlinc. Royal accounts suggest that Levina was highly respected at the English court and that all four sovereigns for whom she worked valued her portrait studies. She also did portraits of people closely associated with Elizabeth and the court. Art critic Roy Strong suggests that the illustrations of Elizabeth in two books by George Turbeville the *Booke of Hunting* and the *Booke of Falconrie*, which are unique in showing Elizabeth in various stages of a royal hunt, are based on drawings by Teerlinc. We know much more about the queen because of the work of a woman artist.

Levina Teerlinc had the status of a gentlewoman and was a lady of the privy chamber of Elizabeth. Each year she did a special picture for Elizabeth for a New Year's gift, and it is obvious that Elizabeth loved miniatures, for that was usually Teerlinc's gift, and she clearly wished to please her queen. Elizabeth in return gave Teerlinc valuable gifts, such as two gilt spoons in 1563. In 1566 Levina's husband George was granted the lease of a property in Stepney where he built a new house valued at £500. The same year George, Levina, and their son Marcus all received English citizenship. Levina clearly lived in comfortable circumstances and had high social status. Some scholars suggest that she helped to train Nicholas Hilliard, the most accomplished miniaturist of Elizabeth's later reign, though in his own writings he praises Holbein as his great predecessor. Teerlinc continued as a court painter until her death and was buried at the parish church of St. Dunstan on 25 June 1576. Her portrait of a lady may be a self-portrait since the sitter is wearing ornamental dice, and the word for "dice" in Flemish is *Teerlinc*.

BIBLIOGRAPHY

Auerbach, Erna. *Tudor Artists.* London: Athlone Press, 1954.
Strong, Roy. *Artists of the Tudor Court.* London: Thames and Hudson for the Victoria and Albert Museum, 1983.

Carole Levin

ELIZABETH JANE WESTON
(1582–1612)
Britain
Exile and Poet

Elizabeth Jane Weston, known as "Westonia," was a brilliant poet, a scholar, an exile, and the stepdaughter of alchemist and magician Edward Kelley. Weston's background is ambiguous, and there seems to be some question over whether Elizabeth and her brother John Francis Weston, two years older, were the illegitimate children of a noble. The father of record, one John Weston, "clerk," was buried near Oxford in May 1582. Kelley may have been paid to marry Joanna Weston and eventually take her children out of the country as a means to avoid aristocratic embarrassment. In the poems Elizabeth wrote in her teens, she referred to a noble background.

Whoever their father was, and whatever arrangement was made, when her children were infants, Joanna Weston married Kelley, an alchemist and medium who was the assistant of the learned magician John Dee, who had cast the horoscope of Elizabeth I. Elizabeth respected Dee enough to have her coronation on the day he suggested. Historians have often characterized Kelley as a charlatan who may have taken advantage of Dee. In September 1583 Joanna accompanied Dee to the Continent with her new husband but left her children in England. They joined their mother in December 1584, and John Francis Weston was registered as a student at the Jesuit Clementine School in Prague in 1585. In Prague, Kelley and his wife had a second wedding ceremony, possibly to have their marriage recognized as Catholic, though they also seem to have traveled in Reformed, humanist circles. Some scholars suggest it is also possible that Joanna Weston was Kelley's second wife, and that Joan Cooper Kelley was a different individual who had either died or gone back to England and the marriage in Prague was not a second ceremony but a second marriage with a different woman who had the same first name. The obscurity of Elizabeth Weston's background makes it difficult to know definitely. We do, however, know that at the time of the Prague wedding, the children also received their middle names, possibly suggesting that they were rechristened as Catholics.

Dee returned to England in 1587, but Kelley and his family stayed on. Kelley received a knighthood from the Emperor Rudolf II in 1589 and soon after moved his family to Jilov. Kelley had convinced the emperor that he could make gold, and Rudolf in return provided Kelley with wealth and a title. Elizabeth was sent to school. Kelley, himself intellectually gifted, insisted on a fine education for both his stepson and stepdaughter.

Despite the knighthood, the emperor eventually became furious with Kelley, and he was arrested in May 1591 and imprisoned in a castle at Krivoklat near Prague. The official charge was that Kelley had killed a court official in a duel, but it is possible that the emperor had lost patience with Kelley's inability to turn lead into gold. It is also possible that Rudolf was worried that Kelley would return to England with his alchemical secrets, and apparently William Cecil, Lord Burghley, was negotiating with Kelley for his return.

After her husband's arrest, Joanna and her daughter eventually moved to Most, where Lady Kelley had property, and Elizabeth continued her education with Jan Hammon, or John Hammond, an immigrant who had been educated at Oxford. By the time she was fourteen, Elizabeth was writing Latin verse and was also fluent in Italian, German, and Czech. Kelley was free between 1594 and 1596, when he was again arrested and placed in prison. The reasons for his second arrest are obscure. Kelley died, possibly by his own hand, after a failed escape attempt in 1597. One legend suggested he died from poison obtained for the purpose from his wife and stepdaughter. All his property was confiscated, leaving Lady Kelley and her children in a terrible situation. Elizabeth's mother briefly returned to England the year after Kelley's death, trying to find some help for her and her children. Their circumstances became even more desperate and tragic when John Francis died in 1600, while still a student at Ingoldstadt. Elizabeth was devastated by her brother's death. In 1601 Elizabeth and her mother moved from Most to Prague. Elizabeth wrote Latin verse seeking patronage from nobles at the emperor's court as a way to support herself and her mother. Elizabeth was also a skilled calligrapher. Some of her poems were somewhat autobiographical, but probably because Kelley had died in disgrace, she never explicitly mentioned him in her poems. Instead, she emphasized the Westons

and what she perceived as her aristocratic background. She also referred to her mother with profound love and admiration. Her skill as
a poet as well as her reputed grace, wit, and beauty led to her success
at finding court patrons.

Though she had left England as a small child, English was spoken
in her family home, and she had a strong identity as an Englishwoman. Especially after the deaths of Kelley and her brother, she
wished to return to England and wrote some poems that she sent in
1603 to the new king, James I. James, however, was appalled by
educated women and suggested that the poems were probably ghost-
written. Elizabeth was deeply hurt when she was informed that this
was his response. It may have been just as well that James's contempt
for educated women meant he did not invite her back. Had she been
able to return to England, her Catholicism would have made her
situation there highly problematic, and early seventeenth-century
England was also not a place that necessarily welcomed and supported
women who expected to publish and make a living as writers.

One of her patrons, the Silesian Georg Martin Von Baldhoven, had
some of her poems published in 1602. Her fortunes improved in
1603 when she married Johann Leo, or Lowe, a lawyer and agent of
the Duke of Braunschweig-Wolfenbuttel at the imperial court, who
aided her and her mother in their legal fight with the emperor to
have Kelley's estate returned to them. Leo also edited her poetry for
publication, and it seems as if Elizabeth married for love. She wrote:
"I think no gift can worthily repay you. . . . So it is, Johann, that love
rebinds the learned" (Schleiner, *Tudor & Stuart Women Writers*,
217). Elizabeth revised some of her poems as well as adding new
ones for a new edition that was probably published in 1607. Elizabeth
had four sons and three daughters in the nine years of her marriage,
but she died in Prague on 23 November 1612 at the young age of
thirty. Only the three daughters survived her.

BIBLIOGRAPHY

Ballard, George. *Memors of British Ladies who have been celebrated for their
     writings or skill in the learned languages, arts and sciences.* London,
     1775. 19–20.
Bassnett, Susan. "Revising a Biography: A New Interpretation of the Life
     of Elizabeth Jane Weston (Westonia) Based on Her Autobiographical
     Poem on the Occasion of the Death of Her Mother." *Cahiers Elis-
     abéthains* 37 (April 1990): 1–8.

Schleiner, Louise. "Elizabeth Weston, Alchemist's Step-Daughter and Published Poet." *Studies in Hermeticism* 10, 2 (Fall 1991): 8–16.

Schleiner, Louise. *Tudor & Stuart Women Writers.* Bloomington: Indiana University Press, 1994. 96–106.

Carole Levin

CATHERINE WILLOUGHBY
(1520–1580)
Britain
Protestant Leader

Catherine Willoughby was the only surviving child of Baron Willoughby and his wife, **Maria de Salinas**, close friend of Henry VIII's first wife, Catherine of Aragon. Although her mother was a devout Catholic, and asked religiously conservative Stephen Gardiner, eventually Bishop of Winchester, to be her godfather, Catherine grew up to be a strong supporter of the Protestant faith and risked her life to stay true to her beliefs.

Catherine's father died on 19 October 1526, and she became Baroness Willoughby and heiress of all her father's lands not entailed to the next male heir, which happened to be his brother, Sir Christopher Willoughby. There was a long struggle between Catherine's mother, Maria de Salinas, and her uncle over her inheritance. After her father's death she became the ward of Charles Brandon, Duke of Suffolk, brother-in-law and closest friend to Henry VIII. Charles's wife was Henry's younger sister, Mary. In 1528 Catherine joined their household and was educated with the Suffolks' own daughters, Frances and Eleanor. A marriage was planned for Catherine and their son Charles; however, three months after his wife's death in 1533 the Duke of Suffolk married her himself. Although Catherine was in her early teens and Suffolk was at least forty-seven, such an age difference was not that unusual in sixteenth-century aristocratic marriages. Suffolk must have hoped his new young wife would be fertile. His son Charles was to die only six months later. The marriage appears to have been happy, and Suffolk was proud of his young wife's beauty and wit. Catherine's first child, Henry, was born in September 1535, and her second, Charles, in 1537.

The England of the new Duchess of Suffolk was rapidly changing. The same year as her marriage, Henry VIII announced his break with the Catholic Church and the annulment of the marriage of his first wife, Catherine of Aragon, mother of his daughter Mary. Henry desperately hoped that his second wife, Anne Boleyn, would give him

Catherine Willoughby. Reprinted by permission of the University Libraries of the University of Nebraska-Lincoln.

the son he craved, but her child, born in September 1533, was another daughter, Elizabeth. Although Anne was executed for adultery only three years later, the break with Rome was complete, though during the rest of his reign Henry shifted back and forth over just how Protestant he wanted England to be in terms of dogma. Catherine, often at Henry's court, listened with fascination to the sermons of Hugh Latimer, who often preached at court during the 1530s, and Catherine was thoroughly converted to Protestant belief.

By the late 1530s it was becoming obvious how interested Catherine was in the Reformed religion. The chaplains appointed to the household were staunch Protestants. In the meantime, Henry VIII himself was more and more conservative and intolerant in his views. In 1539 Henry prohibited Latimer from preaching, as his views were too Protestant for the king. Henry's sixth and last wife, Katherine Parr, whom he married in July 1543, was an old friend of Catherine's. Catherine of Suffolk was one of only seventeen people at the Hampton court chapel when Henry and Katherine married.

Catherine was known for her beauty, charm, kindliness, virtue, and intelligence but also for her ready wit and quick tongue, which sometimes got her into trouble. For example, in the early 1540s the Duke and Duchess of Suffolk gave a large dinner party. The duke asked each lady to take into dinner the man she liked best. Catherine went up to her godfather Stephen Gardiner and explained she was asking him because she could not ask her husband: "Since I may not ask my Lord whom I like best, I ask our Grace whom I like least" (Read, 58). Catherine was upset by Gardiner's treatment of Protestants. She became even more upset later in Henry's reign, when Gardiner's persecution led to the death of **Anne Askew** and other courageous Reformers. Gardiner never forgot this slight.

Catherine was twenty-six when her husband died in August 1545. She was often at court with her close friend Katherine Parr until Henry's death in January 1547. He was succeeded by the Protestant boy king, Edward VI, Henry's son from his third wife, Jane Seymour. Those ruling for Edward sent Catherine's old nemesis, Stephen Gardiner, Bishop of Winchester, to the Tower of London because of the views he expressed in a sermon before the boy king. Apparently Catherine saw Gardiner looking out the window of his room there when she was walking by and taunted him: "It is merry with the lambs now that the wolf is shut up" (Read, 100).

After Henry VIII's death, Catherine spent more time at her country estate of Grimsthorpe, where she ran the estate, supervised the education of her sons, and worked to encourage the Protestant religion in her country. She was very active in supporting the government efforts to abolish unnecessary Holy Days, to remove images and saints' relics from churches, to destroy shrines, to end pilgrimages. She worked to have a Bible in every church and to have strong and effective preaching. Catherine believed that Catholicism placed such importance on the rituals of religion that it impeded people's faith. All that really counted was God and His Word.

Catherine cared deeply for her sons and wanted their best interests. Catherine was highly unusual in not wanting to arrange marriages for them, even if a proposed marriage was materially advantageous, and she turned down a proposal by the Duke of Somerset that Henry marry his daughter, stating they should wait until they were old enough to make up their own minds. Although she had been happy in her first marriage, she was strongly opposed to arranged marriages. She felt people ought to decide for themselves. In the autumn of 1549 her two sons entered St. John's College, Cambridge. Henry was about fourteen and Charles, twelve. Catherine took a house near Cambridge so that she could still see them. In July 1551 the sweating sickness, what was probably a virulent form of influenza, broke out in Cambridge, and both her sons perished. Catherine was devastated. With the extinction of the male line, Edward VI conferred on Frances

Brandon's husband, Henry Grey, the title of Duke of Suffolk. While Catherine was now dowager duchess, she was always referred to throughout her life as Duchess of Suffolk.

In 1552 Catherine began thinking of marrying Richard Bertie, her gentleman usher, a man not of her social standing but someone who had her complete trust. Bertie had great responsibility in running her household and was well educated with a degree from Oxford and fluency in French, Italian, and Latin. He was also the friend of Hugh Latimer, who often visited Catherine's household and preached sermons she loved to hear. In January 1553 Latimer performed a wedding service for Catherine and Bertie. At the end of the year Catherine gave birth to their first child, a daughter Susan.

The year they married turned out to be tumultuous for England. In the summer of 1553 Edward VI died, and John Dudley, Duke of Northumberland, attempted a coup d'état to set aside Henry's daughters in favor of Lady Jane Grey, eldest daughter of Frances and Henry, Duke and Duchess of Suffolk, who had agreed to a marriage between Jane and Northumberland's youngest son, Guildford. The attempt failed, and Mary, a committed Catholic, became Queen of England. Although Frances was Catherine's stepdaughter, and she apparently was very fond of Jane, Catherine had no part in these events. But the outcome would influence her life deeply.

Mary released Gardiner from the Tower and made him her chancellor and began the restoration of Catholicism. Hugh Latimer and other important Protestant clerics were now sent to the Tower, where Catherine sent them anything she could to aid them. Even more frightening for Catherine, early in 1554 Gardiner summoned Richard Bertie to appear before him. Gardiner told Bertie that he as her husband ought to convince Catherine to accept Catholicism. Bertie knew that Catherine would never accept this, and he feared what would happen to her. He wanted to get Catherine and their child out of the country before she could be accused of heresy and told Gardiner that Catherine was owed money from Holy Roman Emperor Charles V, thinking Gardiner would want Catherine to be as wealthy as possible before he might proceed against her. Bertie asked for a passport and went first to the Continent to prepare the way. Catherine, their daughter, and a small retinue of servants secretly fled England and joined him in the Low Countries early in 1555. They lived in disguise in a small town of Santon, near the Rhine, but soon Bertie learned that the bishop of the area suspected who they were, and they had to flee again, especially frightening because Catherine was pregnant again. Catherine and her family were understandably frightened; heretics were being burned in England, including her beloved Hugh Latimer.

They went to Wesel, where they were taken in by the pastor of the town, and a house was found for them. Catherine's son was born in October. They named him Peregrine, a particularly appropriate name for travelers. However, early in 1556 Bertie got word that Lord Paget was in Holland and had convinced the Duke of Brunswick to arrest Catherine and Bertie and charge them with heresy. They fled again to Weinheim, but by 1557, even though they lived as frugally as possible, they were running out of money and did not know where to turn.

Amazingly, the King of Poland had heard of their plight through a Polish Protestant they had known in London. Poland was very supportive of Protestantism and King Sigismund offered them refuge. For the third time Catherine and her family took to the road. In Poland, King Sigismund asked Bertie and Catherine to rule the province of Samogitia (what is now Lithuania) for him. Catherine and her husband put their considerable skills to work to have the province run smoothly.

In November 1558 Queen Mary died and her younger half sister Elizabeth, a Protestant, became queen. Soon the news reached Poland, and in the summer of 1559, Catherine and her family returned to England. Catherine was dismayed that Elizabeth did not pursue a more strongly Protestant church policy. Elizabeth wanted as broadly based a church as possible; Catherine wanted it purified of all popish remnants. Catherine never forgot her conversion by Latimer. Two Elizabethan editions (1562, 1578) of his sermons edited by his Swiss servant Augustine Bernher were dedicated to her.

On their return to England, Catherine and her family divided their time between Grimsthorpe in Lincolnshire and their London house. Richard Bertie was elected to the House of Commons and served for four years. There was definite coolness between the Berties and their queen that continued for the rest of their lives. Their stands on religion were too different, and Elizabeth temperamentally did not like the zealousness of the extreme Protestants.

Catherine allowed both her children to decide on their own marriage partners. Susan Bertie married Reginald Grey in 1571 but was soon widowed. Eight years later she married again, this time to Sir

John Wingfield, a friend of her brother's. Catherine personally did not approve of Peregrine's choice of the Earl of Oxford's sister, Mary Vere. This was not for reasons of status, but rather she was concerned about her personality. Yet since Peregrine was deeply in love, she did all she could to facilitate the marriage. They married in 1578. Two years later, Catherine died. While the young couple did have problems in their early years together, it eventually became a strong marriage and they named their only daughter Catherine, after Peregrine's remarkable mother.

BIBLIOGRAPHY

Bainton, Roland H. *Women of the Reformation in France and England.* Minneapolis: Augsburg Publishing House, 1973.

Bertie, Lady Georgina. *Five Generations of a Loyal House. Part I. Containing the Lives of Richard Bertie and His Son Peregrine Lord Willoughby.* London: Rivingtons, 1845.

Goff, Cecilie. *A Woman of the Tudor Age.* London: John Murray, 1930.

Read, Evelyn. *My Lady Suffolk.* London: Jonathan Cape, 1962.

Carole Levin

MARY WROTH

(ca. 1587–1653?)
Britain
Author and Poet

Lady Mary Sidney Wroth was born into a socially prominent English family well known for their literary accomplishments. Her uncle, Sir Philip Sidney, was a famous courtier during Elizabeth I's reign and the author of an extremely popular romance, *The Countess of Pembroke's Arcadia*, and an important early piece of literary criticism, *The Defense of Poetry* (also called *An Apology for Poetry*). His collection of songs and sonnets, *Astrophil to Stella* (the star-lover to the star), inspired many imitations and created a vogue for Petrarchan love sonnets in late sixteenth-century England. Wroth's aunt was Mary Sidney Herbert, the Countess of Pembroke referred to in her brother's title, herself a poet, translator, and distinguished literary patron. Wroth's father, Robert Sidney, wrote verse, as did her cousin, Elizabeth. The Sidney legacy was important to Mary Wroth, for she continued to use her family's coat of arms after her marriage. Wroth's literary contributions to that legacy are similarly impressive: the first female-authored romance, pastoral comedy, and sonnet sequence in English.

Wroth was the oldest of eleven children. Her mother, Barbara Gamage Sidney, was a wealthy Welsh heiress and a first cousin of Sir Walter Raleigh. Her father, Sir Robert Sidney, assumed his older brother's position as Governor of Flushing after Philip's death in 1586 and remained in the Low Countries for roughly a decade. Mary made several long visits to the Continent with her mother and siblings to see her father, travel, and practice her French. Most of her childhood was spent at the family estate, Penshurst, the subject of the famous poem "To Penshurst" by Ben Jonson, a major English dramatist and poet during the reign of James I. On one occasion, young Mary had the honor of dancing before Queen Elizabeth during her stay with the family.

Mary was married in 1604 to Sir Robert Wroth, one of King James's favored hunting companions; the arranged marriage was not a particularly happy one. Whereas Robert Wroth preferred to hunt on his properties, Mary Wroth participated actively in the artistic and social life of the court. She acted in a masque at court (Jonson's *The Masque of Blackness*) organized by Queen Anne in 1604, a significant honor. Masques were dramatic entertainments with elaborate costumes and scenery, performed for elite, and often royal, audiences. Jonson wrote several poems to Wroth and dedicated one of his plays to her (*The Alchemist*, 1610); he also wrote one poem to Robert. Wroth received a number of other public tributes praising her virtue and her poetic skill.

Wroth's husband died in 1614, and their only son, James, died in 1616. Faced with enormous debts left by her husband, Wroth spent many years paying them off. On several occasions, she was forced to seek protection from creditors as she attempted to repay outstanding claims. Although less active in court circles after 1616, Wroth maintained close personal ties there, and she was invited to participate in Queen Anne's funeral procession in 1619. Between her husband's death and the publication of her romance *The Countess of Montgomery's Urania* in 1621, Wroth had two children, William and Catherine, by her first cousin, William Herbert, who was third Earl of Pembroke and the son of Mary Sidney Herbert. Wroth was one of several female courtiers linked romantically with Herbert during the reigns of Elizabeth and James. Little is known about her children. Wroth's son, William Herbert, became a military officer, serving in the royalist army during the English civil war. He is referred to as "the honorable master William Herbert" in the will (dated 1636) of Wroth's close friend Judith Fox, who left William £10 to buy a ring in her memory. Wroth's daughter Catherine is mentioned in the same will as both a beneficiary and an alternate executrix. A history of the Herbert-Pembroke family refers to Catherine as "the wife of Mr. Lovel near Oxford."

Named for Wroth's close friend, Susan de Vere, Countess of Montgomery, the *Urania* is the first work of fiction by an Englishwoman. It is an enormous work of nearly 600,000 words, almost half of which remained in manuscript until 2000. The printed portion of the romance follows a large cast of noble lovers through their courtships and marriages; the manuscript portrays the main characters in parental roles, while their children pursue knightly and romantic adventures. As Wroth's contemporary readers recognized, the *Urania* alludes to real people and events during James's reign. Some have personal significance, for not only the experiences of the main male and female characters but also those of a number of secondary characters may well shadow Wroth's involvement with Herbert. At the same time, the *Urania* both employs and critiques the usual romance pattern that casts male characters as active, desiring figures and female characters as passive objects of male longing. It devotes considerable attention to the situations confronted by its female lovers and highlights the influence of gender in determining the ways that lovers can speak and act. Wroth's work repeatedly asserts the right of women (as well as men) to choose their marriage partners and criticizes forced matches arranged for familial or political advantage. At the end of the *Urania* is a collection of songs and sonnets entitled *Pamphilia to Amphilanthus*. It is the first English sonnet sequence written by a woman and the first to represent the emotions of an unrequited female lover (Petrarchan courtly lovers are traditionally male).

One of Wroth's contemporary readers, Lord Edward Denny, created a brief social and political scandal upon finding himself unflatteringly portrayed in one episode of the *Urania*. Shortly after its publication, Denny complained to King James and other influential figures about what he saw as Wroth's malicious attack on his honor. He apparently produced such a stir that Wroth felt compelled to stop further sales of the book. A letter written by a contemporary observer states that Wroth targeted "many others" besides Denny with her satire. The episode indeed presents a thinly veiled Denny figure in an extremely unflattering light, but ironically, Denny's response to his characterization essentially proves the accuracy of his portrayal in Wroth's book! An exchange of letters and poems between Denny and Wroth circulated among a select, powerful group of readers. In that correspondence, initiated by Denny, he insinuates a connection between her illegitimate children and her lascivious (in his mind) romance: both are the products of Wroth's unchaste character and are (to him) immoral actions. He urges her either to stop writing entirely or to follow her aunt's example and choose holy works like the Psalms to translate. For her part, Wroth denies any malicious intent to slander Denny and suggests that his public obsession with his honor proves him noble only in name. In his satirical poem, Denny refers to Wroth as a hermaphrodite, because she is a woman and a writer. Wroth's reply, which returns his poem rhyme for rhyme, attacks Denny's social pretensions and asserts that he cannot pass as either a good poet or a true noble. The scandal eventually died down; their letters and poems can be found in Josephine Roberts's edition of Wroth's poems.

Sometime in the early 1620s, Wroth also wrote a pastoral play called *Love's Victory* that may have been performed at private or family gatherings. One scholar calls it the first original dramatic comedy written by a woman in English. It contains several pastoral characters also found in the manuscript section of the romance. After the scandal surrounding the *Urania* subsided, Wroth's name primarily appears in documents related to her efforts to repay her husband's outstanding debts or, in later decades, in Fox's will and papers concerning transfers of property or tax payments. A legal document from 1668 records her death as having occurred either in 1651 or 1653. Wroth has left us an impressive body of work, notably the first fiction by an Englishwoman, and she is among the earliest women to insist on her place as a serious literary author in the predominantly male canon of her era.

BIBLIOGRAPHY

Cerasano, S. P., and Marion Wynne-Davies, eds. *Renaissance Drama by Women: Texts and Contexts.* London: Routledge, 1996.

Lamb, Mary Ellen. *Gender and Authorship in the Sidney Circle.* Madison: University of Wisconsin Press, 1990.

Roberts, Josephine A., ed. *The First Part of the Countess of Montgomery's Urania*, by Mary Wroth. Binghamton, NY: Medieval & Renaissance Texts and Studies, 1995.

Roberts, Josephine A., ed. *The Poems of Lady Mary Wroth.* Baton Rouge: University of Louisiana Press, 1983.

Gwynne Kennedy

KATHARINA ZELL
(1497–1562)
Germany
Protestant Humanitarian

Katharina Zell was a German Protestant activist and reformer in the city of Strasbourg. She came from the respected and politically influential Schutz family of Strasbourg. Her marriage to the clergyman Matthew Zell in 1523 marked the beginning of a life of public activity on behalf of Protestantism.

After a brief tenure as rector at the University of Freiburg (1517–1518), Matthew Zell (1477–1548) had arrived in the city of Strasbourg in order to serve as Roman Catholic priest of the cathedral parish. He also held the office of *poenitentarius* (penitentiary), charged with carrying the bishop's right to absolve grave sins. Zell soon found himself attracted to the views of reformer Martin Luther, and as early as 1521, he began preaching sermons with a Lutheran emphasis. He insisted that he was preaching the "pure Gospel," but the authorities took notice. The Bishop of Strasbourg attempted to have the cathedral chapter oust Zell, but the effort failed in the face of the popularity of the sermons. So great was his reputation that the city council decided to extend their protection to the preacher. Clearly the majority in this sovereign city wanted a reform of the church.

Zell led the movement for reform in Strasbourg from 1521 until 1523, when he was joined by Wolfgang Capito and by the former Dominican Martin Bucer. In 1523 Zell published a defense of the Reformation entitled *Christliche verantwortung* (*Christian Answer*). He followed this in 1525 with the publication of the city of Strasbourg's first evangelical catechism, and he took a principled stand against the use of force in religious matters. Throughout his professional life, Zell focused on preaching and pastoral work. But it was his renunciation of the celibate life that had the greatest impact on the religious life of Strasbourg. Following Bucer's example, Zell broke his vow of celibacy and married Katharina Schutz on 3 December 1523. In response, the bishop suspended Zell and a handful of other married clergymen from their offices, and on 14 March 1524, they were placed under a ban.

Katharina Zell was Matthew's junior by twenty years. She had read Luther's early works before her marriage to Matthew. The priest was attacked as a libertine after their marriage, but Katharina spoke publicly in defense of her husband, even publishing an attack on priestly celibacy in 1524. Bucer had written of the marriage contract as a reciprocal agreement between two free agents who wished to avoid the temptations of promiscuity, and Katharina was no stranger to the aspersions cast upon Bucer's union. In her treatise she argued that the bishop's opposition to clerical marriage was based solely on financial considerations, not spiritual ones. Married priests who left their money to family members would damage the financial standing of the universal church based in Rome. She wrote that her marriage should stand as an example to those priests living in sin with concubines—and with the silent consent of the Church hierarchy. Not willing to accept the Pauline appeal that women should be silent on religious matters, Katharina referred to St. Paul's insistence (Galat. 3) that in Christ there is no difference between Greek or Jew, slave or free, man or woman.

By June 1524 the majority of the Reformed clergy in Strasbourg were married, and these clerical families quickly formed a group dedicated to providing a model of Christian family life for the city as a whole. For her part, Katharina Zell maintained a high public profile in the city of her birth. Without children of her own (two babies died in infancy), she was a tireless worker for the Reformation cause. She was one of the few women to continue writing lay pamphlets on behalf of the Reformers after 1525. And her intellectual efforts were matched by her practical activities.

As one of the free cities in the Holy Roman Empire, Strasbourg became a haven for Lutheran Reformers from nearby lands, especially after the peasant revolt of 1525 was crushed by the authorities. Thousands of refugees flooded into the city of 25,000 in the aftermath of the slaughter. Katharina played a central role in the relief effort until the fighting stopped and the refugees could return to their homes. She also composed a pamphlet aimed at Lutheran women whose husbands had fled to Strasbourg at this time, and in the 1530s, she edited four hymn booklets.

When her husband died in 1548, Katharina continued her benevolent activities. She visited the sick of the city and even took up residence in the syphilis hospital in order to care for a sick nephew. She boldly participated in the service, breaking the traditional injunction that women remain separate from the official ministries. In 1557, angry with the increasingly dogmatic temper of Lutheran pastors in the city, she published *A Letter to all the citizens of Strasbourg* in which she criticized ministers who persecuted Anabaptists and spiritualists. Toward the end of her life, she conducted funerals for two women who had been refused clerical services because of their association with sectarians.

Both Zells were exceedingly tolerant of all who suffered from religious persecution. Katharina went so far as to call for the toleration of Roman Catholics and Anabaptists. At times she and her husband alarmed the city authorities with their insistence that charity take precedence over profit and convenience. They lived the conviction that all work must be spiritualized, and their repeated efforts on behalf of countless refugees and nonconformists linked secular tasks with moral duty.

BIBLIOGRAPHY

Abray, Lorna Jane. *The People's Reformation: Magistrates, Clergy, and Commons in Strasbourg, 1500–1598*. Ithaca, NY: Cornell University Press, 1985.

Chrisman, Miriam U. "Women and the Reformation in Strasbourg, 1490–1530." *Archiv für Reformations-geschicte* 63 (1972): 143–167.

W. M. Spellman

APPENDIX A: NOTABLE WOMEN BY TITLE, OCCUPATION, OR MAIN AREA OF INTEREST

Some names are listed under more than one heading. Not all listings here necessarily appear under the entry head description.

ARTISTIC AND LITERARY PATRONS

Clifford, Lady Anne
Colonna, Vittoria
d'Este, Isabella
Gambara, Veronica
Gonzaga, Giulia
Melisende, Queen of Jerusalem

ARTISTS

Anguissola, Sofonisba
Fontana, Lavinia
Gentileschi, Artemisia
Inglis, Esther
Teerlinc, Levina

BUILDERS

Clifford, Lady Anne
Hardwick, Elizabeth

COURTESANS

Franco, Veronica
Malinche
Poitiers, Diane de

COURT LADIES

Christina of Denmark
Clifford, Lady Anne
The Cooke Sisters
Dormer, Jane
Elizabeth of Braunschweig
d'Este, Isabella
Grumbach, Argula von
Hardwick, Elizabeth
Inglis, Esther
Komnena, Anna
Kottaner, Helene
Margaret of Austria
Marguerite de Valois
Mary of Hungary
Montfort, Eleanor de
Murasaki Shikibu
Ono no Komachi
Poitiers, Diane de
Renée of Ferrara
Salinas, Maria de
Sforza, Caterina
Stuart, Arbella
Willoughby, Catherine
Wroth, Mary

DIARISTS

Clifford, Lady Anne
Halkett, Anne
Izumi Shikibu
Kottaner, Helene
Murasaki Shikibu
Sei Shōnagon

DRAMATISTS

Cary, Elizabeth
Hrotsvit of Gandersheim
Wroth, Mary

MARTYRS

Askew, Anne
Barton, Elizabeth
Porete, Marguerite

MERCHANT'S WIFE

Datini, Margherita

MYSTICS

Barton, Elizabeth
Bridget of Sweden
Catherine of Siena
Christina of Markyate
Elisabeth of Schonau
León, Lucretia de
Mechthild of Magdeburg
Porete, Marguerite

PHYSICIAN

Félicie, Jacqueline

POETS

Akka Mahādēvī
Colonna, Vittoria
Franco, Veronica
Gambara, Veronica
Hrotsvit of Gandersheim
Izumi Shikibu
Labé, Louise
Lanyer, Aemilia
Ono no Komachi
Sei Shōnagon
Stampa, Gaspara

Weston, Elizabeth Jane
Wroth, Mary

POLITICAL ACTIVISTS

Halkett, Anne
Montfort, Eleanor de

POLITICAL LEADERS

Blanche of Castile
Christina of Denmark
Elizabeth of Braunschweig
d'Este, Isabella
Hürrem Sultan
Jadwiga of Poland
Margaret of Anjou
Margaret of Austria
Mary of Hungary
Melisende, Queen of Jerusalem
Nzinga, Queen of Angola
Raziya, the Sultan
Renée of Ferrara
Sforza, Caterina

QUEENS

Blanche of Castile
Hürrem Sultan
Jadwiga of Poland
Juana of Castile
Margaret of Anjou
Marguerite de Valois
Mary of Hungary
Melisende, Queen of Jerusalem
Nzinga, Queen of Angola
Raziya, the Sultan

RELIGIOUS ACTIVISTS

Akka Mahādēvī
Askew, Anne
Barton, Elizabeth

Blanche of Castile
Bridget of Sweden
Catherine of Siena
Christina of Markyate
Clement, Margaret Giggs
The Cooke Sisters
Dentière, Marie
Dormer, Jane
Elisabeth of Schonau
Elizabeth of Braunschweig
Gonzaga, Giulia
Grumbach, Argula von
Hrotsvit of Gandersheim
Jadwiga of Poland
León, Lucretia de
Locke, Anne
Luther, Katherine
Mechthild of Magdeburg
Pirckheimer, Caritas
Porete, Marguerite
Renée of Ferrara
Roper, Margaret More
Willoughby, Catherine
Zell, Katharina

SCHOLARS

Clement, Margaret Giggs
The Cooke Sisters
Dentière, Marie
Komnena, Anna
Locke, Anne
Pirckheimer, Caritas
Porete, Marguerite
Roper, Margaret More
Stuart, Arbella
Weston, Elizabeth Jane

SINGER

Stampa, Gaspara

WRITERS

Akka Mahādēvī
Cary, Elizabeth
Colonna, Vittoria
The Cooke Sisters
Dentière, Marie
Elisabeth of Schonau
Franco, Veronica
Gambara, Veronica
Hélisenne de Crenne
Hrotsvit of Gandersheim
Izumi Shikibu
Komnena, Anna
Labé, Louise
Lanyer, Aemelia
Locke, Anne
Marguerite de Valois
Mechthild of Magdeburg
Murasaki Shikibu
Ono no Komachi
Pirckheimer, Caritas
Porete, Marguerite
Roper, Margaret More
Sei Shōnagon
Stampa, Gaspara
Weston, Elizabeth Jane
Wroth, Mary

APPENDIX B: NOTABLE WOMEN BY COUNTRY OR REGION

Where women are listed under more than one country or region, country or region of birth (*) is distinguished from country or region of influence (†) in parentheses.

ANGOLA

Nzinga, Queen of Angola

AUSTRIA

Kottaner, Helene
Margaret of Austria

BELGIUM, GERMANY, AND THE NETHERLANDS

Elisabeth of Schonau
Elizabeth of Braunschweig
Grumbach, Argula von
Hrotsvit of Gandersheim
Luther, Katherine
Mary of Hungary (Hungary)*
Mechthild of Magdeburg
Pirckheimer, Caritas
Teerlinc, Levina (Britain)†
Zell, Katharina

BOHEMIA

Weston, Elizabeth Jane (Britain)*

BRITAIN

Askew, Anne
Barton, Elizabeth
Cary, Elizabeth
Christina of Markyate
Clement, Margaret Giggs
Clifford, Lady Anne
The Cooke Sisters
Dormer, Jane (Spain)†
Halkett, Anne
Hardwick, Elizabeth
Inglis, Esther
Lanyer, Aemilia
Locke, Anne
Margaret of Anjou (France)*
Montfort, Eleanor de
Roper, Margaret More
Salinas, Maria de (Spain)*
Stuart, Arbella
Teerlinc, Levina (Belgium)*
Weston, Elizabeth Jane (Bohemia)†
Willoughby, Catherine
Wroth, Mary

DENMARK

Christina of Denmark (Italy)†

FRANCE

Blanche of Castile (Spain)*
Félicie, Jacqueline
Hélisenne de Crenne
Labé, Louise
Margaret of Anjou (Britain)†
Marguerite de Valois
Poitiers, Diane de

Porete, Marguerite
Renée of Ferrara (Italy)†

HUNGARY

Jadwiga of Poland (Poland)†
Mary of Hungary (Belgium, Germany, and the Netherlands)†

INDIA

Akka Mahādēvī
Raziya, the Sultan

ITALY

Anguissola, Sofonisba
Bridget of Sweden (Sweden)*
Catherine of Siena
Christina of Denmark (Denmark)*
Colonna, Vittoria
Datini, Margherita
d'Este, Isabella
Fontana, Lavinia
Franco, Veronica
Gambara, Veronica
Gentileschi, Artemisia
Gonzaga, Giulia
Renée of Ferrara (France)*
Sforza, Caterina
Stampa, Gaspara

JAPAN

Izumi Shikibu
Murasaki Shikibu
Ono no Komachi
Sei Shōnagon

MEXICO

Malinche

MIDDLE EAST

Melisende, Queen of Jerusalem

POLAND

Jadwiga of Poland (Hungary)*

SPAIN

Blanche of Castile (France)†
Dormer, Jane (Britain)*
Juana of Castile
León, Lucretia de
Salinas, Maria de (Britain)†

SWEDEN

Bridget of Sweden (Italy)†

SWITZERLAND

Dentière, Marie

TURKEY

Hürrem, Sultan
Komnena, Anna

TIMELINE OF HISTORICAL EVENTS

600–1000	Introduction and spread of Islam in East and West Africa
794–1192	The Heian period of rule in Japan
1066	Norman Conquest of Britain
ca. 1096–1290	European Crusades to regain Christian control of the Holy Lands
1187	Oxford University is founded
1215	King John signs the Magna Carta
1219–1260	Mongols become rulers of central Asia, Iran, Iraq, and eastern Turkey
1233	The Inquisition is established in Spain
1271–1295	Marco Polo visits China, establishing trade routes and cultural ties between East Asia and Europe
1327–1377	Reign of Edward III of England
1338–1453	Hundred Years War between France and England
1347	Outbreak of the plague, known as the Black Death, in Europe

1431	Joan of Arc is burned at the stake for heresy
1450–1600	Portugese explorers on the West and Central Africa coasts
1453	Constantinople falls to the Ottoman Turks, ending the Byzantine Empire
1455	Gutenberg prints the Bible, the first printed book
1455–1485	The English Wars of the Roses
1492	Columbus, in the service of Ferdinand and Isabella of Spain, arrives in the Americas Jews are expelled from Spain
1498	Portugese explorer Vasco da Gama arrives in India, marking the beginning of the European commercial and colonial interests there
1503–1513	Julius II is the Roman Catholic Pope
1509–1547	Reign of Henry VIII of England
1513–1521	Leo X is the Roman Catholic Pope
1515–1547	Reign of Francis I of France
1516–1526	Reign of Louis II of Hungary
1517	Martin Luther posts his ninety-five theses at Wittenberg denouncing abuses of the Catholic Church
1519–1522	Magellan circumnavigates the globe, proving that the earth is round
1519–1556	Reign of Charles V as Holy Roman Emperor
1520–1566	Reign of Süleyman I of the Ottoman Empire
1521	Hernando Cortés of Spain defeats Moctezuma and conquers Tenochtitlan, the center of the Aztec Empire
1525–1526	Tyndale's English New Testament is published
1530–1555	Reformation Wars continue throughout Europe

1533	Fall of the Inca Empire, conquered by Francisco Pizarro for Spain
1543	Portugese arrive in Japan, bringing Christianity and firearms
1547–1559	Reign of Henry II of France
1556	Charles V abdicates and divides the Empire; his son Philip II assumes control of Spain and the Netherlands, and his brother Ferdinand assumes control of Holy Roman Empire
1558–1603	Reign of Elizabeth I of England
1560–1574	Reign of Charles IX of France
1571	Battle of Lepanto: Muslims are defeated by European powers
1572	St. Bartholomew's Day Massacre in Paris: French Protestants are massacred
1574–1589	Reign of Henry III of France
1589–1610	Reign of Henry IV of France
1597	Japanese build a printing press after a Korean model
1598	Edict of Nantes grants full rights to French Protestants
1603–1625	Reign of King James I of England
1607	Founding of Jamestown, the first permanent English settlement in North America
1611	King James version of the Bible is published
1619	Beginning of the African slave trade in North America
1625	Charles I becomes King of England
1633	Galileo is forced by the Inquisition to repudiate Copernican theory that the Earth rotates around the Sun
1642–1648	English Civil War between King and Parliament
1649	Charles I is executed

SELECTED BIBLIOGRAPHY

The bibliography on medieval and Renaissance women is enormous. Each entry contains a brief bibliography on the individual woman. The following suggested readings, some very recent, lead the reader to additional sources of information.

Aughterson, Kate, ed. *Renaissance Women: Constructions of Femininity in England*. London: Routledge, 1995.

Bridenthal, Renate, Susan Mosher Stuard, and Merry Wiesner, eds. *Becoming Visible: Women in European History*. 3rd ed. Boston: Houghton Mifflin, 1998.

Bynum, Caroline. *Holy Feast and Holy Fast: The Religious Significance of Food to Medieval Women*. Berkeley: University of California Press, 1987.

Dronke, Peter. *Women Writers of the Middle Ages: A Critical Study of Texts from Perpetua to Marguerite Porete*. Cambridge: Cambridge University Press, 1984.

Duby, Georges, Michelle Perrot, and Christiane Klapisch-Zuber, eds. *A History of Women in the West, Vol 2: Silences of the Middle Ages*. Cambridge, MA: Belknap Press of Harvard University Press, 1992.

Duby, Georges, Michelle Perrot, Natalie Zemon Davis, and Arlette Farge, eds. *A History of Women in the West, Vol 3: Renaissance and Enlightenment Paradoxes*. Cambridge, MA: Belknap Press of Harvard University Press, 1993.

Echols, Anne, and Marty Williams. *An Annotated Index of Medieval Women*. New York: Wiener, 1992.

Fisher, Sheila, and Janet Halley, eds. *Seeking the Woman in Late Medieval and Renaissance Writings: Essays in Feminist Contextual Criticism*. Knoxville: University of Tennessee Press, 1989.

Gies, Frances, and Joseph Gies. *Women in the Middle Ages*. New York: Crowell, 1978.

Hufton, Olwen H. *The Prospect before Her: A History of Women in Western Europe*. Vol. 1, *1500–1800*. London: Crowell, 1995.

Hughes, Sarah Shaver, and Brady Hughes, eds. *Women in World History, Vol. I, Readings from Prehistory to 1500*. Armonk, NY: Sharpe, 1995.

Hughes, Sarah Shaver, and Brady Hughes, eds. *Women in World History, Vol. II, Readings from 1500 to the Present*. Armonk, NY: Sharpe, 1997.

King, Margaret. *Women of the Renaissance*. Chicago: University of Chicago Press, 1991.

Labarge, Margaret Wade. *A Small Sound of the Trumpet: Women in Medieval Life*. Boston: Beacon Press, 1986.

Larrington, Carolyne. *Women and Writing in Medieval Europe*. London: Routledge, 1995.

Marshall, Sherrin, ed. *Women in Reformation and Counter-Reformation Europe: Public and Private Worlds*. Bloomington: Indiana University Press, 1989.

Mendelson, Sara, and Patricia Crawford. *Women in Early Modern England, 1550–1720*. Oxford: Clarendon Press, 1998.

Raven, Susan, and Alison Weir. *Women of Achievement: Thirty-five Centuries of History*. New York: Harmony, 1981.

Shahar, Shulamith. *The Fourth Estate: A History of Women in the Middle Ages*. London: Methuen, 1983.

Thiébaux, Marcelle, trans. *The Writings of Medieval Women: An Anthology*. 2nd ed. New York: Garland, 1994.

Trager, James. *The Women's Chronology: A Year-by-Year Record, from Prehistory to Present*. New York: Henry Holt, 1994.

Wiesner, Merry. *Women and Gender in Early Modern Europe*. Cambridge and New York: Cambridge University Press, 1993.

INDEX

Numbers in **boldface** refer to main entries.

About the Authors

CAROLE LEVIN is Professor of History at the University of Nebraska, where her specialties are English history and women's history. Her articles have appeared in such journals as *Albion*, *The Sixteenth Century Journal*, *Shakespeare Yearbook*, and *Exemplaria*. She is the author of numerous books and essays in edited collections, has held long-term fellowships at the Folger Shakespeare Library and the Newberry Library, and is a Fellow of the Royal Historical Society.

DEBRA BARRETT-GRAVES is Assistant Professor of English at the College of Santa Fe where she won the Manuel Lujan Award for Excellence in Teaching. Her articles appear in *Shakespeare Yearbook* and *The Early Drama, Art, and Music Review*. She is currently writing a book on servants and service in Shakespearean and Elizabethan drama. She is a member of the Shakespeare Association of America and the North American Branch of the Society for Emblem Studies.

JO ELDRIDGE CARNEY is Associate Professor of English at The College of New Jersey, where she teaches medieval and Renaissance literature. She has published articles in edited collections and journals and is the editor of the biographical dictionary *Renaissance and Reformation, 1500–1620* (Greenwood Press, 2000).

W. M. SPELLMAN is Professor of History at the University of North Carolina at Asheville where his specialties are English history and European political thought. His articles have appeared in such journals as *Anglican and Episcopal History* and the *Harvard Theological Review*. He is the author of numerous books and has held long-term fellowships from the National Endowment for the Humanities and from the Tanner Humanities Center at the University of Utah.

GWYNNE KENNEDY is Associate Professor of English at the University of Wisconsin-Milwaukee, where she teaches early modern literature and women's studies courses. She has written several articles on women writers in early modern England and has recently published a book on early modern English women's anger.

STEPHANIE WITHAM is completing her Ph.D. in English at the University of Nebraska on the topic of Renaissance women writers. She has taught at the College of St. Mary.